D1616954

Denying and Disclosing God

Denying and Disclosing God

The Ambiguous Progress of Modern Atheism

MICHAEL J. BUCKLEY, S.J.

Yale University Press
New Haven and London

T. S. Eliot's poem "The Dry Salvages", from his *Four Quartets*, is copyright 1941 by T. S. Eliot and renewed 1969 by Valerie Eliot, and is reprinted by permission of Faber and Faber Ltd and Harcourt, Inc.

Excerpt from "Watchmaker God" from *Collected Poems* by Robert Lowell. Copyright © 2003 by Harriet Lowell and Sheridan Lowell. Reprinted by permission of Farrar, Straus and Giroux, LLC and Faber and Faber Ltd.

For information about this and other Yale University Press publications please contact:
U.S. Office: sales.press@yale.edu   yalebooks.com
Europe Office: sales@yaleup.co.uk   www.yalebooks.co.uk

Set in Minion by SNP Best-set Typesetter Ltd., Hong Kong
Printed in Great Britain by St Edmundsbury Press Ltd, Bury St Edmunds

Library of Congress Control Number 2004107790

ISBN 0–300–09384–5

A catalogue record for this book is available from the British Library

10 9 8 7 6 5 4 3 2 1

For Tom
Fratri carissimo

Quis ita mihi pernecessarius?
Cui aeque dilectus ego?
Frater est genere,
Sed religione germanior.*

*Bernard of Clairvaux of his brother, "Sermones in Cantica," 26:4, *Patrologia Latina* 183, 905c (adapted)

Contents

Preface

The subject at issue

In the early months of 1950, the *Partisan Review* sponsored a symposium to examine "the new turn to religion among intellectuals." The topic was jarring and unexpected. This initiative seemed to pursue an interest long consigned among the educated and informed to a superseded past. During the opening decades of the twentieth century, in the judgment of the journal, American intellectuals in the main had settled upon a "triumphant naturalism": nature and reality identify, and valid forms of inquiry must be variants of a method recognizably scientific.

Yet by mid-century much of this common conviction was faltering. In increasing numbers, thinkers of moment and of influence in the United States had come to question whether religion was not a necessity for Western civilization, whether society could have any hope of survival "without the re-animation of religious values."

Evaluating this surge in the cultural salience of religion as "one of the most significant tendencies of our times," the journal gave over a number of issues to explore its causes and implications. The editorial board clustered a set of queries under each of five or six general headings. Religion could be examined in its etiology and credibility and as it related to science, culture, literature, and values. The journal invited major thinkers within the United States to contribute their thoughts on this unusual topic.[1]

Among the distinguished contributions was the voice of Hannah Arendt, tough, clear, perceptive. Cutting through the talk about cultural enhancement and political usefulness, she centered on what she took to be the fundamental issue: "The trouble here, as in all discussions of religion, is that one really cannot escape the question of truth and therefore cannot treat the whole matter as though God had been the notion of some especially clever pragmatist who knew what it is good for . . . and what it is good against. It just is not so. Either God exists, and people believe in Him – and this, then, is a more important fact than all of culture and literature; or He does not exist and people do not believe in Him – and no literary or other imagination is likely to change this situation for the benefit of culture and for the sake of the intellectuals."[2] Arendt did not encourage a focus on religion in its elegant or indispensable social uses. She wanted the talk to bear principally on the truth about God. From culture, society, and history, from mores and art, even from "religion," she had selected as inevitable, because foundational, the question about God: the affirmation or denial that God exists. Everything depended on how one came down on that question.

The following pages are an attempt to construe something of this question, both its character and its career. Given originally as the D'Arcy Lectures, sponsored at Oxford University by Campion Hall over the fall of 2000, these six lectures – each now grown in its revisions and additions far beyond the *quantitas debita* of a lecture – are much more an effort to study something of this amazingly tangled subject than to bring it to resolution.

Language here becomes pervasively ambiguous. Hannah Arendt's "God" means many different things and points to widely divergent referents. Upon examination, one man's God turns out to be another man's Satan, and one man's faith is another man's atheism. The quandaries and reversals that figure in methods or arguments and their entailments also tell upon this attempt at understanding. It is remarkable to discover that one member of a contradiction – exists or not exists – can generate the other. One side of the debate can come paradoxically to feed its alternative. The two may even depend upon and assimilate each other. For the alternatives in this great antinomy are not unalterably fixed either in meaning or in consequence. Just as "God" is systematically ambiguous, so also, strangely enough, is the contradiction itself within what exists and what does not exist.

This Preface very consciously, then, enlists such modifying terms as "attempts," "something of," and "suggests", for the subject itself is far too vast for any claim to comprehension or adequacy. However inquiry and conviction come down on one side or the other in addressing such a subject, one is brought before the claim of the infinite mystery that human beings have for millennia called God and what Nietzsche's madman recognized as the "holiest and mightiest of all that the world has yet owned."[3] Failing to see the great significance of the question threatens us as it did the crowd in Nietzsche's marketplace – debasing its discussion to not-very-clever debates and never reaching Nietzsche's understanding of its moment, that to decide this issue in the negative is "to wipe away the entire horizon."[4] Whether one affirms or denies the reality of God, one does not even understand the question if it is reduced to a problem to be solved or a wrangle to be fought out rather than a mystery to be apprehended. For this great question about God also engages the depth of the human person; it shapes the fundamental interpretation of human life and human destiny.

Six chapters, however amplified, should obviously make no attempt to cover such a subject comprehensively. What is told here is only one of the many possible narratives that track the atheism emerging in modernity and that try to search out something of its meaning and its formidable challenge. In what is admittedly so narrow a compass, this attempt attends to the dialectical side of religious concepts and arguments – their inherent contradictions and transitions into their own negations. It further suggests that any negation or contradiction, to realize its own inherent possibilities, must persist into further negation – classically, the negation of the negation – and so constitute an organic development that continues the argument and stamps it as dialectical.

This book, then, proposes an exploration of the internal contradictions in theism, imagined or real, that gave rise to various forms of atheism in modernity. Perhaps an introduction would give some content to what may seem so formal a project.

At the Origins of Modern Atheism *and its problems*

In his extensive lectures on the history of philosophy, Hegel called attention to a radical religious change appearing in the eighteenth century, the conviction that "the great Whole of Nature (*le grand tout de la nature*) is the ultimate: 'the universe displays nothing but an immense collection of matter and motion.'"[5] This identification of all reality with the physical universe and the universalizing of an autonomous mechanics for its study brought for the first time to the modern world a self-confessed and articulately argued atheism. "We should not make the charge of atheism lightly," wrote Hegel, "for it is a very common occurrence that an individual whose ideas about God differ from those of other people is charged with lack of religion, or even with atheism. But here it really is the case that this philosophy has developed into atheism, and has defined matter, nature, etc., as that which is to be taken as the ultimate, the active, and the efficient."[6] The new mechanics of the eighteenth century could become universal and autonomous because the physical universe was comprehensive of all there was or could be.

A previous work, *At the Origins of Modern Atheism*, attempted to address the sources for this conjunction of a universal mechanics with an emergent atheism. It argued that the strategies of theism or religious apologetics in early modernity had led theologians to bracket whatever was of specific religious character or warrant and to rely upon the new and prospering sciences for "the first foundations of religion."[7] The implicit but unrecognized premise in such a strategy, building upon the new mechanics, was that the uniquely religious – in all of its experiential, traditional, institutional, and social forms – was cognitively empty, that religion could not secure its own central assertion, and that it had to appeal to other sciences and disciplines for its foundations and even for its methodology. It was only a question of time until the vacuity of the fundamental religious proposition appeared explicitly, when the various natural philosophies or sciences would indicate that they did not need a divine hypothesis to explain design in the solar system or in organic nature. The more the physical-theologies had in previous centuries insisted that scientific discoveries were to furnish the evidence for the existence of God, the more they unwittingly promoted the inherent contradiction to their own proper and foundational assertion. Nature could no longer serve as religion's evidence. This dawning realization culminated with Paul d'Holbach, Denis Diderot, and the atheism in which Hegel would register them. That is why *At the Origins of Modern Atheism* concluded that atheism as an intellectual conviction in modern Europe was generated dialectically, i.e., that the very efforts to counter it were the forces that gave it ideational origin, enormous intellectual power, and cultural growth in modern Europe.

The following pages support the basic argument of *At the Origins of Modern Atheism* together with its reading of the dialectical genesis of modern atheism. It must, however, be stated here that this conceptual entailment, of course, did not exhaustively explain the origins of the movement that became modern atheism – hence the work was called *At the Origins of Modern Atheism*. Obviously and importantly, countless social, economic and political influences were formatively at play. But this internal contradiction in ideas was present, negating implicitly as inadequate what one was supporting explicitly. This dialectical negation lent to all of these other influences direction and additional strength. In many ways, modern atheism was the self-subversion of this form of theism.

The appearance of *At the Origins of Modern Atheism* provoked some dispute and discussion. Three issues among others figured importantly. A distinguished theologian criticized its conclusions as "dialectical and over neat." Nevertheless, additional research has not weakened the evidence that such a dialectical negation was vitally present. On the contrary, it has strengthened the conviction that this dialectical pattern did in fact obtain and was to be found in the genesis of atheism elsewhere. These various diagnoses were not the supervening product of Absolute Idealism, but – very simply – the history of ideas exhibited in these cases that the arguments of theism, driven by their own interior contradictions, passed over into atheism.

Secondly, some had read *At the Origins* as contending, despite disclaimers, that this dialectical subversion of theism began with Thomas Aquinas. This would have put it in *de facto* agreement with Paul Tillich, who contended that it was in the reliance upon inference that Aquinas "had made atheism not only possible but unavoidable."[8] But there was obviously enough ambiguity in the work that demanded clarification. Further, if one was going to examine the ideational origins of atheism, it would be ill advised not to attend to the thought and the influence of St. Thomas.

Lastly, there was my dawning awareness that the structure within the history that I had examined and presented was still incompletely recognized. *At the Origins* had shown that the initial strategies of theism had generated their own contradictions, subverting themselves dialectically and manifesting their inherent insubstantiality only at a second moment. This would have been sufficient to explain the negation of theistic grammar and apologetics, and the rise of modern atheism as an idea whose time had come, as a self-supporting conviction. But to arrest the career of modern atheism at this stage would seem to lay an unwarranted inhibition on any further development. At least, one needed to ask if there was or was to be a negation even of this negation, i.e., to ask if the dialectical development was to fixate here or to proceed further. At this point, the dialectical pattern of development became heuristic, posing the question: what would such a further negation look like?

Hence, I wanted to explore additional areas in my initial inquiries, and, to my great gratitude, the D'Arcy Lectures enabled me to do so.

Six chapters

It seemed of initial importance to review the hypothesis that it was not the antagonism of the rising sciences that generated atheism in Western religious and intellectual cultures – however popular such a reading of those centuries might be. It was just the opposite. Whatever antagonism rose between the new sciences and religion seemed negligible in comparison with their enthusiastic embrace of religion. Many of the natural philosophers (as they were called at the time) believed that they could ground the apologetic argument better than the theologians. A good number of the theologians seem to have concurred, and with that concurrence they signed on to the history that this dependence would effect. Thus, the first of these chapters presents the three major and very different settlements at the dawn of modernity between the ancient faith and the new sciences, those of Galileo, Kepler, and Newton, not one of which was hostile to religion. These three very different protocols provided something of the context and the possibilities of what was to follow in the history of ideas.

The Newtonian protocol with its inferential argument from design in the universe eventually won the day, and so the second chapter turns to the internal contradiction between bracketing religion, either as content or as form of thought, and the assertion of the reality of the personal God. The atheism that emerged from this set of conventions, as indicated above, thus exhibited a dialectical structure, the negation of an initial position by the contradiction implicit but intrinsic to its character. It seemed very helpful to examine here the important study of James Turner, who, quite independently of my work, discovered the same dialectical structure in the rise of atheism in nineteenth-century America.[9] The second chapter concludes with Alan Kors's magisterial study of the contradiction between the two "theistic" schools in pre-Revolutionary France and his final judgment: "We have seen a complex culture generate its own antithesis, the possibility of which it always had carried within."[10] In the rise of atheism, religion or theology subverted itself. It is not the case that one wishes to apply a "dialectical method" to the history of thought to see if this external, even artificial, schema would yield profitable results. It is rather that one finds this movement in the history of atheism, that theism conceived as it often was in those centuries passes over into its own negation. "If the argument follows a dialectical movement, then this must be in the things themselves, not just in the way we reason about them."[11]

If this was the strategy and its paradoxical results, who set it going? Does it extend farther back beyond early modernity – indeed, to Thomas Aquinas and the intellectual tradition inherent in the "five ways"? What can one say of Paul Tillich's reading of intellectual history here, contending that Western atheism takes its beginnings from the "rational way" of Aquinas? Is God intellectually established for Aquinas not by experience – let alone disclosed in Christology – but only by inference and "natural theology"? The third chapter examines Tillich's claim, arguing that for Aquinas one comes to affirm the reality of God not primarily as a God of inference but as the incomprehensible One who has been irreducibly given within human awareness in a very confused and general way from the beginning of the longings for happiness. The chapter argues further that for Aquinas God is also given historically, normatively disclosed for the Christian, in the reality that is Christ. The circular structure of the *Summa theologiae* allows Aquinas's Christology of the Third Part to feed into the initial affirmations about God in the First Part. So circular is the progress of the *Summa theologiae* that, in an important way, the end of Aquinas's theology can be seen as also its beginning.

Granting to early modernity, then, the temporal origins of modern atheism and the dialectical character of its generation, a seismic shift shook theistic apologetics in the nineteenth century, as the fourth chapter reads that period. The secular autonomy of the sciences, the Kantian critique of any knowledge reaching beyond the objects of possible experience, the rise of evolutionary explanations of design in nature – all combined to displace the area of evidence for the existence of God. This evidence had been nature; it became increasingly human nature. Again, a dialectical contradiction emerged as the explicitly absolute God was argued to be of irreplaceable but derivative value because of the service he rendered human beings and the coherence he offered to philosophical systems. *De facto*, the human being became the unacknowledged or implicit absolute. God was seen first to be a function in modern philosophy, as James Collins contended, and then finally as merging in different ways with humanity itself.[12] One came to recognize that actually the human had been projected as the divine, and the divine, if given autonomous existence, was alienating human beings from their own potential. God became not the enhancement of humanity, but its estrangement. God became "the enemy of human nature" – a term classically reserved for the diabolical. By the latter half of the nineteenth century, humanistic theism had also generated its own negation, its anti-theism.

The first four of these chapters probe certain initial positions, whether philosophical, humanistic or religious, that had been advanced to secure the existence of God. They explore these for an internal incoherence, one that revealed and objectified itself eventually as the overt contradiction of what its argumentation was explicitly advancing or defending. But this recognition does not itself reach the stage of the dialectical if the process is arrested at this second moment, if the disjunction fixates at this point and the initial negation does not generate its own further negation. Hence the fifth chapter explores two different paths that the negation of the religious did take: atheism as the secret of religion; negative or mystical theology as the purification and fulfillment of religion. In both of these very different traditions, the liability of religious discourse to projection is generally accepted. Both are keenly aware that much of what is believed and affirmed is the objectification of human self-consciousness or of human desires for power, security, and love. What Feuerbach and Freud cited as projection, John of the Cross subsumed under the more general maxim: "Whatever is received is received according to the mode of the one receiving it."[13] In this latter tradition, however, the negation of these projections comprises the classical night of the soul, moving beyond the negation of God as projection to the further negation of the negation itself in the affirmation of God, who transcends both "in the brilliant darkness of a hidden silence."[14]

The last chapter suggests one way in which the dialectic of religious argument might pass over to its negation of the previous primacy given to inference and "scientific evidence" by a further negation, i.e., by restoring the religious both in its evidence and in its forms of cognition, i.e., in the content and the form appropriate to questions so inherently religious. This is not a flight into the irrational or the enthusiastic, but the retrieval of a specifically religious intellectuality. If one is to assert the existence of God, then the issue becomes: How is God disclosed to ordinary human life or to reflective con- sciousness? How do human beings come to a responsible awareness of this self-disclosure? Following lines traced out by Karl Rahner, the final chapter explores both the categorical and transcendental components of experiences that are classically "religious." In this restoration of the religious, as a warrant for the affirmation of the reality of God, the dialectical career of atheism has come full and paradoxical circle.

Running through the entirety of this book is the question, as it was initially and inchoatively present at the conclusion of *At the Origins of Modern Atheism*: What can one learn from these reflections on one aspect of the complicated course of religious disbelief? That speculation or inference or metaphysics or even natural philosophy becomes denial when it examines the reality of God – or that such thought is secretly atheistic? This seems quite false. Rather, the lesson that emerges is that one cannot – in an effort to justify, found, or confirm assertions of the reality of God – bracket or excise religious evidence and religious consciousness and the interpersonal that marks authentic reli- gious life and experience. Religion must be allowed to bear the full comple- ment of constituents that Baron von Hügel has argued as essential: the intuitional, emotional, and volitional; the speculative and rational; the insti- tutional, historical and traditional.[15] Excise any of these, and the account of religious affirmations is seriously deficient. One cannot take the place of the other. Inference cannot simply substitute for experience. One will not long affirm a personal God, who is fundamentally inferred as a conclusion rather than disclosed as a presence, one with whom there is no intersubjective communication. The most compelling witness to a personal God must itself be personal. To attempt something else as foundation or as substitute, as has been done so often in an effort to secure by inference the reality of God, is to move into a dialectical process generated by internal contradictions of which the ultimate resolution must be atheism.

Acknowledgments

John Adam Moehler opened the preface to his magisterial work, *Symbolism*, with the observation that every book has a twofold history: "a history before, and a history after its publication."[1] These acknowledgments are a partial attempt to recognize with gratitude that first history.

This book takes it origin, as did Moehler's *Symbolism,* from a series of lectures, but this time at Oxford rather than at Tübingen. A gracious letter from Campion Hall at Oxford and, more specifically, from the Master of Campion Hall, the Reverend Gerard J. Hughes, S.J., invited me to deliver the D'Arcy Lectures during the Michaelmas term of 2000. During those months, I was the grateful recipient of the hospitality of that college and of its Jesuit community, and I remember with fondness that rainy autumn at Oxford, the encouragement of colleagues and the presence of friends, such as Richard and Anne Morris and Michael Gallagher, S.J.

Many were the scholars consulted in the formation of those lectures, and I register their names here with my heartfelt thanks: the late Richard P. McKeon, my mentor during graduate studies at the University of Chicago, whose influence through his lectures, writing and conversations is very much reflected in these pages; John H. Wright, S.J., and the late Clifford Kossel, S.J., teachers of many years ago in whose debt I stand beyond the abilities of a few lines to convey; Michael Himes of Boston College with whom I have conducted a number of graduate seminars on the rise of atheism and to whose massive learning, insightful comments and friendship I am very much in debt; James Turner and Ernan McMullin of Notre Dame, Alan Kors of Pennsylvania, Nicholas Lash of Cambridge, and Brian Davies, O.P., of Fordham University for the openhanded generosity with which they shared their scholarly knowledge through many conversations and correspondence.

My gratitude goes also to my talented and ready research assistants over these years: Brian Hughes, John Hardt, Benjamin VanLandingham, Brian Flanagan and Mitchell Herschbach. Without their responsible, capable and unflagging support, this series of lectures would have been impossible. Equally important was the constant aid offered in so many different areas by the indefatigable Patricia Fleming, my secretary over these years, who gave this project her careful, competent and consistent attention. I should like to express my gratitude to Yale University Press for their help and encouragement.

During these years, I was a member of two very supportive Jesuit communities, one at Boston College and the other at Santa Clara University, and I remember with great gratitude their religious fraternity and continual support as this project gradually took form.

This book is dedicated to my brother Tom, a Jesuit historian who has written books with much more interesting titles than I have been able to field. I dedicate this book to him with an affection and an admiration of many years.

1

The New Science and the Ancient Faith: Three Settlements at the Dawn of Modernity

Prologue

In the development of comprehensive mathematical methodologies for the conduct of scientific inquiry and in the creation of new sciences by which the physical universe and the human body were to be understood, the late seventeenth century came, in the judgment of Sir Herbert Butterfield, to constitute "a civilisation exhilaratingly new." Its scientific revolution gathered strength from year to year and obtained the cultural extension necessary to form a massive landmark, one so conspicuous and so consequential that it could only be compared to the rise of Christianity. Between these two, the ascent of Christianity and the origins and promotions of modern science, one can calibrate much of the intellectual achievement of Europe.[1] To come to terms with the character of modern atheism as an idea and as an argument, then, entails some prior understanding of the intellectual settlements formulated in early modernity between these two radically determinative cultural influences, Christianity and the scientific revolution, as they came to encounter each other and to realize a variety of relationships that would contextualize every constituent element of modern and contemporary culture.

Popular renditions have presented this relationship as minatory antagonism: religious faith, shaken by the aggressive and insistent rationality of modern science, recognized almost instinctively from the beginning an implacable antagonist. The waxing appreciation of its own inadequacies fed the terror and aggression with which religion unavailingly fought its rearguard action and consistently attempted to inhibit scientific advance. A choice had to be made between them. As this persuasion developed, the remarkable polymath John William Draper, American chemist, medical college president, and historian, spoke for many in the nineteenth century: "The time approaches when men must take their choice between quiescent, immobile faith and ever-advancing Science – faith with its mediaeval consolations, Science, which is incessantly scattering its material blessings in the pathway of life, elevating the lot of man in this world, and unifying the human race."[2] Almost at random a century later, one can pick up a similar antagonism in somewhat less strident notes in the antinomy drawn by the distinguished Nobel laureate Steven Weinberg, celebrated for his work on the theory of particles and field. Repudiating anything like a "constructive dialogue" between religion and science, he advocated that "one of the great achievements of science has been, if not to make it impossible for intelligent people to be religious, then, at least to make it possible for them not to be religious. We should not retreat from this accomplishment."[3] The cultural generation of the one seems the corruption of the other.

Such a reading of accomplishments furnishes a second justification for attending to these settlements. For out of these early protocols emerges a paradox to be explored in the second chapter. It was not the opposition of science to religion; it was much more the endorsement of science that generated modern atheism. It was not because science was indifferent or antagonistic; it was because it was too enthusiastically affirmative and comprehensively supportive that atheism emerged. Science smothered religion by adopting it. But to understand this contradiction, it is necessary to grasp something of the settlements that were intellectually available.

The compass of a single chapter allows for only a few soundings, taking measurement in the century from the public works of three of its preeminently formative thinkers: Galileo Galilei, Johannes Kepler, and Isaac Newton – men who lent content and shape to so much of the new culture. Newton was born the year Galileo died, and Kepler was born and died within the years that measured off Galileo's span. For all three, *floruit* can be written for the most part in the script of the seventeenth century. Our soundings must probe their "public works," their books and correspondence, their accessible conversations and recognized influences in contrast to an analysis that postulates and then hunts for the hidden or covert convictions that each held in his heart as a secret faith. Whatever one says about secret beliefs that paralleled or contradicted public profession, they are not the object here. What is under investigation are the common inquiry and the open arguments that it informed and furthered. For, as the late I. B. Cohen has written: "It is this public (published) presentation that has actually conditioned the advance of science in the domain of motion, from Galileo's revolutionary new kinematics to the modern science of dynamics."[4] With all of this as prologue, we may begin with Galileo and his responsibility for "the advance of science in the domain of motion."

Galileo Galilei (1564–1642)

Galileo Galilei considered his dialogue *The Two New Sciences* "superior to everything else of mine hitherto published."[5] Its composition had, off and on, occupied fifty years of the author's life. While it finally appeared in 1638, four years before his death, much of its mechanics – such as the law for freely falling bodies and the parabolic motion of projectiles – had been formulated before his leaving Padua in 1610. *Two New Sciences* is a paradigmatic work, and Galileo's own estimation of this abiding project was that it "contains results which I consider the most important of all my studies."[6] By November 1634, Galileo could write to Fulgenzio Micanzio that "the treatise on motion, all new, is in order, but my unquiet mind will not rest from mulling it over with great expenditure of time, because the latest thought to occur to me about some novelty [repeatedly] makes me throw out much already found there." On 21 December 1634, Galileo was asking Micanzio to arrange for publication.[7]

What Galileo thought constituted the character of these "two entirely new sciences . . . demonstrated . . . in a rigid, that is, geometric, manner" was precisely the introduction of mathematics into physics, without identifying them.[8] The first of the "two new sciences" treated resistance, that property of matter that allowed for construction. Resistance necessitated the differentiation of mechanics from geometry, though the latter would provide the instrument for the former.[9] The second science, which is more to our purposes here, dealt with the very ancient subject of local motion. Galileo saw his contribution to the "new" science of an ancient subject, *de motu locali*, to be twofold: the discovery of certain mathematical properties of locomotion, and the disclosure of an "approach and access [*aditus et accessus*] by which other minds, more acute than mine, will explore [*penetrabunt*] its remote corners."[10] The advance made in his new mechanics, then, lay in new facts framed mathematically, and, what he considered more important, in a new method ("approach and access"). The facts are framed in quantitative measurements and proportions; the method is threefold: to construct and then explore a mathematical definition of what is under study; secondly, to analyze its meaning into axioms and its consequences into theorems and propositions; and finally, to test these consequences to see if they fit the natural phenomena that occasioned the original question.

How do experience and observation figure in Galileo? They occur at two moments of his method: (1) the initial subject matter and some of its properties are given or suggested by experience or even discovered by experiment – and thus he brings to bear his questions on the movement of the pendulum or the motion of projectiles; (2) the conclusions are verified by experiment. But observation alone does not give him the initial principles or sources of his mechanics; mathematics must be present and operative. The subject must be mathematicized. Mathematics allows definitions to be formulated in terms of the reflexive proportions of space and time – velocity, distance, and time – and their consequences to be drawn in axioms and demonstrated theorems.[11] The formulation and application of the definition grounds the apodictic demonstration that Galileo thought essential for science. The definition, then, was an operational formulation of a mathematicized intelligibility. It could be explored in its implications and brought to bear upon the phenomena of observation in order to obtain confirmation and useful results. But the inner structure of the definition was reflexive, for its internal constituents were mutually and internally referential. The "Third Day" begins with these definitions – not with motion as experienced, but motion as mathematicized.

This procedure followed upon an even more fundamental conviction: that mathematics was the language in which the book of nature was written. "The book cannot be understood unless one first learns to comprehend the language and read the letters in which it is composed. It is written in the language of mathematics, and its characters are triangles, circles, and other geometric figures without which it is humanly impossible to understand a single word of it."[12] He thought this conviction fundamental enough to enable him to distinguish between two different kinds of properties that are predicated of sensible things: figures, numbers and motions that truly reside in bodies, independent of sensible perception; odors, tastes, or sound, which in the absence of the perceiving subject are "nothing more than names."[13] There is an ontology behind Galileo's choice of method and definition.

The definition framed for uniform motion, for example, may never as such be precisely realized as a phenomenon in the actual physical universe: "equal distances traversed by a particle in equal intervals of time."[14] Even more, the definition of continually accelerated motion will have to be assumed or extrapolated – at least until Robert Boyle and objects falling in a vacuum.[15] But "if we find that the properties [of accelerated motion] which will be demonstrated later are realized in freely falling and accelerated bodies, we may conclude that the assumed definition [*l'assunta definizione*] includes such a motion of falling bodies and that their acceleration goes on increasing as the time and duration of the motion."[16] A definition was not to be constructed out of whole cloth; nor was it simply a copy of common experience. It is a mathematical extrapolation from – or a mathematical assumption suggested by – experience, and the accuracy of the definition can be tested by its demonstrated results.[17]

Science in the Middle Ages was classically the knowledge of a subject matter through its causes and properties. In Galileo's kinematics, those causes become formal causes, mathematical proportions, which allow for geometric definition and necessary demonstration but omit any consideration of agency. This allows him to demonstrate what may or may not have been observed or approximated in experience, and to demonstrate it as the entailment of a mathematical definition. This methodology seems neither Aristotelian nor Platonic, though affinities exist with both as will be noted. The methodology is what Percy W. Bridgeman and Richard P. McKeon have termed an "operational" method.[18] The definition is not simply given by experience, but hypothesized and then tested for its predictive accuracy.[19]

> When, therefore, I *observe* a stone initially at rest falling from an elevated position and continually acquiring new increments of speed [observation], *why should I not believe* [initial elaboration towards a definition] that such increases take place in a manner which is exceedingly simple and rather obvious to everybody? . . . Thus *we may picture to our mind* [*mente concipientes*], a motion as uniformly and continuously accelerated when during any equal intervals of time whatever, equal increments of speed are given to it.[20]

This use of the active powers of intellect and imagination to frame a definition suggested by observation runs through Galileo's work: for example, "But without depending upon the above experiment, which is doubtless very conclusive, it seems to me that it ought not to be difficult to establish such a fact by reasoning alone. Imagine a heavy stone. . . ."[21]

Such a science of itself says nothing about religion, and this silence occasioned one of the contentious episodes in Galileo's dialogue. The interlocutors are being lured into an argument that would join mechanics and God. Sagredo (one of Galileo's Venetian friends from his days at Padua) had introduced the geometrical generation of a circle either from the center on a horizontal plane or from the top of a sphere, i.e., out of a uniform motion or from a uniformly accelerated motion. Simplicio (an interlocutor, named after a commentator of Aristotle) is quite taken by the demonstration and attempts to raise the dialogue to a higher subject. This geometrical wonder, he suggests, "leads one to think that there may be some great mystery hidden in these true and wonderful results, a mystery related to the creation of the universe (which is said to be spherical in shape), and related also to the seat of the first cause." But Salviati (another former pupil from Padua, and the one who represents Galileo in the dialogues) will have none of this enthusiasm, whatever its influences from the *Timaeus*.[22] Mechanics is not the place for theology. He dismisses the suggestion: "Profound considerations of this kind belong to higher sciences or doctrines than ours [*a più alte dottrine che le nostre*]. . . . Now if you please, let us proceed."[23] Proceed away from theology, they did! Posthaste! Salviati is not denying a *theologia naturalis*, even one that can take mechanics for its evidence. But he is insisting that mechanics is not universal, that it does not encompass among its competencies either natural theology or religious interests, that there is a fundamental and irreducible distinction among the sciences. That conviction had allowed Galileo earlier to write to the Grand Duchess Christina that Copernicus – and hence, Galileo – "never treats matters pertaining to religion and faith," that "he always limits himself to physical conclusions based above all on sensory experience and very accurate observations."[24]

This is the second reflexive limitation of mechanics in the "Third Day." Earlier both Sagredo and Simplicio had introduced a question about agency, that is, about the physical causes of the acceleration of free falling bodies, only to have Salviati respond that such an investigation of the causes of the acceleration of natural motion does not find a place in this work.[25] The kinematics formulated by Galileo is "merely to investigate and to demonstrate some of the properties of accelerated motion (whatever the cause [*la causa*] of this acceleration may be). . . ."[26] This means that Galileo's mechanics will remain kinematics rather than dynamics, a science that attempts to describe mathematically its subject matter, locomotion, rather than to locate and identify its physical causes.[27] In the "First Day," Galileo had insisted that mechanics cannot be reduced to geometry; now he is insisting that mechanics cannot ascend to theology or, as a matter of fact, even to such efficient physical causes as Simplicio and Sagredo would have introduced. On two additional occasions, Salviati dismisses such causes as the "fantasies" of the natural philosophers.[28] But Isaac Newton will give a very different response to these initiatives.

For if the method of Galileo is operational, the principles that ground the method – the definitions – are reflexive, i.e., they are mathematically self-contained and internally interdependent. These principles differ from science to science and consequently mark off one science from another. Mechanics must not become theology. In the science of local motion, motion becomes velocity and velocity is in terms of distance and time (definition); and time is in terms of velocity and distance; and distance is in terms of velocity and time.

The definitions form a reflexive complex – each of the units is in terms of the others – from which the kinematics of the "Third Day" can be deduced and confirmed. That same reflexivity can be found among all of the sciences: they are self-contained. One does not dialectically merge with another. That is why there are "Two New Sciences" in Galileo's greatest work, not one. *The Two New Sciences* insists that these sciences must be distinguished one from the other by their subject matters and principles and that their differences will be registered in their various particularizations of an operational method.

This does not mean, however, that God or religion is absent from the Galilean dialogues on physics and especially astronomy. The heavens are prized as "the creation of the omnipotent Craftsman" and the highest object of philosophy lies in its "turning over the great book of nature."[29] References to God, as indeed references to a personified nature, abound in the great *Dialogue Concerning the Two Chief World Systems*. Further, and in great contrast with his mechanics, Galileo's astronomy makes, as Ernan McMullin noted, "extensive and creative use of causal explanation in cosmology."[30] McMullin employs a term from Charles S. Peirce, "retroduction," for these hypothetico-deductive inferences, when the hypothesis introduces a cause that is then given warrant by the proposition drawn from it.[31]

At the end of the *Dialogue Concerning Two World Systems*, Galileo submitted in the summary of Sagredo three physical phenomena or effects whose causal analysis, he maintained, was "very convincing" in favor of the heliocentric or Copernican system of the world: "those taken from the stopping and retrograde motions of the planets, and their approaches toward and recessions from the earth; second, from the revolution of the sun upon itself, and from what is to be observed in the sunspots; and third, from the ebbing and flowing of the ocean tides." To these Salviati adds the possibilities of the stellar parallax and the change in the meridian line. But even though this dialogue does attempt to locate the physical causes of these phenomena in a heliocentric structure of the universe, the divine never enters into the intrinsic structure of even astronomical argumentation.[32] God and nature, of course, formed part of the atmosphere of the European Christian intellect, and they so staffed Galileo's conversations. But the work of astronomy proceeds with its own autonomy and methodology, making incursions into theology or religion only to counter arguments against astronomical theories taken from sacred scripture.[33]

This basic distinction among the sciences and of the sciences in general from religion tells also in their language. The doctrine of accommodation, found normatively in Augustine's *De Genesi ad literam*, allowed Galileo to distinguish the grammar of religion or of scripture from that which bears upon "physical conclusions." Galileo cites as support the maxim of the contemporary historian Cardinal Baronius, contrasting the purposes of religion and science: ". . . ciò è l'intenzione dello Spirito Santo essere d'insegnarci come si vadia al cielo, et non come vadia il cielo" [The intention of the Holy Spirit is to teach us how one goes to heaven [salvation], and not how the heavens go].[34] Since Augustine, the tradition had held that the language of scripture is adapted to the preconceptions and understanding of the culture in which it was written. Its grammar does not bear upon the issues of astronomical inquiry. The failure of Galileo's theological critics lies in substituting scripture for the components of scientific inquiry, i.e., observation and mathematical definition and demonstrations: "They want to extend, not to say abuse, its [scripture's] authority, so that for even purely physical conclusions which are not matters of faith one must totally abandon the senses and demonstrative arguments in favor of any scriptural passage whose apparent words may contain a different indication."[35]

Out of scripture comes the content of faith – what Galileo called "supernatural propositions." Out of science emerge what Galileo repeatedly designated "physical conclusions."[36] No contradiction is finally possible between these two because "two truths cannot contradict each other."[37] God is the author of nature as well as of scripture, but only confusion can come from the subsuming of the grammar of one by the other, by having science make statements about faith or worship and scripture make statements about the hidden structures of nature.[38]

Do science and theology interact at all for Galileo? It is crucial here to understand one conviction of Galileo: Science entails both purely physical propositions and necessary demonstrations or deductions – neither of which belongs among the articles of faith. Without these, there is no science. Epistemologically, it is not possible for a human being to deny such necessary deductions or careful sensible observations. These, then, must be distinguished from probable opinions and likely conjectures, hypotheses that neither reach the character of science nor demand the accommodation of scripture.[39] That is why Galileo was so insistent – in contrast with Andreas Osiander's Preface to *De revolutione orbium* – that the heliocentric universe was not simply a useful hypothesis but a physical fact with physical demonstrations.

Paradoxically, this demand for the certainty of physical or apodictic demonstrations may well have led both to the exaggerated claims of Galileo for the tides and sunspots as apodictic evidence for the heliocentric universe and to the unconscionable rigidity of the Roman theologians and authorities. Galileo to his death contended that science as certain knowledge and demonstrative method does not contradict religion – however wretched the actual history of his later life. Nor are they simply indifferent to each other. Both make knowledge claims. Both deal with truth about the real. If one finds any contradiction between a statement of scripture and an observation or apodictic demonstration, Augustine, Jerome, and such a contemporary Roman theologian as Benedictus Pererius are cited by Galileo to maintain that in such a case the scriptures have not been correctly interpreted, that accommodation of language is at work, and that no one should impose an interpretation of scripture as if it were a proposition of faith in contradiction to sensory experience or necessary demonstrations.[40] In no way are science and religion at war, but science – like any knowledge that is certain – does deliver a negative norm for the interpretation of the propositions of scripture regarding nature. If scripture is read to contradict science or any certain knowledge, then it has been misread – a common enough conviction of theologians for centuries.

For Galileo, then, religion and science differ in subject matter, purposes, appropriate methods or procedures, and language. If these differences are maintained, each can contribute to the general advance of human beings towards real knowledge.

One last note is necessary to muddy these distinctions that seem so reasonable and suspiciously exhaustive. As remarked, Galileo demanded of science necessary demonstrations. With only probable opinions and conjectures or likely hypotheses, there was no science properly so called. This conviction grounds his enormous resistance to the understanding of the heliocentric system as a mathematical hypothesis, useful for predictions. The Preface of Osiander had introduced such a reading into Copernicus, and led Bellarmine to his understanding of Copernicus, as indicated in his celebrated letter to Antonio Foscarini.[41] The irony is enormous. Bellarmine was correct in insisting that Galileo did not have a physical demonstration for the heliocentric universe or the diurnal motion of the earth; no one did until later centuries. Tides and sunspots just don't do it. But Galileo was correct in insisting that the expressions of scripture were not to be taken as normative pronouncements about the physical structure of nature, but were pervasively accommodated to the grammar and culture of the time – as human beings have no problem saying for all their Copernican convictions that the sun rose at 6:00 this morning. Galileo's relationship with Bellarmine is almost chiastic in its irony: "[Bellarmine] had failed, as a theologian, to grasp as fully as he should have, the consequences of the exegetical principle he was employing.

However, Galileo likewise failed, as a scientist, to grasp what was called for in the way of proof in the context of cosmology or to appreciate the epistemic value of probable reasoning."[42]

But Galileo's *Letter to the Grand Duchess* contained an unresolved tension, as Ernan McMullin has recently pointed out.[43] For Galileo, science as such demanded necessary demonstrations; probabilities were only opinions. What if one couldn't get necessary demonstrations? What if one had only probabilities and useful conjectures? Not enough. Science to be science demanded two components: physical (as opposed to supernatural) propositions and necessary (as opposed to hypothetical) demonstration. If Galileo had stayed with his division and foci of the sciences and his contention that physical conclusions as such are not the concern of revelation, then neither demonstration nor conjecture in the physical sciences would be affected by theological statements. But he did not. He entered into the world of scriptural hermeneutics. So convinced was he of the requirements of science for physical propositions and necessary knowledge that he wrote to Christiana of Lorraine: "Some physical propositions are of a type such that by any human speculation and reasoning one can only attain a probable opinion and a verisimilar [likely] conjecture about them, rather than a certain and demonstrated science; an example is whether the stars are animate. . . . As for the first type, I have no doubt at all that, where human reason cannot reach, and where consequently one cannot have a science, but only opinion and faith, *it is appropriate piously to conform absolutely to the literal meaning of scripture*."[44] I doubt that many scientists or theologians would agree with that judgment today, but Bellarmine and the Congregation of the Index would have concurred, and they did act on some such persuasion, and what ensued was scandal and tragedy.

Johannes Kepler (1571–1630)

Subject-matter, purpose, method, and language can also serve as coordinates to locate the achievement of Johannes Kepler, but they specify a radically different settlement between science and religion. If Galileo had his reflexive principles – and in this, he bore some resemblance to Aristotle – that allowed for distinct kinds of knowledge and sciences according to diverse subject matters, problems, and grammars, Kepler has his Neoplatonic assimilation of all the sciences into a single organic – sometimes seemingly chaotic – whole and a heuristic, even deductive, theological methodology that stands in striking contrast with that of Galileo. Gerald Holton maintains that part of the reason that Kepler has been "strangely neglected and misunderstood" lies "in the apparent confusion of incongruous elements – physics and metaphysics, astronomy and astrology, geometry and theology."[45] One could recognize, however, that this "confusion" of the disciplines always results when one confronts a Platonic, dialectical assimilation with the fixed Aristotelian-like distinctions among the sciences.

Kepler's first work, the *Mysterium cosmographicum*, was annotated and revised over the course of his life, weaving a continuity throughout his scientific project in a manner analogous to the relationship between Galileo's early work *De motu locali* and his *Two New Sciences*. It is in the *Mysterium cosmographicum*, stated I. Bernard Cohen, that "Kepler sets forth a goal, method, and program, which he was to follow successfully throughout the rest of his astronomical career."[46] This seminal, paradigmatic book sets in stark relief the vast differences between Kepler's methodology and that of Galileo. And yet, the *Mysterium cosmographicum* was the first public effort to justify the new astronomical system of Nicholas Copernicus.[47] How did he do it? Theologically.

If Copernicus was right, then the earth moved and was itself another planet, while neither the sun nor the moon could qualify. That meant there would be six rather than seven planets. Was Copernicus right – were there six and only six planets?[48] Yes, there had to be six; there could only be six: Mercury, Venus, earth, Mars, Jupiter, and Saturn, all of which orbit the sun, while the Ptolemaic structure had provided for seven circling the earth, adding the sun and the moon to be among them.[49] But there could be only six: Why? Because of the nature of God! Kepler actually deduces Copernicus's number of planets from the perfection of God. This astonishing feat by one of the geniuses of the scientific revolution deserves scrutiny.

As in Plato's *Timaeus*, so for Kepler, the most perfect God could only create a most beautiful world.[50] How do you determine what is most beautiful in nature? By mathematics. For Kepler had also inherited from the Platonic tradition, especially as influenced by Speusippus and Xenocrates of Chalcedon, its deep reverence for the mathematical truth of material things, its conviction that the final meaning of matter and even of the intelligible forms or formulas is found in mathematics.[51] Mathematics is the inner intelligibility of what is. Kepler frames that tradition within a theological context: "What is there except to say with Plato that God always geometrizes?"[52]

The signature of God is geometry. Thus, the answer to the question about the number of planets must be figure. Six planets (counting the earth) present five interstices or five intervals between their orbits. Correspondingly, Euclid has established that remarkably there are only five perfect geometric solids –

solids that are perfectly symmetrical: the cube, the pyramid, the dodecahedron (12 surfaces), the icosahedron (20 surfaces) and the octahedron (8 surfaces). The Scholium that follows the Eighteenth Proposition in the Thirteenth Book of Euclid's *Elements* had demonstrated that "no other figure, besides the said five figures, can be constructed which is contained by equilateral and equiangular figures equal to one another."[53] Five intervals between the planets; five perfect solids circumscribed by the six orbits of the planets. For each of these perfect geometrical figures has been placed by the Creator within the orbit of one of the six planets. This explains the distance of the planets. "If the five solids are fitted one inside another, with spheres between them and inclosing them, we shall have a total of six spheres" – the exact number of the planets![54]

Hence Kepler's syllogistic defense of Copernicus's heliocentric universe follows: Only that astronomer who formulated the universe as six spheres moving around a motionless sun spoke commensurate with the perfection of the Creator. "But Copernicus has six spheres of that sort. . . . So we must concur with him, until someone has either put forward hypotheses which give a better solution to these problems, or asserted that a system which has *been deduced by excellent reasoning from the very principles of Nature* can creep accidentally into the numbers and into the mind of Man."[55] Kepler saw Copernicus coming upon the brute fact of the arrangement of the universe; he saw himself as giving a reason for that fact. What Copernicus had come upon by observation and argument *a posteriori* "like a blind man leaning on a stick as he walks . . . all that, I say, is discovered to be quite correctly established by reasoning derived *a priori*, from the causes, from the idea of the Creation."[56] Copernicus had given the fact; Kepler with the aid of theology would give the reasoned fact. Kepler had promised to demonstrate by a new procedure or evidence (*nouo argumento*) the truth of the Copernican hypotheses.[57] By bringing the theological into the astronomical, Kepler has given to the simple facts of Copernicus an *a priori* appropriateness that unifies the cosmos. It not only happens to exist that way, it is necessary, with a necessity of appropriateness (*convenientia*), that it exists in that way.

So far, so religious – at least Platonically religious. But Kepler saw the fullest religious disclosures embodied in the dogmas that were peculiarly Christian. His unity between Christian doctrine and science can take as presupposed also for astronomy the Christian dogma that God is love. All explanation would finally lead back to this as a comprehensive methodological axiom: "From love of God for the human being, many of the causes of things in the world are able to be deduced" [*Ex amore Dei in hominem causas rerum in mundo plurimas deduci posse*].[58] The sun became the image of that love. Thus Kepler could argue deductively to the location of the earth within the solar system from the nature of the human being as the image of God as stated in Genesis:

> The purpose [*finis*] both of the universe and of the whole creation is the Human Being. Therefore in my opinion it was deemed by God fitting [*dignam*] for the Earth, which was to provide and nourish a true image of the Creator, to go round in the midst of the planets in such a way that it would have the same number of them [planets] within the embrace of its orbit as outside it. To achieve that, God added the Sun and the other five stars [i.e. planets], although it was totally different in kind. And that seems all the more appropriate [*magis consonum*] because, the Sun above being the image of God the Father, we may believe that by this association with the other stars it was bound to provide evidence for the future tenant of the loving kindness and sympathy which God was to practice towards human beings.[59]

But it was the doctrine of the Trinity that lent wings to Kepler and imparted the confidence that Copernicus had correctly framed the structure of the universe. The Trinity provided the "form and archetype" of the three great stationary realities: the sun, the fixed stars, and the intermediate space. "There were three things in particular about which I persistently sought the reasons why they were such and not otherwise: the number, the size, and the motion of the circles. That I dared so much was due to the splendid harmony of those things which are at rest, the Sun, the fixed stars, and the intermediate space, with God the Father, and the Son, and the Holy Spirit."[60] Here, in the *Mysterium cosmographicum*, he promised to pursue this "splendid harmony" at greater length.[61] At the heart of his astronomy the solar system is homologized to and justified by the Trinity, and thus can explain planetary movement by the force proceeding from the sun. Indeed, because of the revelation of the Trinity, one should have antecedently expected a solar system like that of Copernicus:

> The sun in the middle of the moving stars, itself at rest and yet the source of motion, bears the image of God, the Father and Creator. For what corresponds to creation by God is for the sun to be a source of motion. The sun is the source of movement, however, among the fixed stars, as the Father creates in the Son. For unless the fixed stars provide place [*locum*] by their motionlessness, nothing would be able to be moved. (Even up to today, I hold this axiom of Tübingen.) The sun disperses its power of movement through a medium which contains the moving bodies even as the Father creates through the Spirit or by the power of his Spirit.[62]

Kepler commented about this methodological subsumption of astronomy and mathematics into theology: "You see how near I come to truth. As often as this happens, how can you doubt that I amply shed tears! For God knows, this *a priori* method serves to improve the study of the movements of the celestial bodies; we can put all our hopes into it if others cooperate who have observations at their disposal. . . . I strive to publish them in God's honor who wishes to be recognized from the book of nature."[63]

But Kepler also recognized that these *a priori* arguments from the nature of God yielded conclusions that are in themselves only probable/likely (εἰκότα). It is necessary to do further concrete measurements and mathematical demonstrations before these conclusions can be affirmed with certitude, i.e., it was necessary to "pass to the distances [ἀποστήματα] between the astronomical spheres and the geometric demonstrations."[64] But one should bear in mind two things. First, Kepler is addressing an issue about origination, i.e., he is questioning why something came to be in the way that it did and is. As such, this was the study of becoming, and εἰκότα (likely) was all that Plato also would concede to the stories of becoming, even of cosmogenesis in the *Timaeus*.[65] When one moves beyond becoming to that which is intrinsically stable like mathematics, both Plato and Kepler will claim that certainty is possible. Second, one must also notice the function of observation and actual measurement: they are to confirm the suggestions of theology and a more abstract geometry, for "if they do not agree [*consentiant*], the whole of the preceding work has undoubtedly been a delusion."[66]

Paradoxically, this allowed Kepler to reform doctrine that for centuries had been considered almost sacred. For example: despite some two thousand years of insistence that the orbits of the planets were circular because the circle is a perfect figure – a conviction that enlisted his contemporaries, even the great Galileo – Kepler determined that their path actually described an ellipse. Further, Kepler's great difference from Galileo was not that probabilities were introduced into astronomy or that one began with intellectual structures that needed confirmation, but that these probabilities can be deduced theologically *a Conditore perfectissimo* or *ex amore Dei* and that one looks to astronomical inquiry both to suggest and then to confirm these hypothetical probabilities. To accomplish this transition from theology to astronomy – or better, to respect this unity between theology and astronomy – Kepler transposed into astronomy the classic argument *ex convenientia* from medieval theology. But now this appropriateness was concentrated in geometry. "Geometry, existing before the birth of things, is co-eternal with the divine mind, *is God himself* [*Geometria ante rerum ortum Menti divinae coaeterna, Deus ipse*] (for what is there in God that is not God himself?); geometry provided God with models [*exempla*] for the creation of the world and passed over into human beings together with the likeness [*imaginem*] of God – geometry was not merely conveyed to his mind through the eyes."[67] Kepler argued to this identification of geometry with the nature of God from the divine simplicity, i.e., what exists in God is God. Geometry now takes the place of what for Aquinas were the divine ideas, the creative model according to which God forms and brings into being finite reality. The study of geometry, then, and all of those things whose truth is geometrical, is finally the study of God.

> God wanted us to recognize them by creating us after his own image so that we could share in his own thoughts. For what is there in the human mind besides figures and magnitudes? It is only these which we can apprehend in the right way, and if piety allows us to say so, our understanding is in this respect of the same kind as the divine, at least as far as we are able to grasp something of it in our mortal life.[68]

So the *a priori* movement of the mind of the astronomer is from God to the perfect quantities, from the perfect quantities to high probabilities about the universe, from these probabilities to confirmation through astronomical observation and geometrical demonstration. And this line of development closes in on itself. This *exitus* returns to its source, to God, through the *reditus* of observation and demonstration. There is a pluralism of the disciplines in Kepler, of course, but it is not a fixed differentiation as in Galileo. Each is a moment in the gradual development of knowledge, a moment that yields organically to another in a single progression towards a cognitive fullness. It is this obvious organic movement that Kepler expected from science – here, from abstract geometry to mechanics – a continual movement until one returned to God.

The procedure of astronomy remarkably mirrors in so many ways the stages of divine creation. As Kepler explained in his dedication of *Astronomiae pars optica* to the Holy Roman Emperor Rudolph II: "Neither have I given myself to the speculations of abstract geometry, that is, to pictures καὶ τῶν ὄντων καὶ μὴ ὄντων [of beings and non-beings]. In our day, the most illustrious geometers spend their time on such speculations almost alone; but I have explored geometry through the very formed bodies of the world [*sed Geometriam per ipsa expressa Mundi corpora*], having followed with sweat and panting the footprints [*vestigia*] of the Creator."[69]

This did not mean that Kepler would collapse the distinction between the language of scripture and the grammar of astronomy.[70] As for Galileo, so for

Kepler this issue was raised by the Copernican *De revolutionibus orbium* and resolved by the different methods of these sciences and by the variously accommodated forms of speech. But even here, Kepler's settlement begins with God. God has a tongue and God has a creative finger. "And who would deny that the tongue of God is adjusted both to his intention, and, on that account, to the common tongue of men? Therefore in matters which are quite plain, everyone with strong religious scruples will take the greatest care not to twist the tongue of God so that it refutes the finger of God in Nature."[71] It is not, as with Galileo, that the language of theology is simply distinct from the language of science. It is rather that scripture is only one of the theological languages. Geometry is another. And the knowledge of either bears essentially upon the study of God.

Before one dismisses Kepler's extraordinary writings as theological or scientific fiction, it should be recalled that out of this dialectical integrity of the disciplines came, as Koestler has lined them up, the first articulate and public defense by a "professional astronomer" of Copernicus's heliocentric universe;[72] the "founding" of two new sciences: instrumental optics and physical astronomy;[73] the first accurate explanation of the tides as a "motion of the waters 'towards the regions where the moon stands in the zenith;' "[74] and, above all, the three laws of planetary motion that made possible Newton's "System of the World."[75] These last were the "first 'natural laws' in the modern sense: precise, verifiable statements about universal relations governing particular phenomena, expressed in mathematical terms."[76] It is the judgment of the immensely learned John Heilbron that Kepler was "the greatest mathematical astronomer the world had yet produced."[77]

What might make us pause even more reverentially before Kepler's theological *a priori* is the transposed but emphatic place it sometimes plays in modern science. Paradoxically, Kepler's theological *a priori* has appeared – so radically altered in its reincarnation – as Einstein's impersonal God, the intelligible, determined immanent order of what exists, "the Old One who does not play dice with the universe." Does something like Kepler's theological *a priori* not tell – in a very different way – in Einstein's rejection of the Copenhagen interpretation of quantum mechanics as "not the real thing," his famous debate with Niels Bohr at the Fifth Solvay Congress in Brussels in 1927, the famous "EPR Paper," and so on? His judgment was given in a letter to Max Born in 1926 and repeated again and again in his lifetime: that quantum mechanics was "certainly imposing. But an inner voice tells me that it is not yet the real thing. The theory says a lot, but does not really bring us any closer to the secret of the Old One. I, at any rate, am convinced that He does not throw dice."[78]

This appeal to the divine at least as metaphor – whatever that might mean for Einstein – to justify a fundamental and undeniable character of the universe disconcerted his colleagues and significantly colored the regard in which he was held in the scientific world. Heisenberg, with the uncertainty principle fresh under his academic belt, records the discomfort in a group that included Wolfgang Pauli, Paul Dirac, and himself:

> One of us said: "Einstein keeps talking about God: what are we to make of that? It is extremely difficult to imagine that a scientist like Einstein should have such strong ties with a religious tradition."

"Not so much Einstein as Max Planck," someone objected. "From some of Planck's utterances it would seem that he sees no contradiction between religion and science, indeed that he believes the two are perfectly compatible."

Heisenberg was asked about Planck's opinion and responded that for Planck the two are compatible because science and religion

> refer to quite distinct facets of reality. Science deals with the objective material world. It invites us to make accurate statements about objective reality and to grasp its interconnections. Religion, on the other hand, deals with the world of values. It considers what ought to be or what we ought to do, not what is. In science we are concerned to discover what is true or false; in religion with what is good or evil, noble or base. Science is the basis of technology, religion the basis of ethics. In short, the conflict between the two, which has been raging since the eighteenth century, seems founded on a misunderstanding, or, more precisely, on a confusion of the images and parables of religion with scientific statement.[79]

Heisenberg is transposing Galileo's distinction between physical and super-natural propositions into a diremption between two kinds of knowledge: physical and ethical, factual and evaluative. In contrast, Einstein's *a priori* refusal of the uncertainty principle of Heisenberg, as articulated in the Copenhagen interpretation of quantum mechanics, as not finally and ontologically valid of the sub-atomic, resembles a Keplerian appeal to a "divine order" to decide what is fundamental to the basic elements of matter. "For God does not play at dice."[80] One wonders if the theological *a priori* has not also functioned in an equally curious way as negatively important in science. The astronomer Fred Hoyle is said to have rejected the "big bang" hypothesis because it would suggest the possibility of a creator.[81] The twentieth century also, it seems, has witnessed scientific reflections in which a primacy attributed to what is divine or ultimate has affected significantly what is scientifically acceptable.

Isaac Newton (1642–1727)

Galileo framed sciences intrinsically isolated from the doctrine of God. Kepler framed a science that rationalized, even demonstrated, astronomy within the Christian doctrine of God, integrating both astronomy and theology into a single vision centered on the Trinity and arguing deductively from the triune nature of God to the previously elaborated structure of the universe. Isaac Newton framed a science that was universal in its compass and which argued to the divine reality from the nature of the world and then argued from the divine reality to ground the fundamental coordinates of the mechanical universe. In contrast to Galileo, Newton explicitly affirmed that mechanics was universal and that it gave a foundation to both mathematics and religious belief.

Newton corrected a tradition stemming from the Alexandrian mechanists. To establish the dyadic character of mechanics, they had distinguished rational from practical mechanics. The first, which proceeded by perfect accuracy, came to be called "geometry." The second, which could not lay claim to this accuracy, they called "mechanics."[82] But this division is fundamentally false, judged Newton, and for two reasons: accuracy or inaccuracy has to do with the artificer, not the method or the subject matter; but more importantly, the foundations of geometry lie in mechanical practice. In sharp contrast with Kepler and with most of the mechanical tradition, Newton maintained that geometry does not ground mechanics; mechanics grounds and includes geometry. At the very beginning of the *Principia*, one confronts these startling and critically important convictions in the "Preface to the First Edition":

> The description of right lines and circles, upon which geometry is founded, belongs to mechanics. Geometry does not teach us to draw these lines, but requires them to be drawn, for it requires that the learner should first be taught to describe these accurately before he enters upon geometry, then it shows how by these operations problems may be solved. To describe right lines and circles are problems, but not geometrical problems. The solution of these problems is required from mechanics. . . . Therefore geometry is founded in mechanical practice and is nothing but that *part of universal mechanics* which accurately proposes and demonstrates the art of measuring.[83]

The *Principia*, then, radically recasts the relationship between geometry and mechanics. For one should note Newton's expression: "universal mechanics." Geometry is only a part. Then what subject matter does universal mechanics explore? In this Newton does agree with the Alexandrians: all the phenomena of Nature. And why does he think that mechanics can explain all of nature? "For I am induced by many reasons to suspect that they all depend upon certain forces."[84] The heuristic principle enabling an examination of all of nature and its movements is finally a dynamic one: force. Force was for Newton a comprehensive principle; everything was finally to be reduced to force. Inertial force (*vis inertiae*) is the power of resisting change, and differs only conceptually from mass itself, i.e., the quantity of matter; impressed force, especially as motive force (*vis motrix*), is the power of effecting change.[85] Thus the entire project of the universal mechanics can be described in these terms: "The whole burden [*difficultas*] of philosophy seems to consist in this – from the phenomena of motions to investigate the forces of nature, and then from these forces to demonstrate the other phenomena."[86] These two methodological movements are analysis and synthesis; this method and this understanding of mechanics as universal allowed Newton the possibility of extending mechanics into theology.[87]

For "force" develops conceptually as the *Principia* proceeds. In the definitions, impressed force leads to motive force, and in the first two books impressed force becomes motive force to account for the acceleration or change in any motions occurring in and out of a resisting medium. In Book III, however, in the "System of the World" – the solar system – motive force becomes particularized as gravity, impressed upon all of the planets. Gravity counters the inertial tangential movements of the planets so they do not fly off into space. Gravity balances out the planets into the elliptical orbits around the sun as had been geometrically determined by Kepler. Gravity gives us the continuities that constitute the universe as a system.

Then in the "General Scholium," at the end of the Third Book, Newton pushes the analytic reduction of this great system of planetary motions back to its originating force. Gravity was not enough to explain how the system came to be: "Though these bodies may, indeed, continue in their orbits by the mere laws of gravity, yet they could by no means have at first derived the regular position of the orbits by themselves from those laws."[88] The universe is a system, a unity composed of the sun, planets, and comets whose masses and motions are proportioned so carefully that they "could only proceed from the counsel and dominion of an intelligent and powerful Being." Mechanics, if it is to be faithful to its reduction of movement back to force, must go beyond mechanical causes – and here Newton is again in contradiction to much in the mechanical tradition, especially to Descartes. And his reason: it would be impossible for such a system to take its origin "ex causis mechanicis."[89] "This most beautiful system of the sun, planets, and comets could only proceed from the counsel and dominion of an intelligent and powerful Being."[90] Many, like Edward Strong, have scored Newton for the advance of his mechanics into theology, but for him it was simply a matter of methodological consistency, i.e., the consistent reduction of motions back to their originating forces even when that final force is not mechanical.[91]

God is also named from the mechanics that has furnished the warrant for his existence and attributes. The system of the world leads to the Παντοκράτωρ. He is called God not because of his eternality or infinitude or even perfection, but because of his *dominium*. This vital insight of Newton integrates theology and mechanics: what makes God to be God is his domination. Force has now become no longer simply gravity as in the Third Book, but is, in its highest instantiation, divine domination. So theology itself can be brought within the central concept of universal mechanics, impressed force. "Deity is the domination of God [*Deitas est dominatio dei*]." To see what point Newton is making, one might contrast his position with that of Duns Scotus. Scotus had made the divine infinity the formality of deity; the unique and highest concept of God was that of "infinite being." Newton, in fulfillment of the dynamism of the mechanical tradition, had made *dominatio* or *dominium* the formality of God. As forces are related to mass-objects, so "God is a relative word, and has a respect to servants. . . . It is the dominion of a spiritual being that constitutes a God [*Dominatio entis spiritualis deum constituit*]."[92] *Dominium* or *dominatio* is the final analytic moment in the *Principia*, and it serves as the source of the human knowledge of the further attributes of God: living, intelligent, powerful, supreme, most perfect. Even that attribute which Descartes had made pivotal to the divine reality, its perfection – *ens perfectissimum* – Newton derives from the divine *dominatio*.

As remarked, Newton's method consists of two movements: Analysis and Synthesis. To reduce the system of the universe to its originating dominion is analysis. But God is not only necessary for the comprehensive analysis fielded by the *Principia*; God is necessary synthetically. For from the very beginning of the *Principia* – in order to distinguish true motion from apparent motion – Newton had argued to and insisted upon absolute space and absolute time and distinguished them from their sensible measures. From the everlasting dominion of God, he can now ground true space and true time (duration) as consequences of the divine reality. For God, by existing always and everywhere, constitutes absolute space and absolute time or duration.[93] God, then, functions within the universal mechanics of Newton in two ways: as the terminus of the analytic resolution of movement back to original forces; then, as the source or force whose existence constitutes synthetically the fundamental coordinates of all nature, i.e., space and time. The divine *dominium* or *dominatio* also allows two additional causal principles to be operative within the world, principles the *Principia* could not have asserted up to this theological moment: providence and final causes – as opposed to fate and nature.[94]

It is remarkable to find at the end of this great work on the phenomena of nature the assertion that nature is not enough to explain nature. To talk about nature consistently and coherently, one must also talk about God, not only in his causal interventions but in his attributes. Such a theology is part of universal mechanics: "Thus much concerning God," as Newton wrote, bringing the theological section of the "General Scholium" to its completion, "to discourse of whom from the appearances of things, does certainly belong to Natural Philosophy."[95] Newton explicitly, publicly, and repeatedly asserted that this progression was the "main business" of his mechanics: "The main Business of natural Philosophy is to argue from Phaenomena without feigning Hypotheses, and to deduce Causes from Effects, till we come to the very first Cause, which certainly is not mechanical; and not only to unfold the Mechanism of the World, but chiefly to resolve these and such like Questions."[96]

The unity between the sciences and mathematics and between these and theology or religion does not reduce revelation to philosophy, but it does allow a unity between them as universal mechanics gives a foundation for an assertion of the God of revelation. As Newton wrote to Richard Bentley – the formidable discoverer of the lost digamma and first of the Boyle Lecturers: "When I wrote my treatise about our Systeme I had an eye upon such Principles as might work wth considering men for the beleife of a Deity and nothing can rejoyce me more then to find it usefull for that purpose."[97]

These distinctions within the foundational unity of mechanics and theology also tell upon the language of both. Human beings do not know the real substance of things, but perceive only their figures, colors, sounds, outward surfaces, and so on. So also they do not know the substance of God, but only the system of the world that reveals his power, his wisdom, and purposes. But just as human beings come to form ideas through what can be perceived, so *per allegoriam* can they speak about the actions of God from what can be perceived in the actions of human beings – an imperfect but valid similitude.[98] The language about God is adapted, as in Galileo and Kepler, to the human possibilities.

But Newtonian natural philosophy can go even farther than this. It can establish what Newton called "fundamental religion."[99] Universal mechanics can ground assertions not only of the divine reality and attributes, but of human morality and its duties, what Newton would call Godliness and Humanity: "For so far as we can know by natural Philosophy what is the first Cause, what Power he has over us, and what Benefits we receive from him, so far our Duty towards him, as well as that towards one another, will appear to us by the Light of Nature."[100] This "fundamental religion" prior to all revelation "consists of two parts, our duty towards God and our duty towards man, or piety and righteousness, which I will here call Godliness and Humanity."[101] Following rigorously the methodology of the universal mechanics, one is led not only to theology, but to a way of life that could also be termed a spirituality, and yet a spirituality of natural or "fundamental religion."

Like the other two settlements, those of Galileo and Kepler, Newtonian universal mechanics has also found new life in the scientific traditions that have emerged from its inspiration. Paradoxically, the cast of thought it represents emerges as the most truculent: science – rather than mechanics – now becomes universal. Science can be popularly and naively supposed to be one in its methods or structures and to constitute the only valid or the most fundamental and comprehensive form of knowledge. Under such a persuasion, it sometimes subsumes the function of religion, at other times it provides the foundations for religion, and still at other times religion is excluded as illusion or myth. Sigmund Freud, John Dewey, and Paul Dirac all furnish examples of this exclusion. Paul Dirac, showing obvious influences of both Marx and Freud, gives no quarter to any understanding that would validate religion as knowledge: "If we are honest – and scientists have to be – we must admit that religion is a jumble of false assertions, with no basis in reality. The very idea of God is a product of the human imagination."[102] Science is universally competent to handle human questions; religion is universally fraudulent.

It is not a great step to move from a universal mechanics to the hegemony of science. In such a reading of the emergence of science, religion forms an outdated stage in the movement towards the omnicompetence of science. Carl Sagan engagingly represented this conviction on popular TV and in his paperbacks, and it shapes the hermeneutic of the history of science advanced not infrequently in the American media. It enlisted such seminal thinkers as the microbiologist Jacques Monod in *Chance and Necessity* and the sociobiologist Edmund O. Wilson, the latter writing that "the power of religion will be gone forever when religion is explained a product of evolution; it will be replaced by a philosophy of 'scientific materialism.'"[103]

On the other hand, it was in *Science and the Modern World* that Alfred North Whitehead wrote of the evidence for God: "Nothing, within any limited type of experience, can give intelligence to shape our ideas of any entity at the base of all actual things, unless the general character of things requires that there be such an entity."[104] Steven L. Bernasek, Professor of Chemistry at Princeton University, maintained that the existence of God "is apparent to me in everything around me, especially in my work as a scientist." The distinguished novelist and critic Dan Wakefield noted in the *New York Times* that science is "one of the major factors making the idea of God a serious subject again." He cited with approval the judgment of physics professor Chet Raymo that "scientists are wresting from philosophers and theologians the biggest question of all: why is there something rather than nothing."[105] The physicist Paul Davies, in *God and the New Physics*, gives the summary claim for science taking over the function of religion: "It may seem bizarre, but in my opinion, science offers a surer path to God than religion."[106] The God that emerges in Davies's study is impersonal. This allows for statements to be made about the divine, but not for the interpersonal engagements of Christianity.

For all of the variations, there is sympathy extending back in a very meandering way from such contemporary convictions to the universal mechanics of Isaac Newton.

A final word

At the dawning of modernity, then, one comes upon three distinct settlements negotiated between the new knowledge and the ancient faith: in Galileo, they are separate enterprises, neither contradicting the other and neither having a place within the other. Where certainty is found, the one will correct the other as is the case with any knowledge. In Kepler, they are finally a single enterprise, a deduction of what is likely and appropriate within the universe from the triune nature of God and the suggestion or the confirmation of that deduction from observation and mathematics. In Newton's universal mechanics, science gives to religion crucially important evidence, its methodology, and its foundation in fundamental religion.

The significance of Galileo, Kepler, and Newton is not that their universe was better organized and more automatic than Ptolemy's. The crucial thing lay in their influence on modernity. Mechanics supplanted what had classically been called "physics." Aristotle had implicitly ruled out a mathematical physics in the Second Book of the *Physics* because the necessity it embodied was quite contrary to the necessity found in nature. Necessity was one of the characteristics of any authentic science, and inquiry became scientific only when and if it reached the necessary. But the necessity of one area of knowledge would differ from that of another. Necessity in mathematics is *a priori*, i.e., necessity issues from its principles, its definitions, axioms, and postulates, while the conclusions and theorems result necessarily from these causes.[107] Such a necessity is "simple" or absolute (ἁπλῶς). The necessity in nature and in the physics that studies nature is just the opposite. The necessity lies in the effects, i.e., in the purpose or results that govern the natural processes and necessitate the constituents. Such a necessity is hypothetical (ἐξ ὑποθέσεως). In physics, one argues back from the effects (and consequent purpose either of nature or of art) to the causes that were necessary if these effects were to be brought about. If one mixes up these two different sciences, one will lose the sense of nature with its final causes and the interactions within its operations of art, chance, and fortune, and be left with only a mechanical universe. Physics itself will become – as it *de facto* did become – mechanics.[108]

These three settlements, however, open up to an immense historical problem, one that this book hopes to explore somewhat. How was it that modernity moved from these various forms of concord between science and religion to such an accepted putative hostility, formulating an antinomy so profound that something genuinely novel appeared within Western intellectualism: modern atheism? If the discoveries and procedures of science in any one of its major and creative protagonists did not generate the denial of God, what did? How did Western intellectual culture become able, in Nietzsche's words, to "wipe away the entire horizon?"[109]

2

A Dialectical Pattern in the Emergence of Atheism

Prologue: History and its discovered structures

It is commonplace to assert that the study of history figures very differently in theology, in philosophy, and in the sciences. Indeed, historical inquiry appears still more differentiated within each of these forms of knowledge. A particular historical analysis specifies its individual character or mode of exploration through the determination of its subject matter, its crucial questions, its principles, and its method. Yet, taken quite simply as the actual processes of human events and ideas rather than as their interpretation or written record, history obviously tells in all three disciplines. Their concepts and methods, their issues, facts, and influences are formulated, affected, and evaluated by cumulative experience and evolving reflection. These parameters obtain their specific character as they are developed over time and applied in determined historical circumstances.

Even further, the analysis of such a history can at times disclose an internal configuration in the process that is studied – a "one" that makes sense out of the "many." History – however differentiated, in the fashion of Richard P. McKeon, among epochal, causal, disciplinary, and exemplary histories – can manifest structures and dependent interrelationships among its components. A pattern or a direction or a set of proportions can be discerned in the process studied, one generated by the interactions or dependencies between repeated, albeit analogical, factors. Michel de Certeau has wisely warned that a radical finitude and consequent pluralism will always resist any tendency to totalize such taxonomies or to claim comprehensiveness.[1] For in a very particularized research, an individual history as an actual process is always single and never simply repeated. But in a more generalized examination, history can exhibit reoccurring structures as similar antecedents produce their necessary or natural or compatible consequences. These commensurate patterns can exhibit what is actually contained implicitly in the initial or fundamental concepts, postulates, and methods as consequences spell out what is entailed in antecedents.[2] Such corresponding or homologous patterns, elaborated over time, reveal more clearly perhaps than any other experience what is at stake in the beginnings that have been chosen. Events become ideas. In this way, as Jacques Barzun has recently written, "our distinctive attitude toward history, our habit of arguing from it, turn events into ideas charged with power."[3]

Classically, historians have been interested in homologies – whether in events or in thoughts. Thucydides judged his *History of the Peloponnesian War* to be a "possession for all time" because knowledge of the causal relationships discovered in the past would aid "to the understanding of the future, which in the course of human things must resemble if it does not reflect it."[4] Thucydides would himself be an example of "causal history," and the pattern he attempted to establish emerges as similar causes are seen to originate or to evoke similar effects. Aristotle prefaced to his major tractates a "disciplinary history" whose pattern consisted of the development of problems or subjects or principles to be treated in a particular inquiry because "he who thus considers things in their first growth and origin, whether a *polis* or anything else, will obtain the clearest view of them."[5] The beginning is coordinate with the end, and the end reveals what was contained within the beginning.

In the history of philosophy, Etienne Gilson maintained that the development of doctrines makes philosophical sense only if the internal necessity of their development is grasped.[6] The debasement of doctrine and ideas to mere epiphenomena of the political or social or industrial or racial prerequisites for their emergence is historicism, not disciplinary history as such, while the concatenation of ideas, with their own ideational necessities, forms patterns that Gilson called "philosophical experiments." Augustine's *City of God* and Bossuet's *Discourse on Universal History* bear eloquent witness that the tradition of concern for proportions and unity, for presupposition and consequence, has not been absent from "epochal history." Their reach was massive: to trace out the developing gradations in the comprehensive providence of God as it worked itself out in historical processes. From the results of history, both judged the validity of initial theological principles and settlements. Whatever the different forms of history – causal, problematic, or epochal – or whatever the variety of ideas, acts, events, and processes studied, inquiry into a particular history has from the beginning attempted to perceive, to elicit or even to impose a schema or a pattern whose unity draws the facts and data under scrutiny into intelligibility and relevance. It is hard to imagine a philosopher more different from Gilson than Jacques Derrida, but even Derrida argues that "to 'deconstruct' philosophy . . . would be to think – in the most faithful, interior way – the *structured genealogy* of philosophy's concepts [with all the slippage ingredient to their formation]."[7] "Structured genealogy" is not that far from patterns in intellectual history.

Either in personal history or in the study of the ways of human beings, one comes upon such proportions in experience or in ideas or in the human narrative – in things, thoughts, or words – accepted rather than imposed, often initially suspected and feared for the strange and added clarity they offer to the chaos of immediate experience. One learns from history. *Telling the Truth About History* contends that the "didactic function of history has long been recognized as valid. Voltaire gave classic expression to it when he referred to history as philosophy teaching by example."[8] T. S. Eliot recognized this search for meaning through experience and pattern:

> It seems, as one becomes older,
> That the past has another pattern, and ceases to be a
>   mere sequence –
> Or even development: the latter a partial fallacy
> Encouraged by superficial notions of evolution,
> Which becomes, in the popular mind, a means
>   of disowning the past.
> The moments of happiness – not the sense of well-being,
> Fruition, fulfillment, security or affection,
> Or even a very good dinner, but the sudden illumination –
> We had the experience, but missed the meaning,
> And approach to the meaning restores the experience
> In a different form.[9]

The pattern with its interrelationships of components is the intelligibility of events and thoughts and words – whether one discerns that structure in the form of a sonnet or the strategies of battles or the cycles of goods and services or the forms within the *étude* or the conditions, causes, and results of effective history. In any pattern the beginning insinuates the end; the end elucidates the beginning. The beginning and the end call to each other, fit together, and reach a new understanding through each other. Arthur Schlesinger, Jr. recorded how the drive for "big theories, deep structures, conceptual frameworks" led the new generation of social historians, but who in their turn "failed to come up with the analytic synthesis that would absorb chaotic social data in a 'deep,' all-embracing conceptual structure."[10] The dream was for an integration of all the factors into coherence that could be called something of a unified pattern, what to the scholastics would have suggested form.

Nothing so grand is attempted here. Henry F. May maintains that any study of history depends upon an act of faith. A faith that human beings can "achieve some meaningful relation with it [the past]. That words have some meaning. That a usable pattern will emerge from one's reading and note-taking. That this pattern will have meaning to some people beside oneself."[11] Somewhat along this line: this chapter simply advances the claim that the remarkable and unprecedented emergence of atheism in modern Western civilization exhibited its own "structured genealogy", its own "usable pattern." The intellectual configuration attended to here is not so much in the social events, economic pressures, and usages of power that always contextualize and energize such an emergence. Our focus and questions bear upon the appearance and development of ideas that constituted it, justified it, and gave it intellectual density – the ideas and their history that made atheism make sense.

This is not to assert that a discovered pattern is universal, i.e., that this particular relationship among ideas always occurs when human beings finally conclude to God as bogus, preposterous, injurious, or incredible. There is no claim that this pattern invariably informs all similar arguments in the history of ideas. The claim is much more modest: that this pattern has recurred often enough and in social contexts different enough to warrant attention and to call for analysis and reflection. Perhaps, as May says, it may prove to be a "usable pattern." John Dewey calls such an effort at interpretation "the search for the pattern of inquiry."[12] Something like that is what this chapter is all about.

Some thirteen years ago, the book *At the Origins of Modern Atheism* argued that the emergence of modern atheism was driven in a dialectical pattern, i.e., that atheism as an argument and theorem was generated by the very intellectual forces enlisted to counter it. Theologian John Milbank criticized this thesis as dialectical and over-neat, citing Michel Foucault and Gilles Deleuze to encourage suspicion "of any approach concentrating on contradiction and negation." Milbank seems to agree with them that any dialectical approach "must always in the end promote an identity or a set of 'proper' positions which transcend historical process. Dialectics, therefore, prohibits a radical historicism."[13]

When so distinguished a theologian raises such an issue, one is bound to pay attention. I do not think that one can simply identify dialectics with a fundamentalistic reading of Hegel's metaphysics. Dialectics has a much longer history, a broader meaning, and exists in many more philosophies than that of Hegel, as enriched by Hegel as it has been, both as content and as method. To speak of positive assertions, concepts, and arguments as generating their own negations and so constituting or exhibiting contradictions within an initial subject – which is all that is meant by "dialectics" here – is not to suppose that anything finite is not liable to its own finitude, to its own inadequacies and incompletions. In the dialectical movement, the finite, inadequate determinations or characterizations of any subject supersede themselves and pass over into their opposite. This need not mean that this development reaches some atemporal *stasis*. But Milbank's caveat is well taken.

It should be noted, however, that once one starts to think about or comment upon any historical process, one has somewhat transcended the radical and intractable singularity of that process. Simple apprehension, affirmation or negation, interpretation, and application – all involve some mode of transcendence. Even to level a predicate at a subject is to transcend the subject by including it under a more general attribute. Further, perhaps prohibiting a radical historicism – depending upon the meaning of that phrase – is not all that deplorable if "radical historicism" *a priori* fails to recognize any claim to analogous universality and resemblance or to the common-sense experience that one can learn much for the present from the past.

This concern affords – in the rhetorical tradition of *urgeo* – an opportunity to consider, reargue, and extend even further the basic thesis of my previous book, i.e., that the remarkable development of atheism in modernity exhibits a dialectical structure. To explore and apply that judgment, this chapter will first retrieve or summarize in brief the interpretation found in *At the Origins of Modern Atheism*; then, attend to a study that appeared some twelve years ago, Professor James Turner's *Without God, Without Creed: The Origins of Unbelief in America*; and finally, refer very briefly to Professor Alan Kors's monumental study, *The Orthodox Sources of Disbelief*, the first volume of his continuing study, *Atheism in France, 1650–1729*. Subsequent chapters will seek to extend this same reading in the history of ideas – with a few further distinctions.

One must be afraid that any pattern – and even more, its outline – is "overneat" in the interpretation of a history, but only if one confuses the pattern with the history, the structural outline with the messy and vastly complex historical reality, and fails to allow, as much as Derrida would, for the great slippage in any structured genealogy. With this in mind, let us turn to three great "theological experiments" whose attempt to justify in modernity the existence of God ideationally did so much to generate the denial of God.

The first experiment

This first experiment can be observed in its rise over the early seventeenth century. In those stirring times, "atheism" was a disparaging epithet, not a personal signature. "Atheists" were what your enemies were – albeit faithful believers by their own profession. As such, atheists were to be found every-where.[14] The sixteenth century detected a hidden, but ubiquitous atheistic pres-ence – not unlike the forebodings of a covert, pervasive communism in the United States of the 1950s. Among the works composed to confront this puta-tive atheism was that of Leonard Lessius, a Flemish Jesuit, *De providentia numinis et animi immortalitate*, a book written in 1613 explicitly "against Athe-ists, Polititians of these days." Its serviceable Latin was quickly turned into Recusant English, to appear in 1631 as *Rawleigh: His Ghost*.[15] This seventeenth-century polemic is symptomatically important, as Lessius formulates and fur-thers a line of argument from which very few theologians will retreat in the century of battles ahead.

One should take note that there are three oddities about Lessius's volley against the atheists and the politicians. The Flemish theologian could cite his politicians among contemporaries. He was talking about Machiavelli and those who took religion as *conducibilis* (useful) for political persuasion, but of no intrinsic value. But who were his atheists? Lessius could name no contempo-raries. He had to reach back into classical antiquity to find them supplied by the canonical lists drawn up by Cicero, Sextus Empiricus, and Claudius Aelianus: Diagoras of Melos and Protagoras; Theodore of Cyrene and Bion of Borysthenes; and Lucian. Not really the long-ball hitters of antiquity! With them Lessius grouped the eminent atomists who denied divine providence: Democritus, Epicurus, and Lucretius. One should note, then, that with all of the alarms sounding through Europe about an insidious if latent atheism, Lessius had to reach back some sixteen hundred years to garner names for his list.

Now the second oddity follows upon the first. The typical atheists are ancient philosophers – atomists, sophists, and skeptics. Hence, Lessius took up the issue as if it were a philosophical, rather than a religious, question. He wrote as if atheism were not a repudiation of the God and the intellectual, reli-gious world of Judeo-Christianity, but simply a seventeenth-century recovery of the Epicurean and Academic traditions found in Cicero's *De natura deorum*. Lessius argued as if Christianity had not significantly affected the grammar of "God." The demonstrations of the existence of God must proceed from *rationes philosophicae* – but only from obvious sources, like those from design in nature, leaving out those which "are more obscure, which can be explored in [Aristotle's] *Metaphysics*."[16] It is critically important to understand that Catholic theologians were writing against atheists who did not seem to have existed. Some might even say: those are the best kind! Well, they are certainly the easiest to write against! And these theologians had decided further that this mortal religious combat was essentially philosophical.

This decision about the appropriate discipline or mode of inquiry shifted the topics from religion to philosophy not merely because the ancient adversaries were philosophers, but also because confessional Christianity was gradually discrediting itself among the thoughtful. Its many divisions – sanguinary as well as ideational – were seen to furnish the soil of atheism. As Francis Bacon put it: "the causes of atheism are divisions in religion, if there be many."[17] Alan Kors records a similar judgment from France of the same century. In 1578, Guy Lefèvre de la Boderie wrote of his "'unfortunate century, with its corruption of laws, customs, good morals, and the chaos and confusion of sects which gush forth and multiply rapidly from day to day' as one that 'nourishes, like the serpent in its breast, Atheism, which secretly creeps into the hearts and minds of several voluptuous and depraved men.'"[18] Theologies and confession were endlessly and hopelessly pitted against one another. Major thinkers in Europe could turn to philosophy as to a neutral ground, open to all confessions and related to all disciplines, to ground the common and central assertion of religion. And the arguments to which Lessius turned were those of Quintus Lucilius Balbus in Cicero's *De natura deorum*. Not only were his adversaries pre-Christian; so were his arguments for the existence of God. The topics of the Stoics allowed him the resources to invent and to order his arguments.[19]

Now, it is amazing to see how many of the Stoic topics reemerge in *De providentia Dei et animi immortalitate*, and the competent manner in which they gathered to themselves the inventions and the discoveries of early modernity. One finds here the universal consent of humankind, especially of the wise, the motions of the heavenly bodies, the existence of bodily things, the beauty of things and the structure of their parts – a gaggle of arguments encompassing the parts of the world and diversities of faces – some fifteen arguments in all. All of these are but variations on a single theme: from some particular instance of obviously contrived and intelligible structure one argues to a creative, conserving intelligence. Like the Stoics, Lessius would find intelligence within the universe, embodied either in mind – the common belief of human beings – or, more, in the manifold structures in astronomical and biological nature. For organization or design demanded an intelligence to account either for the coming together or the being together of coordinate constituents that do not explain one another. Structures bespoke contrivance; contrivance, intelligence; and these structures could be found omnipresent in mind and nature. Into the wineskins of the Stoic *loci communes* or "commonplaces," Lessius was able to pour the discoveries of the Renaissance.

The Stoic argument from universal consent, for example, now can assimilate the extensive sea voyages that have recently established that even the "Indians, the people of China, Japonians, Tartarians, and all others" confess a belief in God.[20] The Stoic demonstrations from the movement of the heavenly bodies subsume the new factual data from the recently celebrated telescope. Here in 1613, about two years after Galileo's *Siderius nuncius* had published the discovery of the uneven face of the moon, the four Medicean satellites around Jupiter, and the phases of Venus – and thus destroyed much of the Ptolemaic or Aristotelian argument for a geocentric universe – this Flemish theologian speaks about his own use of the *fistula dioptrica*, which was, after all, invented in the Netherlands and not in Italy, to observe these astronomical structures and to enlist them as further evidence of design.[21] The same line of reasoning runs through all fifteen topics. As the theologians applied to astronomy to bulwark their beginnings, so they also called upon any number of structures in biological nature to fortify the battlements of Christian faith and theology.

And this brings us to our third oddity: the union between "science" and "religion." In the seventeenth century, not only was science (or natural philosophy as it was called through the time of Newton) not opposed to confessional Christianity; it often believed that it could and should do the foundational thinking for Christianity. Religion, of course, had to become philosophy in order to defend itself against atheists who do not seem to have existed, and philosophy, with its battery of Stoic topics and under the heady impetus of the great discoveries in technology, territorial exploration, mathematics, anatomy, and (above all) mechanics, was becoming most popularly natural philosophy. And all of this became a natural theology, foundational for the assertion of the existence of God against its putative denial.

We might pass by Lessius now to devote one paragraph to Paris and to the great Minim theologian and polymath, Marin Mersenne, and allow him to serve as a second symptomatic thinker of the early seventeenth century, both in his massive commentary on Genesis and in *The Impiety of the Deists, Atheists, and Libertines of this time.* Lessius might not have been able to indicate contemporary atheists; Mersenne more than made up for this failure. His *Quaestiones in Genesim* asserted with enviable panache that the Paris of the seventeenth century alone numbered 50,000 of them among its denizens. Who were his atheists? If Lessius had to summon up antiquity, Mersenne could bring before the court anyone whose thought was found dangerous. Three names stand out before all others: Pierre Charron, a skeptical fideist who had himself analyzed and written against unbelief with arguments based upon scripture; Geronimo Cardano, who had contributed significantly to algebra, mechanics, philosophy, and medicine; and Giordano Bruno, a thoroughgoing rationalist and metaphysical mystic. Each of these would have repudiated the convictions with which Mersenne burdens them. But however different their systems and persuasions, they were all read as philosophers. And so in this enterprise Mersenne will engage the issue of God with something of a Platonic version of Epicurean mechanics: from mechanics one argues to the necessity of the infinite plenum as the explanation of the existence of the finite, building up to the evidence provided by *le bel ordre que est au monde*, and this line of mechanical argument is brought to its conclusion by the Neo-Platonic philosophizing of Augustine and Anselm.[22]

This strategy of the Catholic theologians became, with rare exceptions, the protocol of European Christianity. The existence of God was taken primarily as a philosophic question and defended through the evidence provided by the new learning. Philosophy itself, then, became either the Universal Mathematics of René Descartes or the Universal Mechanics of Isaac Newton. And these, the most influential philosophers of that age, not only accepted the assignment from the theologians, they introduced and defended this allocation of duties. To the faculty of theology at Paris, Descartes dedicated his greatest work, his *Meditations on First Philosophy*, but in that very dedication distinguished his responsibility from theirs: "I have always been of the opinion that the two questions that have to do either with God or with the soul were the chief among those that ought to be demonstrated by the power [*ope*] of philosophy rather than by that of theology."[23] Which is Descartes's nice way of saying to the theologians that to establish the existence of God is his responsibility, not theirs.

It is not as if Descartes had read Lessius. It is rather that this division of labor had become so axiomatic that a great philosopher could cite it to the most distinguished assembly of theologians in Europe and simply expect it to be acknowledged. In one respect Descartes paralleled the settlement of Galileo, insisting upon this differentiation of the disciplines by various subject matters, methods, and languages. But he had carried his philosophy up into the giddy heights of metaphysics, and so distinguished kinds of philosophy and their proper subjects: God would be treated in first philosophy or metaphysics, while mechanics (in sharp contrast with Newton) would have only mechanical principles. This differentiation of the disciplines allows for the decision that mechanics was to have simply mechanical principles. This decision was to play a critically important role in the centuries that succeeded him.

Europe and its intellectuals were, however, to be captured by the almost immeasurable genius of Isaac Newton and the towering place which his *Principia* assumed in the development of natural philosophy. Newton's settlement, as was traced out in the first chapter, came to prevail eventually even on the reluctant Continent. Mechanics was to be universal, not only to ground all mathematics and to explore "all of the phenomena of nature," but to provide the very foundations of religion. Theologians had not only prepared the way for these critical movements in Western apologetic thought; after they had occurred, theologians enthusiastically followed suit. Descartes begat his Malebranche, and Newton his Samuel Clarke. All of the factors were then in place for the Enlightenment to formulate the first articulated atheism in modern times.

Whatever social structures or economic movements and power blocs encouraged this quiet revolution can be left for another analysis. What happened in the progress of ideas, however, is critically important but basically quite simple. Two of the most influential agents of this revolution were the great founder of the *Encyclopedia*, Denis Diderot, and the other, the engaging *salonier*, Baron Paul d'Holbach. [24] But their common resources were Newton and Descartes, the very ones celebrated by different theologians as guardians of the foundations of religion.

From Newton, Diderot and d'Holbach accepted the universality of mechanics, that the mechanical method could deal with all of reality from mathematics to theology; what they rejected of Newton was his claim that the mechanical study of natural phenomena necessarily leads to a non-mechanical principle, to a transcendent source above nature, i.e., to God. From Descartes, Diderot and d'Holbach refused his metaphysics or first philosophy as nonsense – as Newton had before them; but from Descartes, they accepted the autonomy of mechanics, i.e., that all physical reality was mechanical and must be explained through mechanical principles. In many ways, Diderot and d'Holbach synthesized Descartes and Newton. The synthesis was a universal mechanics (à la Newton) with only mechanical principles (à la Descartes).

They effected this synthesis by making one revolutionary change. They radically altered the understanding of matter. Both Descartes and Newton had understood matter as inert. Descartes identified matter with the extension that made geometry possible; Newton identified matter with mass, and found matter to differ only conceptually from inertial resistance to change. How did matter get motion? How did it begin to move? Descartes relied upon momentum to generate motion; Newton relied upon force.

Now Diderot and d'Holbach revolutionized natural philosophy by making matter no longer inert, but dynamic. They made motion part of matter's very existence. They insisted that movement was not an addition to matter by some external agency, but a necessary attribute of matter. Descartes had said that with matter and the laws of motion he could explain everything in the universe, design and all. But he needed God to give the initial motion to matter; the rest happened of necessity. Now Diderot and d'Holbach made such an initial endowment unnecessary. No one needed a god to give the first impetus to matter. It is there already; it has been there forever; motion and matter are inseparable. Matter is the creative, dynamic source of all physical reality. Motion is the manner in which matter necessarily exists. It is no great wonder that Diderot was Karl Marx's favorite prose author.[25] A devout Marxist might read this history as the injection into the contradiction of a theologically oriented mechanics of a revolutionary principle, dynamic matter. God became otiose in both astronomy and natural philosophy as he figured less and less as an explanation in natural philosophy and mechanics.

The dialectical unraveling or emergence of this negation bears remarkable resemblance to Mircea Eliade's reading of the career of the primordial high god. Andrew Lang's recasting of the preanimistic history of religion had suggested an original high god, "not at the end of religious history, but at its beginning."[26] But over time this primordial high god, once pervasively present and influential, became progressively more distant, less and less operative in the explanation and understanding of the world and its worship. One understood the world and dealt with human interaction without the invocation of such a god. It became gradually the *deus otiosus*, the idle god, not so much denied as unattended to, detached and uninvolved, not influential in the world of nature and of human beings, and finally yielding to oblivion. He was "believed to have retired to the highest heaven, quite indifferent to human affairs."[27] In other words, the high god was removed from any religious involvement. Finally it fell "into total oblivion."[28] So also ran the history of the God of mechanics in early modernity. The disclosure of his idle, unnecessary presence led to indifference, even ridicule, rejection, and final oblivion. Robert Lowell caught something of this declination in "God," if one may change only one proper noun for station identification:

> There's a pale romance to the watchmaker God
> of Descartes and [Newton]; he drafted and installed
> us in the Apparatus. He loved to tinker;
> but having perfected what He had to do,
> stood off shrouded in his loneliness.[29]

This very sketchy outline in the history of an idea suggests that the origins of atheism lie with a development in natural philosophy or physics, and so has it often been taken in popular accounts. But physics or mechanics did not argue that God did not exist. It simply said that it did not need the theological hypothesis in order to explain the development and design of the universe or the movement of matter into particular configurations. Dynamic matter would supply all the causality that was needed. Mechanics in the intoxicating days of its triumphs needed no longer to conclude theologically and thought itself better for this independence. It did not require theology to be complete and coherent. But this removed what had been taken by many as the foundational warrant for the existence of God.

Mechanics may not have needed theology, but theology in its apologetics had come to need mechanics, whether in astronomy or biology. Theology had become addicted to it. The pivotal theological assertions that had so relied upon mechanics became gratuitous assertions, and it runs as a classic maxim in logic, as well as in history, that "whatever is gratuitously asserted can be gratuitously denied." The obvious next stage was denial, the contradiction of a demonstration that had ceased to be a demonstration. What was actually demonstrated was the intrinsic self-subversion that had been with it from the beginning.

For the contradiction was not new. Atheism simply disclosed the contradiction latent in these original moments of mechanical demonstration.

THE CONTRADICTION

At the first stage of this strategy, there had been implicit but lethal contradictions both in evidence admitted to provide for these foundational apologetics the warrant that God existed and in the manner of thinking by which this evidence was assessed.

(1) In evidence the impersonal was taken as the foundational warrant for the personal. The intellectual credibility of the existence of God had been made to depend fundamentally upon the inference in philosophy or natural philosophy or mechanics – as if nothing more pertinent were available. The contrast was stunning: All appeal to a religious experience of God was omitted, and the infinite mystery that was God had in effect become a corollary of a particular configuration of the solar system or of the human body. The unspoken assumption was that one had to turn to such impersonal evidence because there was nothing specifically religious or personal cogent enough to support a demonstration of the reality of God. There was nothing in the grammar and usages of religion

that contained anything convincing and more immediately pertinent such as the experience of the absolute claim upon conscience or the lives and narratives of holiness or the person of Christ or the drive towards the horizon of truth or religious traditions and experience. In the great debates about the existence of God, one can not attend to them. They are not rigorous and compelling. Mechanics, not any religious dimension of life, supplied the principal evidence upon which the foundationally religious could be reasonably asserted.

In the dialectical development out of this initial moment of strategy, the contradiction that had been implicitly present emerged. For to bracket the specifically religious in order to defend the God of religion was to assert implicitly the cognitive emptiness of the very reality one was attempting to support. The unexpressed though vitally present conviction was that this religious life of the human being or of the human community did not have the resources to secure its own case. In implicit recognition of this insufficiency, it had to turn to other evidence to ground itself, to establish its own reasonableness. What the rising atheism simply did by its negation was to make explicit the contradiction that had been implicit from the beginning. Theism so internally conflicted and contradicted passed over into its negation. It passed over into atheism.

(2) There was a further contradiction implicit in this strategy, a contradiction between the various forms of thought, between religious assent and inference. In religion, God is experienced or worshipped as a presence and asserted in a real assent; in mechanics and in philosophy, God is inferred as a conclusion from what is more evident. John Henry Newman has developed this at great length so I shall not delay on it here, except to note that as one insists upon the primacy of inference, one makes assent that much more difficult.[30] In the strategies of early modernity, however, this was precisely what was being done: inferential forms of thought were introduced as foundational demonstrations because the religious experience and reflection was not read to possess adequate intellectual cogency, certainly not what one would find in natural philosophy and mechanics.

As a form of thought, religious recognition and assent were read as intellectually soft. To give substance and seriousness to its presuppositions and conclusions, the form of thought must become scientific inference as one found it in the *Principia* and *Opticks* of Newton. God was not encountered as a presence; God was inferred as a conclusion from what one did encounter. Newman put his finger on the fatal contradiction: "Arguments about the abstract cannot handle and determine the concrete. They may approximate to a proof, but they only reach the probable, because they cannot reach the particular. . . . Science, working by itself, reaches truth in the abstract, and probability in the concrete; but what we aim at is truth in the concrete."[31] Inference may prepare for assent, indeed, it often does, but its conditionality distinguishes it irrevocably from assent.

Both in evidence and in mode of thought, the gap widened between God received as a living and self-communicating presence and the God of the physico-theologies who was at best, in Gilbert Murray's elegant dismissal, "a friend behind the phenomena."[32]

One must stress that it was not what this strategy included that worked its own reversal. It was what was omitted as irrelevant, and what was substituted in its place. It was not that Christian philosophy argued the import carried by the conjunction of diverse elements that bespeak design – not in this or that particular thing but in nature itself – or the need to find a postulate that made sense of the ethical drive towards duty or a metaphysics of being that questioned why there was something rather than nothing. It was rather the omission of the manifold that is religious life and experience and the substitution of natural philosophy or mechanics as what was foundational that was so self-contradicting. This was a strategy that was implicitly asserting at the absolutely fundamental moment of reflection the cognitive emptiness of the actual Judeo-Christian assent.

Such a strategy, then, was to introduce an intrinsic contradiction both within the evidence for God and within forms of the assertion of God. Eventually the scientific inference and the scientific evidence moved towards their own autonomy, to resolve these contradictions by enclosing the world within themselves. Mechanics would be both universal and possessed of only mechanical principles. It could then dispense with the sovereign architect so skilled in geometry, and reassert its own integrity. The historical pattern in the seventeenth and eighteenth centuries indicates that at least in the case of Western civilization such a contradiction lay at the ideational generation of atheism. To assert that this generation of atheism was dialectical is simply to maintain that the denial of God was generated by the very strategies that were constructed to combat it.

But did such a dialectical pattern obtain elsewhere? Let us look at the second experiment and the work of Professor James Turner.[33]

The second experiment

For this second attempt, let me invite you to travel to the New World. Puritan New England did not have a Leonard Lessius, but it did have its Cotton Mather.

Both were theologians of unquestionable orthodoxy and influence within their Christian denominations. Lessius could distinguish between the way of faith and the reasons of philosophy and locate the arguments for the existence of God within the latter. Cotton Mather could distinguish with John Chrysostom *The Twofold Book of God* into the Book of the *Creatures* and the Book of the *Scriptures*, and maintain that the former will "help us in reading the Latter." For God "having taught first of all us, διὰ πραγμάτων, by his *Works*, did it afterwards διὰ γραμμάτων, by his *Words*."[34] This recognition lent character and even wings to his book that appeared in 1721: *The Christian Philosopher: A Collection of the Best Discoveries in Nature, with Religious Improvement*. It is critically important to recognize with Kenneth Silverman that this was "the first general book on science to be written in America," and it was written in the interest of what today would be called religious apologetics.[35] If Lessius could draw upon contemporary astronomy and summon the Stoic topics to the court, Cotton Mather's Newtonian century would enable him to do all of this, but also to make use of the physico-theologies of "the Industrious Mr. Ray, and the Inquisitive Mr. Derham; *Fratrum dulce par*."[36] For both Leonard Lessius and Cotton Mather, design was everywhere to be explored for religious purposes. Thus "*Philosophy* [contemporary science] is no *Enemy*, but a mighty and wondrous *Incentive* to *Religion*."[37]

Indeed, Mather believed that God had first employed the scientists to make their discoveries and had then moved the physico-theologians to collect them, so that the entire universe could then be seen as what it was: the temple of God, "*built* and *fitted* by that Almighty Architect."[38] These discoveries and these collections generated what Mather called a "philosophical [i.e. scientific] religion," one whose universal scientific warrant placed it beyond the wrangles of conflicting sects: "Behold, a *Religion*, which will be found *without Controversy*; a *Religion*, which will challenge all possible Regards from the *High*, as well as the *Low*, among the People; I will resume the Term, a Philosophical Religion: And yet how *Evangelical!*"[39] Evangelical and Philosophical: those two adjectives set in motion so much in the centuries that were to follow. Evangelical, it may well have been, but what made it philosophical, i.e. scientific, was its concentration upon design within the universe and the inference from design to intelligence, indeed to the Supreme Intelligence.

It is staggering to recognize that for this New England divine, this religion was open to Christian and to Muslim alike.[40] Newton had formulated his "fundamental religion;" Cotton Mather had his "philosophical religion," one that would aid the theology that was the exploration of divine revelation. The book could be indifferently entitled "Religio Philosophica; or, The Christian Philosophy," and its very first chapter is given over to Newton's Three Laws of Motion and the Law of the Inverse Square, for these bespeak their divine origin: "These are *Laws* of the Great GOD, *who formed all things*. GOD is *ever to be seen* in these *Everlasting Ordinances*."[41]

What was the purpose of this remarkable philosophical religion? Positively, it was the inculcation of piety, "piety" being almost a synonym at that time for "religion." Negatively, it was that "*Atheism* is now for ever chased and hissed out of the World." Philosophical religion had confirmed that "everything in the World concurs to a Sentence of *Banishment* upon it [atheism]."[42] Indeed, the metaphors became more emphatic as "every Part of the *Universe* is continually *pouring in* something for the *confuting* of it; there is not a Corner of the whole World but what supplies a *Stone* towards the Infliction of such a *Death* upon the *Blasphemy* as justly belongs to it."[43] The collection of such stones was the task of philosophy become natural philosophy become philosophical religion, a discipline "without any *Teacher*, but *Reason* in a serious View of *Nature*, led on to the Acknowledgment of a Glorious GOD."[44] For to this discipline belonged the question and the defense of the existence of God.

It should then be no surprise that this reliance upon science grew, even while the sturdy Calvinism of the Mathers – with all of its double predestination and the paucity of the saved – abated into a dogmatically weakened Congregationalism and Unitarianism scarcely distinguishable from the respectable "American Way of Life." The two books of Cotton Mather passed into their own histories of development. The American Enlightenment seized upon the book of creatures as foundational – even exhaustive – a decision that reached its full stature in the various "deisms" of Thomas Paine and Ethan Allen, of Benjamin Franklin and Thomas Jefferson.[45] This deism, in its turn, evoked its opposite, i.e., the revival of Evangelicalism in the early nineteenth century, rising out of the Pietist movements from the mother countries of the previous centuries and drawing much of its strength by absorbing while taming Enlightenment rationalism. This revival with its emphasis on conversion, morality, and a personal commitment to Jesus, swept the country in the early decades of the nineteenth century, but paradoxically it won its victories among prominent Church leaders and theologians only because it subsumed into itself the previous generation's reliance upon science as foundational for the affirmation of God.

God might indeed be asserted by the heart, but that assertion saved itself from irrationalism by assimilating the confirming findings of science. The scientific was to do two services: it would provide the fundamental evidence for the existence of God, and it would supply the form of thought by which this evidence would be argued to its conclusion.

But this covenant contained its own internal contradiction. The tradition of the two books eventuated in a god for each. Nature entailed a god, impersonal and remote, one who governed the universe through such universal, necessary, and mechanical laws of physics as Mather's Newtonian Laws. Scripture, conversion, and personal religious experience pointed to God and to a particular providence by which God moved the heart, called sinners to repentance, directed the congregation, and empowered the moral life.[46] Added tension occurred as the first was made to stand warrant for the second.[47] Kenneth Silverman finds in this displacement the dialectical contradiction already latent in the settlements of Cotton Mather's *The Christian Philosopher:* "The very piety evident in such thinking – widespread among Christian scientists in the eighteenth century – obscured its dangerous implications, and unwittingly led Mather close to irreligion. Although the physico-theological disclosure of an intricately contrived universe was meant to provide a rational foundation for Christianity, it tended in practice to displace it. . . . Mather shared unawares in some of this subversive shift in emphasis."[48]

Such a dialectical contradiction within the first moments of this apologetics would necessitate its own subsequent resolution, a movement through negation that became more inevitable as Evangelicalism insisted upon its strong dependence on science for its foundation. Indeed the new Evangelicalism became the popular medium for this use of science. It was through this American version of Pietism that Paley could guarantee for many the existence of God and God could guarantee nineteenth-century morality.[49]

This strategy, however, was confirmed in its usefulness in nineteenth-century America as higher criticism increasingly undermined the inspiration of the scriptures, as anthropology located the idea of God not in revelation but in cultural evolution, as the comparative study of religions shook the uniqueness of the Christian claim, and an increasing sensibility to justice and human pain drew into furious question the doctrines of original sin, atonement, special election, and the perpetuity of hell.[50] In that welter of direct and atmospheric criticisms, the religious intellect looked perhaps even more emphatically than in the past to science for reassurance of its most fundamental belief, the existence of God, and also for its methodological guide by which sound belief could be guaranteed.

This foundational settlement lasted until the middle of the nineteenth century.[51] "Before 1859, believers could rest secure in the conviction that the evidence for God was as certain as science itself. God remained central to thinking about important scientific questions."[52] This god was actually the god of the gaps, brought in to explain such facts as the origins of life, the design of the individual species, and the correlation between organic life and supportive environment.[53] Francis Ellwood Abbot spoke for so many of that generation when he warned: "Theism and Atheism are in the scales, and Science holds the balance."[54]

But then, as Laplace in astronomy, so Darwin in biology: God was not necessary. God was not even implied by the designs either in the heavens or in organic nature. Whether nebular hypothesis or natural selection, science increasingly had nothing to say about the existence and character of God. Order came out of chance, if chance was given sempiternity to evolve a planetary system or a complicated organism by natural selection. Mather's *Twofold Book of God* was illegible. The reliance upon scripture was ravaged in the nineteenth century by the new historical criticism, and the book of creatures was closed by an evolutionary enthusiasm. The scientific evidence claimed by the theologians had disappeared, leaving them with statements that had become gratuitous and empty. For many educated Americans of the second half of the nineteenth century, the honest – the moral – resolution of the contradiction that was groundless affirmation lay with either agnosticism or atheism. A theism built upon the discoveries of science eventually generated its own negation.

For others, the escape was achieved by a flight into a religion privatized beyond social recognition, conflated with feeling and intuitions, one that made few if any dogmatic claims and considered itself justified or confirmed by its welcomed encouragement of bourgeois morality.

As in celestial mechanics, now in geology and biology, God as the corollary of science yielded to evolving matter dominated by chance. God became again *Deus otiosus*. Dynamic matter could explain both design and every form of evil. In fact, evolution proved more comprehensive than providence: the blind struggle for life could explain evil far more competently than could the providence of a loving God. Evolution made evil as equally understandable as good.

Once more, religion was not undermined by science; the religious assent was undermined when theologians excised the specifically religious and came to rely upon scientific evidence and procedure as foundational. The more that theologians insisted upon such a foundation, the more they discredited belief. Professor Turner traced his own discovery in these words:

As I began to trace the origins of unbelief, it slowly dawned on me that the *pattern* I was seeing did not fit conventional expectations, including my own. . . . Though both science and social transformation loom large in the picture, neither caused unbelief. . . . On the contrary, religion caused unbelief. In trying to adapt their religious beliefs to socioeconomic change, to new moral challenges, to novel problems of knowledge, to the tightening standards of science, the defenders of God slowly strangled Him. If anyone is to be arraigned for deicide, it is not Charles Darwin but his adversary Bishop Samuel Wilberforce, not the godless Robert Ingersoll but the godly Beecher family. [55]

The patterns, whether at the dawn of modernity in Europe or in post-bellum America, were analogous. The great differences between the seventeenth century and the nineteenth, of course, affected profoundly the manner in which this pattern was concretely realized. One must recognize, for example, in the later period that "the more widespread popular enthusiasm for science (identified with technology) . . . , the greater faith in progress (understood as moral advance, afforded by science) . . . and the vastly larger proportion of literate people made it easier for unbelief to spread and root itself widely in the nineteenth century, whereas it did not do so in the seventeenth. The pattern of ideas recurs, but its cultural consequences differ."[56] Mather had made the scientific reading of the book of nature a propaedeutic to the book of scripture. As in Europe, so in America, the *praeambula fidei* changed to become foundation, and this foundation changed from being one confirmation to the only credible support in both evidence and procedure. And when it could no longer sustain this theological task, the failure was taken as enmity.

The third experiment

If the compass of a chapter, however expanded, were still not so constricted, we should review in some detail the emergence of atheism among the devout and learned in eighteenth-century France, an emergence so carefully traced out by Professor Alan Kors in the first volume of his prospected two-volume study. Here one can only follow the central thesis of this capacious work of painstaking scholarship and register agreement. Atheism in Catholic France came to its ideological birth or its intellectual availability obviously from within the learned community – this was true of the Enlightenment community that numbered Diderot or D'Holbach as well. But the "overarching argument" which Kors's study advances is that atheism was generated from within Catholic France neither by the enemies of Christianity nor by those alienated from any religion, but by the religiously "orthodox culture itself."[57] No pattern in history has anything but analogical similarities to another, but here again the analogy tells. The pattern in the France of the seventeenth and eighteenth centuries resembled in its own way the basic dialectical structure present in modernity in general and later to be found in the United States in the nineteenth century: out of intrinsic contradiction issued negation. But there is a significant difference. In Catholic France the issue was not fed so much by the rising mechanics and the illation from design in nature to God. It was insistently a philosophical debate, and the contradiction in the first stage was between two battling philosophical schools, both professing the same final conclusion.

Within the protocols suggested by Lessius, the internal and original contradiction lay between the profoundly religious question and the displacement of the religious both as evidence and as a mode of thought by what came to be generally designated as natural philosophy. Eventually Newton was to name this religious employment of mechanics "fundamental religion." Cotton Mather conjoined two books and did not see how very gradually the book of creatures was to displace the book of the scriptures as foundational in what he called "philosophical religion." In Catholic France before the Revolution, the fundamental contradiction was not between two disciplines or between two books; it was between two schools.

Two different sets of Catholic protagonists divided the Catholic academy: the scholastics, tracing their lineage through the medieval schoolmen back to Aristotle, and the Cartesians, newly arrived on the scene. In 1701, the Jesuits' *Journal de Trévoux* stated that "the whole world of learning [which, for that distinguished journal, may well have meant educated France!] 'is now divided between two kinds of philosophers . . . those who call themselves disciples of Aristotle and those who have embraced the new opinions.'"[58] Both took up the task that Descartes had earlier assigned to philosophy, and emphatically not to theology: to demonstrate the existence of God.[59] The reliance upon philosophy made philosophic debate inevitable. God was someone whose evidence one worried about and contested in order to achieve a sure foundation for Catholic faith. But two schools meant inevitably that each side would hammer out arguments against the other. This was not another example of clerical or academic petulance. It was essential to the task of foundational apologetics. In the effort to secure the existence of God, it was necessary to demolish those demonstrations that were unsound. For, as N. Herminier had written in his commentary on the *Summa theologiae* at the turn of that century, arguments that are poorly done "caused the greatest harm and prejudice to theology and gave the greatest comfort to incredulity."[60] Contrary to their interests and intentions, however, this contradiction between the warring schools generated a negation that would undermine both. It negated not only the methods, evidence, and arguments they leveled at each other. Its effective history went far beyond that. What was eventually negated was the conclusion the two schools shared in common: the existence of God.

For these intractable and endless battles between the two schools supplied the tools for their collective demolition by an atheism taking the field against both in the name of natural philosophy. The rising unbelief had only to avail itself of these arguments so paradoxically formulated by the orthodox against each other. This facilitated in Western culture that purported hostility between faith and learning or science, commonly today accepted as a classic division of the struggle. Kors cited Abbé de Gérard writing in 1679 that "learning [*la science*] produces atheists and impious men."[61] Learning, scientific learning, had begun to turn from the support of religion to becoming its contradiction. The French debates, attempting to discover – each in its own school – the most telling arguments from philosophy for the existence of God, actually passed over into the contradiction of what both were attempting to defend. Once more, the process of apologetics that made this kind of evidence or philosophical arguments absolutely foundational gave birth to the intellectual and skeptical processes that led to their own denial:

> The emergence of atheism in France would not be an affair of merely nominal Christian culture, but, rather, in very large part, an affair precisely of the Christian mind or soul. "Theism" entails the concept, if not the categories, of "atheism." It is a believing culture that *generates* its own antithesis, disbelief in the principles of its own belief. Early-modern theists, Catholic, Protestant, and heterodox, sought to reassure themselves that no one could give doubts about God's being coherent argument or positive content. *They, themselves, however, were the source or conduit of such argument and the discoverers or creators of such atheistic teaching. Such an argument may sound paradoxical, but, we shall see, it restores both the potential and reality of atheism to the culture of which they were themselves a living part.*[62]

This claim is made prospectively as the study advances, but at its end, Kors can state as the major conclusion of this first volume: "We have seen a complex culture *generate its own antithesis*, the possibility of which it always had carried within."[63] The contradictions within the religious culture moved dialectically into this comprehensive negation. It was in its debates self-destructive. The schools had insisted that their task was the verification of the existence of God. Not only were the devices they employed judged inadequate by others, but the arguments they had forged to counter their adversaries were turned against the both of them.

In insisting that natural philosophy or first philosophy must justify the fundamental assertions of religious belief or provide both the evidence and even the form by which fundamental religious or theological convictions could be asserted, theologians were again confessing to the cognitive insufficiency, even emptiness, of religious beliefs and experience. The primary evidence for God is asserted as impersonal: either the content of ideas in Descartes or the content of nature as in the scholastics. The mode of the assertion of God is entailment or inference.

A final word

In all three of these theological experiments, the fatal contradiction lay with the bracketing of the religious, the displacement of the religious either as a mode of thought or as evidence to be explored. In all three, the stratagems employed dialectically generated their own negation. Atheism, either as theorem or as argument, did not arise in its strength primarily from a purported opposition of science or from the rich discoveries of that period or from the intellectual movements skeptically antagonistic to any claim for certainty. It arose from the contradiction immanent within the orthodox tradition itself and its apologetic strategies. As dialectical, these three enterprises embodied an initial contradiction both in content and in form: the impersonal was made the fundamental warrant for the personal; inferential reasoning substituted for disclosure, communication, and real assent. As dialectical, the fatal contradiction was not mounted from the outside; it was immanent within the total career of the argument. It was with the strategy from its beginnings, and the resulting negations merely realized the internal insufficiency of the subject in that initial stage. The second stage of denial merely developed this subject explicitly into its truth: The dialectical method "does not hold the position of external reflection; it draws the determinate element directly from the object itself, since it is the object's immanent principle and soul."[64] This is not to claim, as did Hegel, a universality for dialectic – nor is it to deny it. It is simply to assert that it did obtain a number of times in the emergence of modern atheism.

But the question must then be asked: Does not Thomas Aquinas set the stage for much of this with his reliance upon what is given in sense perception and inferential argument to answer the issue: "utrum Deus sit [whether God is]"?[65]

Does the *Summa theologiae* not encourage such a strategy – with its employment of the inference of the *quinque viae* to demonstrate the existence of God and to buttress philosophically the self-revelation of God, with its reliance upon metaphysics in its treatment of the nature of God and of the trinity itself before any consideration of the mysteries of Christ, indeed, with its postponement of the mysteries of Christ until it has completed an exposition of the character of creation, the nature of the human being, the constitution of human destiny, of human virtues and vices? Only when this is done does the *Summa theologiae* turn and attend to the mystery of Christ, the personal manifestation of God within history. Can one honestly say that Christ enters into the intelligibility or even the manifestation of the existence of God – of even the nature of human beings, for that matter? Do the history and the strategy we have related not number Aquinas as one of its principal progenitors and is he not honestly liable to the strictures we have leveled against them? This is the question I hope to explore in the next chapter.

3

Thomas Aquinas and the Rise of Modern Atheism

Prologue: The argument to date and the issue

THE ARGUMENT TO DATE

Modernity initially commended to the European intellect at least three alternative settlements between the theological enterprise with its ancient faith and languages and the new knowledge with its mathematized evidence, methods, and conclusions. A single term could fix each of these settlements: separation, subsumption, and foundation; a single figure could successfully represent each: Galileo, Kepler, and Newton – granted that these resolutions, sometimes extensively modified, have endured through the subsequent centuries in protean careers and with divergent acceptance. So ran our first thesis in the history of ideas.

The ideational genesis of modern atheism, i.e., atheism as a theorem, argument, or ideology, owed much especially to the last of these three settlements, the Newtonian. Paradoxically, it was easily the one that at first blush extended the most promise for mutual concord and support. Laying "the first foundations of religion" deep within the competence and commitments of the new mechanics or within another form of scientifically disciplined inquiry, this settlement contributed the evidence and the inferential methodology for asserting the existence and nature of God most in harmony with the genius of the age. Thus the Newtonians generated their numerous physico-theologies and converted the primary "evidence" of the divine reality into something other than the religious and argued to the reality of God as a conclusion to be discursively drawn rather than a presence of which to become progressively aware or with which to be in communion. The religious was not a world or a community of interpersonal relations that one lived within and within which one looked for justification as its validity was challenged. The religious was fundamentally a deduction that one reached from evidence afforded by mechanical inquiries as these were brought to bear upon particular examples of design in the universe.

This strategy carried hidden within itself a double contradiction, one that would eventually bring these initial moments into the denial of what they had been at pains to advance. For in its evidence and in its discursive attainment of knowledge, this protocol implicitly asserted the inner cognitive vacuity of Judeo-Christian or religious experience – however that engaged the person of Christ or the immanence of the Spirit or the summons of an absolute or the grammar of God or such manifestations as those repeatedly offered within various traditions and narratives of sanctity that proposed a response to the self-communication of God. This strategy accepted implicitly that the religious itself was without the intellectual cogency to justify itself or to ground its staggering claims. For this, one must go elsewhere. Thus unrecognized, but operative, in the beguiling support extended by the new sciences for both the fundamental evidence and the procedures leading to religious convictions was the unrecognized denial of the intellectual density or cognitive seriousness of the very realities that were to be affirmed and the world in which such an affirmation would have made sense. The god reached by continuing the analysis of mechanics or science was at best – as noted in the elegant phrase of Gilbert Murray – a "friend behind the phenomena."[1] *Deus* became *deus otiosus*, and like this distant figure from out of the history of religions, to whom Eliade gave its name, this god also eventually perished. So ran our second thesis in the history of ideas.

The second chapter ended, however, with a question: If this was the apologetic strategy and its paradoxical result in much of Europe, who set it going and patronized its progress in the West? Was it not Thomas Aquinas with his celebrated *quinque viae*, the *doctor communis* of Catholic theology and of much of Europe? Paul Tillich, at least, thought that it was indeed Thomas Aquinas! In May of 1946, Tillich published in the *Union Seminary Quarterly Review* an essay entitled "The Two Types of Philosophy of Religion," resuming reflections first introduced with his essay "Estrangement and Reconciliation in Modern Thought."[2] There are two ways of approaching God, maintained Tillich: one is the process of overcoming estrangement and the other is "the way of meeting a stranger." The first was that of the Augustinians and the early Franciscan scholastics of the thirteenth century, the theologies of Alexander of Hales, Bonaventure, and Matthew of Aquasparta; the second entered Western theology with Thomas Aquinas and advanced in its deadly progress more radically with Duns Scotus and William of Occam.

Augustine and the early Franciscans had realized the inescapable and pervasive presence of Truth, of *Veritas*, in every human project. "*Veritas* is presupposed in every philosophical argument; and *veritas* is God. You cannot deny truth as such because you could do it only in the name of truth, thus establishing truth. And if you establish truth, you affirm God." This Tillich denominated the "ontological way" of the philosophy of religion, embodied in the maxim that "God can never be reached if he is the *object* of a question, and not its *basis*."[3] It claims an immediacy for the knowledge of God; indeed the very thought about him contains its own necessity, as Alexander of Hales insists: "The divine substance is known in such a way that it cannot be thought not to be."[4] Even to question or to deny the existence of God is to affirm him. God is inescapable, for God is immediately given as Truth.

For a contradicting contrast, Tillich pointed the finger at Thomas Aquinas. His was the "rational way," in stark opposition to the ontological way. "The rational way to God is not immediate, but mediated. It is a way of inference." Truth and indeed all of "the *transcendentalia*, are *not* the presence of the divine in us, they are *not* the 'uncreated light' through which we see everything, but they are the created structure of our mind." Aquinas's "sense-bound epistemology" can only infer God; it cannot experience God. There is no immediate presence of God to human awareness. What human beings know are only those created things that point by their ontological deficiencies to an unexperienced other. Aquinas "brings God's existence down to the level of that of a stone or a star, and it makes atheism *not only possible, but almost unavoidable,* as the later development has proved."[5] It is from Aquinas that we derive the present empirical or experimental philosophy of religion, in which God emerges as "the best explanation of man's general experience," and the "theistic hypothesis" as the "most reasonable belief."[6] Tillich placed Aquinas at the origins of the vast drift in Western culture towards atheism, the one who made "atheism not only possible, but almost unavoidable." Tillich even approved of atheism as the correct response to the God of Aquinas: "to such a concept and to such attempts atheism is the right religious and theological reply."[7] God as discursive conclusion should be denied.

This basic attack on any demonstration for the existence of God runs through Tillich's later work. Thomas Aquinas and the schoolmen tradition he fathered "perverted their insight [into the identity of essence and existence in God] when in spite of this assertion they spoke of the existence of God and tried to argue in favor of it. . . . God does not exist. He is being-itself beyond essence and existence. Therefore, to argue that God exists is to deny him." Each of Thomas's "five ways" is reduced to "the 'missing link,' discovered by correct conclusions." In such arguments, Tillich judges, the idea of God emerges at "the end of the causal regression in answer to the question, 'Where from?' (Thomas Aquinas)."[8]

Tillich's explicit and fundamental indictment bears upon both the form of thought and the evidence by which God is asserted: the ontological vs. the rational, God as immediately given in experience vs. God as inferentially argued from external evidence. The second of each of these antinomic pairs suggests the resource that must be substituted for faith: ecclesial authority. Any inference is always open to doubt. Ecclesiastical authority must compensate for the lack of certainty inherent in all inference, and, in turn, it converts the Bible into "a collection of true propositions instead of a being a guide book to contemplation as in Bonaventura."[9]

Tillich did not, however, extend the lines of his attack to their full capacity. For such a theology as is attributed to Aquinas, one insistently grounded on inference and posed against the immediacy or givenness of God, necessarily implicates the character and place of Christology in Christian theology. For in Christ one encounters the givenness of God in incarnation and history.

Christ classically figures in Christian theology as the categorical and normative revelation – and, hence, manifestation – of the reality of God in history. But just as Aquinas is charged with removing God from the immediacy of human experience at the beginning of the *Summa theologiae*, so has he been charged with removing Christ effectively from the shaping and denomination of the content of theology. Aquinas does this by placing Christology at the very end of the *Summa theologiae*, after the great questions about God and the human person's movement to God have been explored. Over the centuries, theologians have framed these two indictments against the theology of St. Thomas: In Aquinas, God is given neither transcendentally nor categorically – to use these two terms in the meaning offered by Karl Rahner – i.e., neither in human interiority, human nature, and human experience nor in human history. The two criticisms are mutually entailed. To gauge the influence of Aquinas in the generation of modern atheism, it is of critical importance to explore both of these issues.

The "ontological" and the "rational"

With care and precision, a small prologue opens the way to the Second Question of the First Part of the *Summa theologiae*. It first outlines Aquinas's study of God and what pertains to God in the three parts that constitute the *Summa theologiae*. The First Question of the *Summa* had laid out the character of *sacra doctrina* – God's teaching the human race about God and whatever relates to God – and had established a human theology that pertains to *sacra doctrina*. Now the principal intention of *sacra doctrina* is to give to human beings a knowledge of God – not only as God is in himself, but as God is the source and end of all things, especially of the rational creature. Consequently, Aquinas's *expositio* of *sacra doctrina*, i.e. his theology, will parcel out its own progress accordingly. To introduce the theological inquiries that follow, the student is given this schema. First, this theological *expositio* will treat of God; then of the movement of the rational creature to God, then of Christ, who, as a human being, is our path or way to God.

The *consideratio* about God will itself have three parts, taking up the divine essence, the distinction of persons, and the procession of creatures from God. Within the consideration of what belongs to the essence of God, one must first examine the question: "whether God is."[10]

This initial inquiry into the existence of God must weigh two alternatives for asserting that God is: it is either evident in itself or evident because of something else, i.e., God is either given or inferred.

So the First Article of this Second Question runs: "Is it self-evident/evident in itself [*per se notum*] whether God is?" Thomas is going to answer in the negative, but he notes that there are three possibilities for an affirmative answer: the judgment that God exists could be supplied immediately either by the experience it specifies; or by the meaning of the terms of the proposition in which it is expressed; or by the truth it realizes. In each of these three objections, the "self-evidence" could be something in the nature of things or in the grammar of language or in the immanent content of thought. Bonaventure had advocated all three of these possibilities, as did medieval masters before him. But for Aquinas these three constitute what are today unhappily called "objections." Actually, what these "objections" do is to fill out the problem the article is to address. One should notice carefully how Aquinas formulates this First Objection.

> *Obj. 1*: It seems to be self-evident [*per se notum*] that God is. [Why?] Because those things are said to be self-evident to us, whose knowledge is naturally

present [*naturaliter inest*] within us. This is obvious, for example, in the case with first principles. But, as Damascene says at the beginning of his book, "The knowledge that God exists is naturally implanted [*inserta*] in everyone." Therefore, that God is, is self-evident.[11]

The intellectual tradition that John Damascene represented here, as understood by St. Thomas, is far more ancient than Christianity. The Epicureans, for example, explained universal consent by an internal πρόληψις – a basic and undeniable, conceptual and self-justifying pre-apprehension – that made all subsequent thought possible. This was the position that the Epicurean Gaius Velleius had proposed and defended in Cicero's *De natura deorum*.[12]

Now the answer that Aquinas gives to this objection is remarkable – and also remarkably different from his previous treatments of this same issue in earlier works.

> *Res. 1*: It should be said that to know in some general way and under a certain kind of confusion that God is, is naturally implanted in us [*cognoscere Deum esse in aliquo communi, sub quadam confusione, est nobis naturaliter insertum*], namely, in so far as God is the happiness of the human being [*hominis beatitudo*]. For the human being naturally desires happiness. And what is naturally desired by the human being is naturally known by him. But this is not to know simply [*simpliciter*] that God is – just as to know that someone is coming is not to know Peter, although the one coming is Peter; for many think that the perfect good for the human being, which is happiness, is riches; others, indeed, think it is pleasure; still others think it is other things.[13]

It is imperative to note very carefully how Aquinas deals with this objection. In no way does his response simply dismiss it. Nor does he distinguish two *kinds* of knowledge, one of which apprehends God and the other does not. At issue here, and they are internally differentiated, are two different *stages* of knowledge – as the figure approaching is apprehended first in the most general, incomplete way and then as the individual person, Peter. In both of these developmental stages, God in some way emerges in human awareness and judgment.

Aquinas's response was initially to develop the cogency of the objection further with the axiom that "what is naturally desired is naturally known." Now human beings naturally desire happiness – not simply some form of contentment however mindless, but the fulfillment of the human desires for knowledge and love, for meaning and communion. Happiness is the complete human good, and thus the longing for happiness is inherent in a human being. But God specifies or constitutes or "informs" human happiness. God discloses, realizes, and constitutes the meaning and joy for which human beings were made. Thus, when human beings naturally long for happiness, they are actually and naturally longing for God.

But whatever is naturally desired/longed for is naturally known. Thus and in this way, God actually is known – even if unknown! God is given to human awareness in the human longing for happiness. Human beings naturally and primordially know God in their longings – but they may be without the intellectual and religious acuity to recognize the character of what their drive towards happiness is fixed upon. If human happiness is given as possible, then God must be given as actual – otherwise human happiness is not even possible. His actuality is the condition for and the specification of human happiness.

Aquinas agrees that to know in this way that God is (*cognoscere Deum esse*) is naturally implanted (*naturaliter insertum*) in us. This real but very primordial stage of knowledge (*cognoscere*) has two significant, modifying characteristics. It is very general (*in aliquo communi*) and it is indistinct or confused (*sub quadam confusione*).[14] The knowledge that emerges out of natural desire is not "simpliciter" to know that God is. It is to know "in aliquo communi, sub quadam confusione." This is an imprecise, rudimentary, and inchoative human awareness of God, and Aquinas clarifies it with a crucially important example: If you should see at a great distance someone approaching, you do not know exactly who it is, even though it is Peter. You can mistake his figure for any number of other persons or other things. It is only gradually that Peter becomes clearly figured as the thing that is approaching. But it is crucial to note that one does not deduce or infer Peter from the initial experience of an approaching figure. Rather in one way or another, the confused and general object, which could be interpreted in so many different ways, gradually clarifies itself in experience, perhaps in multiple experiences. So also, human beings in their inescapable longing for happiness are actually desiring God and aware of God in this primitive beginning of awareness, though in a very confused and general way. But such inchoate knowledge is so primitive that it is open to many errors. Indeed, rather than necessarily identifying happiness with God, human beings can and do identify happiness with riches, pleasure, and other things.[15]

At this very beginning of his treatment of the existence of God in the *Summa theologiae*, Aquinas is advancing an alternative in knowledge other than the absolute divide between inferential knowledge of God and immediate vision.

He is differentiating two developmental *stages* or moments within knowledge – rather than *kinds* of knowledge – and asserting the rudimentary, very imperfect beginnings of knowledge, a stage that is grounded on a fundamental human orientation towards God prior to any inference or demonstration – an indistinct and confused givenness of God in human longings for happiness.

This introduces a knowing compenetrated with unknowing: an inchoate, confused, vague knowledge of God, but one that is inescapably part of human experience, as it is disclosed in the human desire for happiness. One really does not know specifically what one already knows in this confused way until it comes into a more articulated focus. One does not know what one is already in intentional contact with. This confused and general knowledge is inherently incomplete, but its presence makes it legitimate to assert that at this fundamental moment of human longing, God enters as a horizon and direction of human awareness – as final cause, if you will – an awareness that is vague, confused, general, atmospheric, but enough so that Aquinas can use the word *cognoscere.*

Very few have given this response of Aquinas the understanding attention it deserves. One can take for an example the writings of the great Domingo Bañes – the one whom Etienne Gilson judges the greatest among the classic commentators on St. Thomas. Bañes reduces the content of this response to inference: it is discursive knowledge, bearing directly upon similitudes, effects, created participations in the highest good, and from these one can argue to God. What one is desiring is not God (in his essence) but the similitudes/likenesses of God. But that is not what St. Thomas is asserting. Aquinas is asserting that in desiring happiness, human beings are actually desiring – and hence, actually (albeit confusedly) knowing – God. Bañes states explicitly that God and all God's excellences can be known only by inference or by faith, *ex discursu* or *ex fide humana vel divina.*[16]

Aquinas certainly maintains that to know and to love anything created is to know and to love God implicitly, the way that one comes to know and loves a cause from its effects. But that is not what he is stating here. Here, at the very beginning of his treatment of the essence of God, St. Thomas is saying something much more and something that will at this juncture contextualize everything else that follows: namely, that there is a comprehensive desire that is crucially human, a desire whose focal object we call happiness or the complete human good, and the specifying cause of that happiness is God, although not necessarily apprehended as God. To desire in this primordial way is to long for God and hence to know God – in a confused, general, inchoate, incomplete way, granted, modify it as you will, but still in some way to know God, so much so that nothing else will ever satisfy, unless one negates or suppresses this desire.

Even more: human beings first know God in this way – not by arguing from a similitude or by inferring from effect to cause, but far more directly, as they long for happiness, albeit (again) in such confusion and so vaguely. This is obviously not to say that the metaphysical proposition, "God is," has been demonstrated. Even less is it any claim to discursive knowledge about the divine nature. But, on the other hand, neither is it nothing! It is for human beings the first and inescapable stage of their knowledge of God. Subsequent experience, the acceptance of faith, analysis, and inference will clarify this awareness, demonstrate what is true about the One whom human beings already reached so vaguely and inchoatively in their longings, and move in a thousand ways in knowledge from what is so profoundly imperfect to a greater actualization. As reflection and inference proceed, they are not introducing a simply new reality into human awareness, they are not introducing a stranger as Paul Tillich would have it. Thomas is not proposing a knowledge of God as one would come to argue to the existence of Neptune because of the pertur-bations on Uranus. He is rather moving towards greater clarity about One who has always been so indistinctly and vaguely given and present in experience. As Etienne Gilson commented: "God was that which, under the name of hap-piness, [the human being] was always pursuing as his ultimate end. When a man knows that God has always been the end of his desire, he cannot help feeling that he has *always known* God."[17]

This aboriginal awareness of the divine, however, is not the beatific vision – just as it is not a conclusion emerging out of argumentation. There must be a mediation, a finite modification of the intellect that makes it possible for the human being to possess such awareness, a medium that so modifies human consciousness as to have it intentionally focus upon the reality of God – as confused and general as such focal awareness is. For Aquinas, the medium is the appropriation of human longings, the human yearning for happiness. God is known *in* the awareness of these human longings. "Whatever is naturally desired is naturally known." God is known in this vague and general way as purpose, as direction, as specifying final cause.

There are two things Aquinas is not saying; there are two kinds of media-tion he is ruling out. First, human longing does not serve simply as evidence for God, evidence from which one reasons or argues to something of which one has no experience, i.e., the way one would see smoke and infer that there must be a fire (*signum quod*). Second, human longing is not a modification of human awareness of which human beings are simply unaware as their long-ings mediate an awareness of God – as the image in the eye makes it possible to see the trees (*signum quo*). Both of these are foreign to Aquinas's argument. It is rather that human beings know both their own comprehensive longing for happiness and *in it* at the same time they know (in a very confused and vague way) the God who specifies this longing, makes it to be what it is.[18] Thus it is *in the desiring* (*signum/medium in quo*) that we know both the longing itself and the God who is mediated in it as its specifying object, "as the reality itself that we desire to possess."[19] God is given to human beings in their desire for happiness in a mediated immediacy.

Human happiness is a single, but dyadic reality, essentially constituted by the (1) reaching and possession "of the [2] reality we desire to possess." Human happiness entails two components, uncreated and created, divine and human: the God reached (*finis cuius*) and the human possession of God (*finis quo*).[20] Just as words are media in which one is aware both of the sounds and of the meaning they convey or just as a hug or embrace conducts both the physical experience and the friendship it embodies, so do fundamental human long-ings for the possession of happiness mediate the reality of God primordially. In knowing them and as we know them, we know God confusedly, vaguely, and very imprecisely – God as the reality that specifies the character of human happiness. God is known in our longings.

PARALLEL TEXTS

To understand how radically different was the position advanced here by the *Summa theologiae* and how considered was Aquinas's departure from his pre-vious judgment, one must review something of his prior exploration of this issue. His repeated treatment of this objection in his prior works indicates that he had given it continual reflection, while the changing character of his treatment indicates that he was never satisfied with previous arguments. An analysis of "parallel texts" in other works may prove instructive.[21]

Dealing with the knowledge of God offered in the fundamental human desire for happiness, Aquinas's early *Commentary on the Sentences* also acknowledged the "*auctoritas Damasceni*," but its response distinguished two kinds of knowledge of God, i.e., two different "objects" of knowledge rather than two stages of knowledge. There is the knowledge according to his like-nesses (*secundum ipsius similitudinem*) and the knowledge of God according to God's nature, in God's self (*secundum quod est in sua natura*).[22] A similitude of God is anything effected by God. "Those things that come from God are like him [*assimilantur ei*] in so far as they are beings [*entia*], as God is the first and universal source of all being [*totius esse*]."[23] Similitude is that which an effect possesses from its cause and that which bespeaks this cause. The effect is in this way symptomatic of its cause. Knowledge can be obtained inferentially from similitudes as one explores an effect for intelligence about its cause. This distinction between knowledge of God through his effects and knowledge of God in his nature is one that Bañes introduced to deal with *Summa theologiae* 1.2.1.ad 1. But Aquinas had not applied this distinction in the *Summa theologiae*; he had used it in his early *Commentary on the Sentences*. In this way, Aquinas's commentary asserted, God is desired implicitly in everything that is desired and known in everything that is known. This is the way that a cause is known implicitly through its effect.[24] Thus his *Commentary on the Sentences* held that "we do not come to God except by inferential argument, and nothing such [as God] is evident in itself [*per se notum*]."[25]

The *Quaestio disputata de Veritate* formulated virtually the same response. The Objection cited again the classic text from John Damascene as one part of the statement of its problematic and argued from Boethius that all human beings necessarily desire the *summum bonum*. "But only God is the *summum bonum*. Therefore all desire God. But what is not known cannot be desired. Therefore, there is a common conception [*conceptio communis*] that God is." But here Aquinas interpreted John Damascene as laying the foundation for a process of reasoning to the reality of God. What is *naturaliter insertum* in every human person is not a knowledge or awareness of the divine reality – however general and confused – but "something from which one can come to the knowledge that God is."[26] Again the distinction is drawn between desiring God in God's nature or essence and in his likeness. It is only in this latter way that all desire the *summum bonum* because nothing is desirable except insofar as in it the likeness of the *summum bonum* is found.[27]

The argument developed somewhat further in the *Summa contra Gentiles*. The human being naturally knows God as he or she naturally desires God. But what the person desires is not the divine goodness in itself, but a human happiness, which is again *quaedam similitudo divinae bonitatis*. Thus it is not God who is naturally desired and known, but God's likeness and God only by implication. And the human task is "through [*per*] his [God's] likenesses found in effects to come by reasoning [*ratiocinando*] to the knowledge of him [God]."[28] In these three earlier and somewhat different responses of Aquinas, inference seems to be the only alternative to the beatific vision. But this does not reach the more subtle resolution offered by the *Summa theologiae*.

COORDINATE TEXTS IN THE *SUMMA THEOLOGIAE*

In the First Question of the *Summa theologiae*, Aquinas did, indeed, treat a knowledge somewhat similar to this when he described knowledge from inclination (*per modum inclinationis*). The chaste man, he wrote, recognizes what actions are chaste, not because he can define or analyze the virtue of chastity. He does not perceive the presence of chastity because he can define it conceptually, let alone conclude to it by argument. He knows by a kind of connaturality. His own desire for chastity, his chaste life, and his inclination or orientation towards chastity disclose its presence or its absence in a particular choice or action. The chaste person is able to identify the chaste correctly "insofar as one is inclined towards a life of chastity."[29] It is out of this inclination that one comes to the recognition of its presence or absence. So also in all connatural knowledge, one knows connaturally insofar as the character and the desires of the knowing subject are coordinate with the object known.[30] You know as you are what you are. One does not prove its presence, but recognizes it. But there is also a connaturality in the inclination that is the human natural desire for happiness and the God who specifies that desire as an object specifies an act and its potency. God is intentionally present in the inclination for happiness, and "what one naturally desires, one naturally knows."

The *Summa theologiae* came back again to this primordial knowledge of God in its treatment of the first principles of the moral or ethical order. There is a very strange problem raised here. An Article poses this question: whether one can commit a venial sin with only original sin on his soul.[31] This may not be a raging issue troubling the ranks of contemporary theology, dividing its practitioners into intractably warring camps, but Aquinas did think it important and answered it emphatically in the negative. The *determinatio* maintained that when a human being enters into the very first use of reason – before any rational inference or argument – the person in some way begins to become aware of herself, to reflect or deliberate about or appropriate herself. As this deliberation emerges in her consciousness, she either turns – however imperceptibly and gradually – to the appropriate purpose or the end of her human life (*ad debitum finem*) or she does not. If she does turn towards this end (again, one must stress, however vague and confused) she is graced and original sin remitted – whether baptized or not. (In this, Dante's first circle of the *Inferno* could not be more distant from St. Thomas's theology.) But if someone fails to turn *ad debitum finem*, she sins mortally in choosing to turn away from the purpose of her life; she chooses "not to do what lies within her capability."[32]

Now there is no doubt for Aquinas that the end of human beings is God, and this because of the divine goodness.[33] In moral deliberation, therefore, Aquinas seems to posit a pre-inferential awareness similar to that given in the primordial desire for happiness: a vague, very general and confused, apperception of God, as final and specifying cause. In this way, at the radical beginnings of conscious human life, God is given as present, not simply inferred.

Granted that God is in some way prediscursively apprehended, what can one say about the character of this apprehension? What is the knowledge that exists in some "general way and under some confusion?" What can this very odd language mean?

Later in the First Part of the *Summa theologiae*, similar wording appeared in another Article.[34] Again, the issue was knowledge, and again the example will be given of Peter coming – only this time, it is not Peter; it is Socrates! Aquinas is asking whether the more universal is prior in human knowledge:

> Our intellect proceeds from potency into act. Anything that proceeds from potency into act arrives first at an incomplete act [*actum incompletum*], which is midway between potency and act, before arriving at the complete [*perfectum*] act. Now the complete act at which the intellect arrives is complete knowledge [*scientia completa*], through which it knows things distinctly and determinately. The incomplete act is imperfect knowledge, through which it knows things indistinctly and under some confusion.[35]

As in his previous response to the objection taken from John Damascene, Aquinas is here distinguishing explicitly not two kinds of knowledge, but two stages in the development of knowledge. He is distinguishing the complete act of knowledge "through which things are distinctly and determinately known," from "imperfect knowledge, through which things are known indistinctly and under some confusion [*scientia imperfecta, per quam sciuntur res indistincte et sub quadam confusione*]."[36] (One must remember that "imperfect" for Aquinas means "incomplete;" it carries here no moral implications.) This second is not another kind of knowledge; it is rather an incomplete stage in the process towards complete knowledge. It lies between potency and act. What is known in this manner is "in a way known actually [*in actu*] and in a way known potentially [*in potentia*]." This is the way, for example, that one knows a whole, without a distinct knowledge of each of the parts. Here one knows, but in general and with the parts confused. Aquinas reaches back to Aristotle and the opening of the *Physics* for the experience and tradition out of which he is speaking:

> Now what is plain and obvious at first is rather confused masses [τὰ συνκεχυμένα], the elements and principles of which become known to us later by analysis. Thus we must advance from generalities [ἐκ τῶν καθόλου] to particulars; for it is a whole that is best known to sense perception, and a generality is a kind of whole, comprehending many things within it, like parts.[37]

Then Aquinas comments: "It is manifest that to know something in which many things [*plura*] are contained, without having a proper knowledge of each of these constituents, is to know something under a certain confusion [*sub confusione quadam*]." Confused knowledge is indistinct knowledge, an imperfect stage of knowledge. This is how human beings know the parts of a whole without perceiving each by itself.

The language and the example return one to the response of the First Article of the Second Question. For this is the kind of knowledge, St. Thomas had maintained, in which human beings first know God. God is given in the whole of their experience of a longing for happiness, but given generically and indistinctly. The actual example Aquinas gives here of imperfect knowledge is the match of one we have seen in the previous one:

> When a thing is seen from afar, it is seen to be a body before it is seen to be an animal, and to be an animal before it is seen to be a man, and to be a man before it is seen to be Socrates or Plato.[38]

It is not the case that this *cognitio indistincta* results from seeing the similitude and arguing from it to the hidden object, as Bañes would have it. Rather, Aquinas asserts that one sees or even (in this way) experiences the object from the beginning, but confusedly. As this knowledge grows, and however it grows, the basic focus has not changed to something else. It is rather that human awareness focuses upon the same reality and distinguishes increasingly the characteristics that reveal it – first as it is very imperfectly known and continually as that imperfection yields to increased realization of its distinctive aspects or components. Knowledge here grows to its completion within an experience that is already there.

Nor should St. Thomas's nuanced position, of an imperfect stage of knowledge that is neither distinct vision nor inference, come as a surprise, different as it is from the response given in earlier texts to similar objections. For the Question here is "An Deus sit?" In a much earlier work, his *Expositio super librum Boethii de Trinitate*, Aquinas had stated that "we cannot know *that* a thing is without knowing someway *what* it is, either perfectly or *confusedly*."

Again the distinction is between two stages of knowledge: complete and incomplete or confused. He applied this general statement to the human knowledge of God (and all immaterial substances): "Similarly, therefore, we cannot know *that* God and other immaterial substances exist unless we know somehow, in some *confused* way, *what they are*."[39]

This seems to me a crucially significant text. Confused knowledge comes first – as it does in the *Summa theologiae*! But where is that confused knowledge of God to come from as the *Summa theologiae* moves to consider the proposition, that God is, unless it comes from something prior to demonstration, i.e., from that vague, generic awareness – given in experience – of what God is to specify the character of human happiness?

However encased in scholastic precisions and vocabulary, Aquinas's developed position on the initial human awareness of God is of immense importance, an awareness awakened in human beings within the primordially human, within the desire for happiness. Aquinas does not present human beings coming to God as to Tillich's stranger. They come to God as to the incomprehensible, granted. But this mysterious God has always been given to human awareness in those longings that are the confused beginnings of the exercises of humanity.[40] God was, thus, not primordially reached as a conclusion – the religious act is not inference – but as a presence, there from the beginning of human awareness and gradually coming into focus, even in its increasing incomprehensibility. The metaphysical inferences from the finite universe serve this movement into a more articulated awareness, but it does not serve as its first moment. The first moment is given by human longings and loves.

Christology in the Summa theologiae

But that still leaves open the question of how Christology figures in the *Summa theologiae*. Christian theology insists that the normative historical revelation and witness of the reality of God – and indeed, of the meaning and destiny of all things – is Jesus Christ.[41] In Jesus, God is giving himself. But the structure of the *Summa theologiae* does not make it immediately evident that this tells in the theology of St. Thomas. Moving through this work for beginners, the neophyte would treat in the First Part the existence of God and then the divine essence, the trinity of persons and then the procession of all things from God including the creation of angels and human beings. The Second Part takes up the movement of the human person to God, and hence the character of human happiness and fulfillment, human virtues, vices, law and grace, and so forth. And only when all of this inquiry into the divine reality and human life has reached its conclusions does the student begin finally to consider *ex professo* the incarnation and the mysteries of the life of Christ. This appears to allot a very secondary, hardly definitive role to Christology. No surprise is it to find that so devout a Thomist as Anton Pegis can omit any questions dealing with Christology entirely from his two volumes proudly presented as *The Basic Writings of Saint Thomas Aquinas*.[42] Obviously Christology is not to be reckoned basic! Can one not push this further and suggest that absence of Christology in the discussion of God opens the field to other normative options by which the assertion of the reality of God is to be secured, which is the history of later centuries?

The great Père M. D. Chenu, O.P., schematized the *Summa theologiae* in terms of the Neo-Platonic *exitus* and *reditus*. All things proceed from God in the First Part; all things return to God in the Second Part. Variations and modifications of this scheme have been presented by many other commentators, but this will do for our purposes. But what does Chenu say about the Third Part, the Christology? He presents the problem starkly, even if phrased in the subjunctive: that "judging in the *abstract*, [Part III] would seem to play the role of no more than a part added to the whole as an afterthought."[43] Abstract or concrete, that would be an extraordinary position for any Christian theologian to occupy, and it is not Chenu's. He explains the position of the Third Part in this way: the "transition from the *Second* to the *Third Part* is a passage from the order of the necessary to the order of the historical, [which he explains as] from an account of structures to the actual story of God's gifts."[44] These latter are "the contingencies of God's free will." Thus theology in the three parts of the *Summa* "unites, amid sensitiveness to God's transcendency, a science of the necessary [the first two parts] and the respect for the contingencies of a love which is eternally free [the third part]."[45] The distinguished Dominican moralist Benoit Henri Merkelbach is praised by Ignatius Theodore Eschmann, O.P., for another very similar suggestion: the Christology understood as the "incidental (that is, the historical)" contingent means for achieving what had been already explored and what is essential to theology.[46]

One hesitates to disagree with scholars who have made such major and insightful contributions to the study of the text of Aquinas, but I must confess that I do not find this explanation of the location of the Third Part persuasive nor does the language of "contingencies" and "incidental" – abstract or concrete – strike one as adequately representing the place of Christology within any presentation of *catholica veritas*. The free choices of God are as crucially present throughout the earlier sections of the *Summa theologiae* as they are in the latter. One recalls, for example, the temporal missions of the Son and the Spirit; the decision to create; the specification of that creation to be of angels and of human beings. It is hard to predicate historical and contingent of the Incarnation in the Third Part and not of original sin in the *Prima Secundae* (1–2.81.1). The gratuity of grace runs through the entire *Summa*, as Thomas O'Meara, O.P., has recently pointed out.[47] The incarnation is no more contingent than is creation. Both are pure gifts, coming out of the freedom of God.

But that only underscores the question at hand: If Aquinas as a *catholicae veritatis doctor* is going to talk about God, what about Christ, the paradigmatic manifestation of God? Why are Christ and the mysteries of Christ introduced so late after so many of the principal theological questions have already been resolved – questions into whose resolution Christology should have entered?

It is, of course, important to remember, as the very First Question of the *Summa* insists, that the theology in the *Summa theologiae* is derivative from and belongs to *sacra doctrina*, and that *sacra doctrina* is effectively God's teaching as found in the Bible, especially the New Testament. There the position of Christ is obviously of central and critical importance. One must further recognize that the treatments of the New Law (1–2.106–114), of Original Sin (1–2.81–85), and of the Gifts of the Holy Spirit (1–2.71–80) are earlier than the Third Part and are not intelligible apart from Christology.[48] But this acknowledgement simply intensifies the problem about the place and weight of Christology in the *Summa*. Why does the explicit theological attention to the reality and meaning of Jesus appear so late in a study whose inquiry and conclusions should be so fundamentally dependent upon God's self-revelation in Christ? Why does the problem of the existence of God not engage the witness of Christ?

To get some purchase on this question, it might help to consider the three prologues that introduce and outline the three parts of the *Summa*. For there is a remarkable parallelism among them. Each of these prologues begins with a substantial reality and then moves to what emerges from its freedom. So the First Part takes up God, whose being, essence, and triune nature are necessary and from whose free choice comes the procession of all created things. So the Second Part takes up human beings and the things that issue from their "free decision [*liberum arbitrium*] and the power over their own works."[49] Now in the Third Part does not a similar structure obtain? Only here one is dealing neither with the divine necessity of God nor with the human being, the created image of God, but with *convenientia*, what is appropriate, what is profoundly fitting, i.e., Jesus, the Savior, and those "benefits that he has extended to the human race." "Benefits" designates the things that proceed from his power and freedom, namely (here) the sacraments, and the goal of eternal life.

But even more: St. Thomas does not say that this consideration of Christ comes as incidental or as something of an appendix to the steady progress of the *Summa*. He states just the contrary: Christology comes as the fulfillment of all that has gone before in theology. The Latin is quite strong: "It is necessary that, for the consummation of the entire enterprise of theology [*necesse est ut, ad consummationem totius theologici negotii*], after the consideration of the ultimate end of human life and of the virtues and the vices, our consideration [*nostra consideratio*] about the Savior himself and about his benefits to the human race follow immediately [*subsequatur*]."[50] "Consummatio" is a very strong word in Thomistic usage, indicating accomplishment or completion or perfection. And understandably so. Completion is a very strong theme in the Aristotelian tradition because one only knows something in its completion. "For what each thing is when fully developed, we call its nature, whether we are speaking of a man, a horse, or a family. Besides the final cause and the end of a thing is the best."[51] The consummation of theology indicates what theology is or should be.

The *Summa theologiae* must be conceived or read in a manner that does justice both to its internal structure of *exitus/reditus* and to the "consummate" character of Christ's revelation of God and, hence, of the entire theological project. Paradoxical as it may seem, each of these requirements reinforces the other, i.e., the very *exitus/reditus* dynamic of the *Summa* allows the Christology to illumine uniquely what has gone before as completion illumines preparations. This is to claim more than that this completion of the *Summa* by the Third Part, like any completion, discloses the potencies and the promise of prior sections. There is a further and unique contribution the *exitus/reditus* structure makes to this explicit consideration of Christ and of what issues from his freedom. For this *exitus/reditus* schema forms a circle. The consummation of theology is made possible by a circular structure in which the *reditus* returns to the beginnings of the *exitus*, in which created reality is united to God. Such a circular structure was of the essence of completion or perfection.

Only here does the completion become one with the beginning. "For the ultimate perfection of a rational creature is in the principle/source/beginning of its being. For each thing is perfect/complete insofar as it attains to its principle/source/beginning."[52] "Ad suum principium attingit:" The *Summa theologiae* achieves this circular completion in and through Christ.

Jean-Pierre Torrell, O.P., has drawn attention to Aquinas's statement in the *Compendium theologiae*: "The totality [*universitas*] of the divine work finds its completion [*perficitur*] when the human being, the last creature created, returns to his source by a kind of circle, when *through the work of the incarnation*, the human being finds himself united to the very source of things itself."[53] Christology is the consummation of theology because Christ is the consummation of the divine action of uniting the world with himself. What began in the creation returns to God in the incarnation. Such an understanding of the incarnation as the circular perfection of creation had been with St. Thomas from the beginning of his teaching. Commenting upon the problem whether human nature, more than any other nature, can be assumed, Aquinas remarked in his *Commentary on the Sentences*: "Because the human being is the last of creatures, as it were the last one created, when this nature is assumed, the last is joined to the first principle in the manner of a circle, which is the perfect figure because it does not admit of increase."[54] "The last is joined to the first." Christology completes the lines of the two previous parts in this circle of knowledge, joining God with the human both in the work of the incarnation and in the work of salvation. It is, therefore, the consummation of theology. *Exitus/reditus* forms perfect reflexivity, a circle brought to its completion in its Christological *reditus*, as in Christ, all things return to God.

Thomas has said that in the work of salvation, Jesus showed himself to be the way of truth (*viam veritatis*). The way to the truth both about God and about the human is to be finally found in Jesus.[55] If this claim is to be realized, the Third Part must illumine the First Part. And that is precisely what happens, because the line of inquiry is circular. Very early in the First Part, for example, Thomas had argued to the goodness of God. This goodness is both manifested in creation – because God is the first cause of all things – and constituted in itself by the divine perfection in being.[56] But if one would come to a deeper manifestation of this same divine goodness, now as *self*-communication, *self-giving*, one must move beyond the creation and contemplate the incarnation. The initial evidence for the goodness of God was the created world; the final evidence is Jesus. Now in his Christology, Thomas makes his own the maxim that "it belongs to the very character of the good that it communicate itself to others [*pertinet autem ad rationem boni ut se aliis communicet*]." He applied this metaphysics of the good to the goodness of God. Now, the *Summa* grounds the entire tractate on the incarnation upon the goodness of God, the goodness constituted by and revealed in self-communication.[57] To make this statement clearer, one could say that in the earlier parts of the *Summa* each created thing reveals God as evidence *from which* one can argue to the existence and attributes of God. But Christ reveals the actual goodness of God in his incarnation, his attitudes and actions. God is present and active and self-manifesting in the mysteries of Christ's life. In the *Summa theologiae*, the First Part is the first word about the divine goodness, but the more definitive word about the goodness of God – in which the first comes to its fulfillment – is Christ. Thus the *Summa* actually embodies in its *ordo* what St. Thomas had made a criterion for the perfect, for completion: "Each thing is complete or perfect, only insofar as it reaches its beginning or source [*in tantum enim unumquodque perfectum est, in quantum ad suum principium attingit*]."[58]

One further example: the First Part of the *Summa* takes up the nature and character of divine providence, but if one would apprehend the depth of providence in its unspeakable commitment and care for human life and eternal destiny, one must contemplate the purpose and the hypothetical necessity of the incarnation and of the passion, death, and resurrection. These great mysteries are the concrete components or content of divine providence. In the *Summa theologiae*, one comes to the consummation of the self-manifestation of God as one meditates upon the reality of Christ and finds them revealed *in Ipso*.

Christology brings the First Part to a consummation, to a unique manifestation. Thus Aquinas can and does make his own in the very First Article of his Christology the statement of John Damascene that through the incarnation "is *shown* [*monstratur*] the goodness and the wisdom and the justice and the power or strength of God: goodness, for he did not despise the weakness of his own handiwork; justice, because he vanquished the tyrant by none other than man and yet did not snatch man away by violence; wisdom, for he found the most apt payment for a most exacting debt; power or strength that is infinite, for nothing could be greater than for God to become a human being [*nihil est maius quam Deum fieri hominem*]."[59] The incarnation is for Aquinas "quo maius nihil." So it is in Christ that one perceives in some normative and definitive way the attributes of God: what is God's goodness and wisdom, God's providence and power. It is in Christ that we understand the depth and the great promise that is initially present in the First Part and revealed Christologically in the Third Part.

Christ comes, then, at the consummation of theology in Aquinas, a culmination in which everything else about God and about human beings must be reviewed and reread. All other things are propaedeutic to Christ's revelation of God as Christ is the revelation also of the final meaning and destiny of all things. The end of theology is in this sense its beginning.

The separation of Christology from classical theology is not the fault of the *Summa theologiae*. The fault has been to read or hand out the *Summa* so piecemeal that the circular nature of its *exitus/reditus* schema, its *ordo disciplinae*, is broken and lost. In this dismantling, each part is made to stand autonomously on its own and the sections that should be mutually elucidating are not able to offer one another their reciprocal intelligibility. But the issue of the structure of the *Summa* is not simply an interesting, even fascinating puzzle for specialists. Its resolution indicates the way the book should be read, the mutual support offered by its various parts, and the "way of learning" students should assimilate. This circle embodies the *ordo disciplinae*, which is, after all, an order of learning. The entire study of theology is itself a part of this *reditus*, a return to God. The project of reading the *Summa* is part of the return of creatures to God. For the *Summa* originates in the most primitive experience of longings and awareness of God, and it moves towards a developed understanding. For this understanding, the Third Part maintains, there is that which "Jesus Christ has shown us in his own person."[60]

A final word

For Aquinas, God is *given* initially or primordially in his effects, rather than simply *inferred* from his effects. God is a presence, not simply a conclusion. This "givenness of God" is crucially affirmed in at least two ways in the theology of the *Summa theologiae*.

God is given to human beings in their primordial experience of longing for human happiness, in their experience of a human yearning they may come to recognize as desire for a comprehensive, personal love, meaning, and communication. God is given – so vaguely and incomprehensibly – as the focus of these desires as human beings appropriate into a dawning consciousness the happiness to which they aspire and the purpose that draws them. In Rahnerian language, God is given transcendentally as the direction and the drawing of that fundamental love which underlies all others and is present in them.

Secondly, God is given to human beings historically, as part of human history, in Jesus of Nazareth – as one learns to read in him the manifestation of the presence of God. Human beings come to recognize God in Jesus in a manner not totally dissimilar from the way they recognize another as a person, and as they come into this knowledge, they assimilate more profoundly the presence of the attributes and providence of God.

One recognition of the mediated immediacy of God issues from the ontological structure of the human being; the other is empowered by the grace of that faith that transforms the knowing subject and discloses realities that would otherwise be opaque. But in both instances, human knowledge of the presence of God emerges not as the conclusion of inference, but as manifested in – not simply by – pervasive human longing and the person of Jesus. And in this, the *Summa theologiae* charted a radically different course from the one taken by the rationalist tradition traced in the seventeenth and eighteenth centuries.

4

God as the Anti-human[1]

Prologue

The religious intellect confronts in the nineteenth century a unique situation, unprecedented both in the depth of its challenge and in the extension of its claims. During that period, the denial of the reality of God rose to achieve an articulate and powerful presence within the intellectual culture of Western Europe that has never diminished. The nineteenth century watched "the eclipse of God" deepen over Europe, descending massively upon modernity and upon the worlds it embraced as non-European nations fell under the influence of Western thought. Its darkness comprised an absence of religious faith or of any living theistic affirmation together with an alienation, skepticism, or hostility towards religious doctrines and institutions. Atheism with its cognate indifference or militant contempt for the religious was unique in the public acceptance it secured during that century, in the ascendancy within particular subcultures it accrued, and in the rapidity of its increase among intellectuals and the formative agents of culture. This eclipse fell upon all ranks of society in Europe, from workers to bourgeoisie to intellectuals, gathering strength to spread over into the twentieth century with an ideational force unmatched since the Protestant Reformation.

Perhaps more than any previous theologian, Henri de Lubac accurately read the atheistic dynamism of that century as it developed its unexampled repudiation and attack and as it gained in its formidable protests legitimacy and prominence in the intellectual culture of Europe. Those years of passion and revolution were not the recrudescence of a disinterest that in one mood or another has variantly visited humankind in every age. Nor did the century simply retrieve the disdain of the French *salonniers*, of Paul d'Holbach and Denis Diderot, and "the pure critical atheism so fashionable in the last two hundred years."[2] A far more urgent spirit began to drive the repudiation of the God of Christianity, a prophetic humanism whose religious passions were to subvert and replace what from time immemorial had given energy and organic unity to Western culture. The call to this new vision found both articulation and specification in the positive humanism of Auguste Comte, or in the dialectical humanism of Feuerbach and Marx, or in the impassioned advocacy of some form of the Nietzschean or Wagnerian transvaluation of values. But whatever its species, atheism in the nineteenth century bent its considerable energies to apotheosize the human; and for this mission, it was held necessary to counter, overthrow, and supersede the Judeo-Christian worship of God. Under this persuasion, atheism grew into a fanatical anti-theism.[3]

During this steady devolution of religious affirmation, not only the validity of religious belief fell under suspicion and question, but the nature or content of religious ideas themselves. The religious culture of Europe was being reconfigured because the notion of "God" was being reconfigured. God was coming to be seen now as the alienation of the human in favor of an imaginary subject or as the structure of the human society now writ large or as the projection out of fear and longing of Oedipal necessities. Each of these reconfigurations affected in some way political economy, theology, literature, philosophy, and rhetoric. Emerging in the psychological theories that explained religious ideas were such terms as *Vergegenständlichung* and *Entäusserung*, objectification and alienation, and the face of God changed as in some way the hermeneutics of suspicion registered the human interests that had created it.[4]

One wonders how it came to this, how atheism precisely as humanism amassed such strength that European culture became unthinkable without this as a constituent. This is not to ask how social, economic, and political realities gave these ideas their time and their support, but rather how the ideas themselves garnered such credibility in the world of intellect, idealism, and culture of the nineteenth century that in the twentieth century they would shadow great masses of peoples in some way derivative from this culture and touched by the European mind.

"Our first enquiry"

As has been suggested already, a single chapter, no matter how amplified, can only address such questions in a limited and profoundly inadequate way. But even at that, it must begin two centuries before Feuerbach, Comte, and Nietzsche, and consider those previous figures, as Jacques Derrida suggested, in whose wake they wrote.[5] Those prior centuries provided the shaping context for what was to follow. It is necessary to appreciate the change in fundamental thinking that early modernity introduced.

"Fundamental thinking" designates that disciplined reflection within an intellectual period which provides and explores the foundation for all subsequent sciences and arts. It recognizes the general area that a culture regards as fundamental and elaborates the discipline or disciplines that are to investigate this general area. From this, the basic terms and categories are derived; by this, all other human inquiries are finally explained and justified. Such inquiries that exhibit the fundamental thinking characteristic of an era would be the metaphysics of Aristotle or the critiques of Kant. "Fundamental thinking" establishes what one must understand "before" – as the grounding for all other disciplined inquiry – although one often comes upon that "before" long after other disciplines have been pursued. One often comes upon the first last.[6]

In the seventeenth and eighteenth centuries, the focus of fundamental thinking was on the reality that confronted the thinking subject, whether as the content of ideas with Descartes or as the things of the physical universe with Thomas Hobbes. Though he prefaced a "Logic" to the rest of his works, Hobbes named as "The First Grounds of Philosophy" that which deals directly with the physical universe and so combines the geometry that studied simply the motion of things, as in Galileo's mechanics, and the physics that bore upon the general properties of bodies. After this foundation is laid in a grasp of the nature of things, one can go on to study the human person and political society or the state.[7]

The change in the focus of fundamental thinking might take its beginning with an episode that John Locke thought consequential enough both to instigate and to introduce his great project, *An Essay Concerning Human Understanding*. Locke sets the stage at Exeter House in London in the early months of 1671. He and some five or six friends had gathered at the home of his patron, Lord Ashley. One of those present, James Tyrrell, reported that they were discussing "the principles of morality and revealed religion." Now when a group is collectively exploring morality and revealed religion, and especially when it is focusing upon the "principles" of either, i.e., upon their fundamental sources, the discussion is attempting something like ethics and theology. But Locke wrote that "they found themselves quickly at a stand, by the Difficulties that arose on every side."

For some time, they struggled to resolve these "difficulties," but the problems proved intractable. At this point, Locke discerned their common miscalculation. The discussion remained sterile because the order of the inquiries was skewed. Before the group could explore ethics and theology, a prior inquiry was required – a foundational inquiry. The group must talk about the human capacities for this discussion before entertaining it. So Locke proposed, and the entire company agreed, "that, *before* we set our selves upon Enquiries of that Nature [ethical and theological], it was necessary to examine *our own Abilities, and see, what Objects our Understandings were, or were not fitted to deal with.* This I proposed to the Company, who all readily assented; and thereupon it was agreed, that this should be our *first Enquiry.*"[8] Locke's *Essay Concerning Human Understanding* took its birth from that winter conversation, and a whole world was beginning to turn.

What Locke was proposing to his companions and what he formulated in his *Essay* was a quiet revolution. He was urging that one must not investigate any subject matter until one has first ascertained what human beings have the capabilities to know: "Abilities" and "objects" – these must be established first; then one can look among the possible "objects" to decide what they comprise and can disclose of morality and religion. Locke does not introduce the first formulation of a theory of human knowledge; theories of this kind of knowledge pervade the history of Western philosophy. What Locke decided and introduced into modernity was that the theory of knowledge must be foundational to all other knowledge human beings could legitimately claim. This shift was revolutionary in modernity, but in the history of philosophy it was retrieval.

To understand the radical nature of this change in fundamental thinking, one could profitably scrutinize the Hellenistic period, an intellectual world that also came to place before the study of things the epistemological exploration of the ability to know. For the Epicureans, the Stoics, and the Academy agreed that human intellectual capacities also had first to be determined – the possibilities of knowledge, sense perception, judgment and certitude – before an inquiry into any other subject matters of philosophy such as physics or ethics could be engaged. Sextus Empiricus recorded: "The Stoics themselves, too, say that Logic comes first, and Ethics second, while Physics occupies the last place. For the mind must first be fortified for the task of guarding its heritage impregnably, and what thus makes the intellect secure is the Dialectical section."[9]

Epicurus generally accepted the atomic physics of Democritus, but as Sextus Empiricus noted, the Epicureans formulated as primary and fundamental a Κανών καὶ Κριτήριον, and this "canonics," which secured the three criteria for truth – sensation, concepts, and feelings – allowed one to continue on to physics and from there to ethics.[10] In a few pages, Theophrastus recapitulated the Aristotelian division of the theoretical sciences, but epistemologically recast their proper subjects: nature, quantity, and first principles or god become denominated also as the objects of sense (αἰσθητά), objects of knowledge (νοητά) and the object of desire (ὀρεκτόν).[11] As the original Platonic Academy developed into the Second Academy with Arcesilaus and the Third Academy with Carneades, the basic questions became epistemological as they battled skeptically with the Stoics about the validity of sense-perception and the possibility of certitude.[12] Finally, the Sophists' reduction of all human knowledge to perspectival discriminations gave way to Pyrrho's assertion that "things are unknowable" and so judgment must be suspended, a suspension buttressed by the contradictions between sensation and understanding and induced by the ten modes of antinomies.[13] No matter how far these great schools of Hellenistic philosophy differed among themselves, to provide a foundation for all inquiry and reflection necessitated initially securing the epistemological possibility or impossibility of valid knowledge.

As is so often the case in the history of thought, revolution followed the institution that had once been revolution. The Hellenistic world eventually yielded to the Roman with its fundamental emphasis given to *verba et facta* (language and deeds), and this Roman revolution shifted the focus of fundamental thinking from epistemological inquiries to semantics and pragmatics as absolutely foundational to disciplined knowledge.

Each of these changes in fundamental thinking gave its specific features to the age and its philosophies. "The foci of divergent philosophies are formed by the dominant intellectual tendency of an age to converge its [foundational] inquiries either upon the structure of things or the processes of thought or the expressions of men in language and action."[14] Each of these foci, in turn, stamped its character on the subsequent reflection and inquiry of the period; each had emerged as a necessity because of the deficiencies of its predecessor.

Locke was signaling a similar need, here, to turn from the immediate consideration of the nature of things or the imperatives of human morality to the epistemological as foundational for any such consideration. Thomas Langan and Etienne Gilson could justly remark about that moment: "The day it occurred to Locke to ask *What can we know?* criticism was born into the modern tradition."[15]

This was to begin philosophy with the human knowing subject, as had Descartes. But Locke parted company with Descartes. Descartes attended to the content of the ideas grasped by thinking: doubting has thinking within its own content, and thinking similarly contains personal existence. Locke would also begin with the thinking subject, not to examine particular ideas, i.e., the content of thought, but the human process of thinking itself, the human capacity for understanding. And from this, he would justify its objects, the things that could be known. Locke was not to establish the entailments of their content, but to give warrant to this content's even being entertained. With Locke, Western philosophy began once more – as in the Hellenistic period – to shift its foundational thinking from "things" – from the realities given in nature or the ideas confronting the thinking subject – to the actual capacities of thinking subjects themselves.

God in evidence and function

This shift worked its concomitant effect on Locke's natural theology. "Morality and divinity" had occasioned the project of the *Essay*, and they also constituted those "parts of Knowledge, that Men are most concern'd to be clear in."[16] Locke would continue the ancient tradition of finding that through design the "wisdom and power" of God "appears plainly in all the works of the creation."[17] But that was not to be the first or primary demonstration. Locke's "First Enquiry" bore upon the thinking subject, and this allowed him to transpose the traditional demonstration from the contingency of things to the cognitive appropriation of the contingency of this thinking subject. One knew that one was contingent. One's own existence embodied a contingency recognized in intuition and reflection: "To shew, therefore, that we are capable of *knowing*, i.e. *being certain that there is a* GOD, and how we may come by this certainty, I think we need go no farther than ourselves, and that undoubted Knowledge we have of our own Existence."[18] This is not a Newtonian appeal to design. Locke moves to the existence of the thinking subject – again, not in the manner of Descartes – as the fundamental evidence for the existence of God. This is to sponsor within modernity a new natural theology commensurate with the new Enquiry. We begin with the knowledge of our own existence. One begins with the self-knowledge of the thinking subject.

A human being (1) "knows certainly, that he exists, and that he is something." Now, if "he is something that actually exists," (2) something must always have existed, for nothing cannot produce anything real. Thus (3) "from Eternity there has been something; since what was not from Eternity, had a Beginning; and what had a Beginning, must be produced by something else."[19] The contingent thinking subject, the one who "knows," gives the warrant for an eternal being as its source.

Now further: (4) human "capacities" and their "objects" allow some knowledge of this eternal source since "all the Powers it [the thinking subject] has, must be owing to, and received from the same Source . . . so *this eternal Being must be also the most powerful.*"[20] So also "a Man finds within himself *Perception*, and *Knowledge*," and this entails "*a knowing Being from Eternity.*" (5) And to conclude this line of thinking: "thus, from the Consideration of ourselves, and what we infallibly find in our own Constitutions, our Reason leads us to the Knowledge of this certain and evident Truth, That *there is an eternal, most powerful, and most knowing Being,* which whether any one will please to call *God,* it matters not."[21] This is all "from the Consideration of ourselves and what we infallibly find in our own Constitution." Human beings "cannot want a clear proof of him, as long as we carry our selves about us."[22] For proof, all we need is ourselves! This seems an inconsequential enough and minor adjustment of a standard demonstration, but actually it is a revolution in natural theology.

This gradual shift to the thinking subject as (1) the primordial object of inquiry and as (2) the foundational evidence for God was taking its solitary beginnings just as the theological reliance upon mechanics, biology, and astronomy with their uncovering of designs in the universe was reaching its theological peak. In a few years, Newton would write the "General Scholium" at the end of the *Principia* and the Queries after the *Opticks* – both with their inference to One "very well skilled in Mechanicks and Geometry."[23] Enthusiastic decades would follow of numerous physico-theologies.

But within little more than a century, the argument from design was to yield its pride of place. Kant, Herschel, and Laplace found in the nebular hypothesis quite an adequate explanation of the system of the world and took for granted the rising autonomy from theology of all that could be called natural philosophy. In a few more decades, the Darwinians would explain design in nature through the evolutionary hypothesis and the principle of natural selection. Since neither in the heavens nor upon the earth could one find contrived design to function as theological evidence, the shift in strategy suggested by Locke and his successors was to gain increasing welcome. One must turn from the external world to the inner world of the thinking subject. In greater and greater numbers, Western thinkers shifted from nature to human nature in order to ground their science, morality, and religion.

As urbanely skeptical as was David Hume about any inference to the existence of God, he recognized that Locke and those who followed him "have begun to put the science of man on a new footing." He agreed that the science of man – not natural philosophy – "is the only solid foundation for the other sciences." [24] The study of human nature is *central* – to switch the metaphor – and so the philosopher is now able "to march directly to the capital or center of these sciences, to human nature itself, which once being masters of, we may every where else hope for an easy victory."[25] Inquiry into human nature grounds and provides a critique of all of the sciences and of natural religion as well, and this inquiry into human nature is primarily epistemological:

> It is impossible to tell what changes and improvements we might make in these sciences were we thoroughly acquainted with the *extent and force of human understanding*, and could explain the *nature of the ideas* we employ, and of the operations we perform in our reasonings. And these improvements are the more to be hoped for in natural religion, as it is not content with instructing us in the nature of superior powers, but carries its views farther, to their disposition towards us, and our duties towards them; and consequently we ourselves are not only the beings, that reason, but also one of the objects concerning which we reason.[26]

While the epistemological inquiries concerning "capacities" and "objects" was assuming a foundational importance, the relevance of God was concomitantly changing from that occupied in classical metaphysics and natural theologies. With the Continental philosophers, a new calibration of the agency of God was emerging, as James Collins has perceptively noted. God became a necessary functionary within the philosophical systems themselves. His was a function so crucial that the systems could not operate without that contribution.[27] In Descartes, for example, God's veracity made possible the scientific or certain knowledge of the world. Why? Because the divine truth, the perfection of God, guarantees that the sensible universe is actually reached by human perceptive powers. It is not the sensible universe that stands warrant for the existence of God, as in the classical natural theologies; it is rather the function of God to stand warrant for the sensible universe.[28] In Spinoza, the continuity of the system had to mirror the continuity of being. God, then, becomes the beginning and the end of the entire system, the first principle from which everything is to be deduced and the final term that gives to this ethical-metaphysical-religious inquiry its fulfillment in intellectual happiness. God makes the system possible. He functions necessarily within it.

> At no time before or since has God occupied such an important position in philosophy. This does not mean that the rationalist systems were religious or theocentric in structure. Quite the contrary. God was made to serve the purposes of the system itself. He became a major cog, but still a cog, in the over-all program of answering skepticism, incorporating the scientific spirit, and building a rational explanation of the real. It is this functional attitude towards God which characterizes the rationalist movement in the century of genius.[29]

Without this divine contribution to the philosophical system, the system col-
lapses. But with the assertion both of the primacy of the epistemological and
of the ready functionality of God within a system, philosophy was ready for
its Kant and theology for its Schleiermacher.

The emphasis that Locke gave to the processes of thought gathered force in
the years that followed and reaches full strength in the works and subsequent
influence of Immanuel Kant. In Kant, the concerns and commitments of
England and of the Continent converge. His three *Critiques* were to transpose
all fundamental reflection into this new key: "I do not mean by this a critique
of books and systems, but of the faculty of reason in general, in respect of
all knowledge after which it may strive independently of all experience. It
will therefore decide as to the possibility or impossibility of metaphysics in
general."[30] Before one launches into metaphysics or natural theology or universal mechanics, one must analyze the knowing of the knower to determine
what could be known; otherwise human inquiry would yield only transcendental illusion. Before one explores the objects of morality and ethics, one
must analyze the practical intellect or *Wille* and the human ability to choose
in accordance with the demands of the moral law. Before one deals with the
beautiful and the sublime, with taste and genius, one must understand the
reflexivity or harmony that is possible between the imagination in its repre-
sentations and the understanding in its judgment.

Again, Kant did not originate this flood; he augmented and sanctioned it
for the century that was to follow. Under his blessings, these waters became
holy. Disciplines bearing such names as epistemology or criticism or
phenomenologies of spirit or cognitional theory became prevalent and foundational in the nineteenth century. When the epistemological was secured, one
could entertain questions of inquiry and decision without the dangers of irresolvable contradiction and conflicts. One must gauge the human first.

This insistence upon the foundational importance of the self-appropriation
of the knowing subject carried also into theology, into the inquiries of
the greatest Protestant theologian of the nineteenth century, Friedrich
Schleiermacher. Here one finds a primordial dependence of all discussion
of theological subjects or of the propositions of religion upon the prior
appropriation of immediate consciousness, variously formulated as either the
feeling and intuition of the infinite or the feeling of absolute dependence.

Kant and Schleiermacher, as Professor Fred Lawrence has so well maintained, represent two distinctly different kinds of foundational consciousness.
Kant tethered reason, understanding, or judgment to consciousness as a perception of objects; like Rousseau, Schleiermacher rooted them in the percep-

tion of feelings, the feeling of feeling, which he sometimes referred to as "sentiment."[31] What Kant was for philosophy, Schleiermacher was for theology. Both gave a foundational priority to human subjectivity – not in the sense of an arbitrary imposition of meanings, but in the sense of the subject as agent, possessing its own internal structure of mind or spirit, whose capacities must be determined as the fundamental security for subsequent affirmations. For both, the human subject came first; the human subject would measure the things that it would engage. Not nature, but human nature had become fundamental if one was going to discuss God.

Theistic argument in a new key

As this revolution swept through modernity, Kant and Schleiermacher transposed the arguments for the reality of God into a new key. They shifted the issue of God to human subjectivity for its fundamental point of departure. Kant provided critiques, while Schleiermacher explored "religion." In both God emerged as a necessity to deal with human life and experience. God was an entailment, not of design in nature, but of the human.

For Kant, the coherence of the entire ethical enterprise, i.e., for human life to make sense morally, dictates that one must postulate the existence of God. The austere ethical imperative is to choose freely – with the freedom of autonomy – to do one's duty. But duty dictates that one strive for the highest human good, the *summum bonum*. This object conjoins virtue (dictated by duty) and happiness (which objectively ought to be united with virtue). The virtuous deserve to be happy. If this highest human good is commanded by the ethical imperative, this union of virtue and happiness must be possible.

But the fact of the matter is that no human effort can guarantee that conjunction. What is more: the events of history show its realization to be random and even happenstance. Either duty commands human beings to act toward what is statistically absurd – and consequently discredits itself and the entire ethical enterprise – or one must postulate, by a subjective necessity, an intelligent God who will effect this union between moral worth and happiness.[32] Thus, if the ethical enterprise is to make any sense, "we must postulate a higher, moral, most holy, and omnipotent Being which alone can unite the two elements of this highest good."[33]

Without such a God, the ethical is absurdity. Morality is only rationally possible if the object of morality is itself seriously possible. Thus what human beings cannot effect must be within the power of another. God must exist to sanction the validity of the moral life. "Morality thus leads ineluctably to religion, through which it extends itself to the idea of a powerful moral Lawgiver, outside of mankind, for Whose will that is the final end (of creation) which at the same time can and ought to be man's final end."[34] In this way, God must make morality possible, and Jesus Christ is the exemplification of this morality. Human morality gives the warrant for the existence of God because God gives the possibility for human morality.

In Friedrich Schleiermacher, "the Kant of Modern Protestantism," as Richard H. Niebuhr called him, the human becomes both (1) the interest or motive by which a commitment to religion is evoked and (2) the criterion for what we know of God – since we never know God in himself but only what God is for us.

(1) Schleiermacher's early apologetic work, *Über die Religion*, had summoned the romantics to religion – what he would later call "piety" – because here above all one celebrates and enhances the human, "the holy mysteries of humanity." The value of religion is its unabashed and unique enhancement of the human; the infinite is to awaken the intuitions and feeling that constitute religion, and thereby disclose the human to itself.

(2) Even further, the appropriation of God in the *Glaubenslehre* bears upon a similarly immediate self-consciousness, the consciousness of self as absolutely dependent, an experiential consciousness that both identifies with the fundamental relationship to God and discloses the nature of the human. The revelation of God emerges most basically as this feeling/immediate consciousness of absolute dependence that is native to humanity. The acceptance and certitude of this sense of absolute dependence is faith in God.[35] But the focus is upon the experiencing subject.

It is important to notice that the experience of absolute dependence does not tell us what God is in himself – God never reveals himself in this way in Schleiermacher – but what he is doing for us, what he is for us, and what is the nature of our humanity. Nor should one confuse this experience of absolute dependence – which is much more like a "fact" – with the Christian personal interchange that, in the words of Teresa of Avila, constitutes a conversation with God. Absolute dependence is not the Judeo-Christian communion of word and response. For Kant, a human being cannot live in a coherent ethical world without postulating God; for Schleiermacher, one can only appropriate God in terms of the human being.[36] The critical issues for both are the entailment and the enhancement of humanity.

For Schleiermacher, "religion" provided the foundation for dogmatics and for his greatest work, *Die Glaubenslehre*. Kant had deliberately excluded experience from the exercise of human freedom because "the philosopher, as teacher of pure reason (from unassisted principles *a priori* [in Ethics]), must confine himself within the narrower circle, and, in so doing, must abstract from all experience."[37] For Schleiermacher, there is no similar bracketing of experience in favor of illation. On the contrary, one appeals to the fundamental experience that underlies all inference and even differentiated thought. Whether that immediacy be grasped by "intuition" or "feeling," the experience denotes a fundamental awareness, an immediate self-consciousness given in every act of cognition. Now this self-consciousness is inseparable from God-consciousness – as doubt in Descartes is inseparable from existence:

> To feel oneself absolutely dependent and to be conscious of being in rela-
> tion with God are one and the same thing; and the reason is that absolute
> dependence is the *fundamental* relation which must include all others in
> itself. This last expression includes the God-consciousness in the human
> self-consciousness in such a way that, quite in accordance with the above
> analysis, the two cannot be separated from each other. . . . God is given to
> us in feeling in an original way.[38]

God is a necessary postulate of ethics in Kant, making duty's object, the highest good, realistically possible; God is a given of the primordial experience of human self-consciousness in Schleiermacher.

Through the influence of both thinkers, a new and critically important reconfiguration was taking place in the philosophy and theology of modernity, one that would resituate foundational thinking about the divine reality, a shift that Tennyson would both celebrate in *In Memoriam* and comment upon at the end of his life. He saw that the days of the religious use of nature were passing or at least diminishing. Charles Lyell's *Principles of Geology* (1830–3), with its demonstrations of the great age of the earth and the successive and massive extinction of species, had left "Nature red in tooth and claw/With ravine." Tennyson found that nature "shriek'd against his creed," leaving those who depended upon Nature's witness convinced that they must regard "life as futile, then, as frail."[39] He must turn elsewhere:

> Yet God *is* love, transcendent, all-pervading! We do not get *this* faith from
> Nature or the world. If we look at Nature alone, full of perfection and imper-
> fection, she tells us that God is disease, murder and rapine. We *get this faith
> from ourselves*, from what is *highest within us*, which recognizes that there is
> not one fruitless pang, just as there is not one lost good."[40]

"This faith from ourselves. . . ." Nature – for all its designs and universal mechanics – executing its history of destruction and deaths, could not provide the warrant for the existence of God. One must rather go to the postulate

inferred by the *Critique of Practical Reason* or to the experience fundamental
to religion. For all of their contrasts and even contradictory procedures, what
both critique and religion have in common, what they both necessitate as
foundational, is what they interpret as the radically human – in contradis-
tinction to subhuman nature. The Kantian critique recognized that ethics
engages an activity that is uniquely human, the way human beings should
decide and act and live; Schleiermacher saw that human passivity is engaged
in religion, suggesting the influence of an object that reveals its existence to
the inner consciousness.

> The same is true for religion. The same actions of the universe through
> which it reveals itself to you in the finite also bring it into a new relation-
> ship to your mind and your condition; in the act of intuiting it, *you must
> necessarily be seized by various feelings.* In religion, however, a different
> and stronger relationship between intuition and feeling takes place, and
> intuition never predominates so much that feeling is almost extinguished.
>
> On the contrary, is it really a miracle if the eternal world affects the senses
> of our spirit as the sun affects our eyes? Is it a miracle when the sun so blinds
> us that everything else disappears, not only at that moment, but even long
> afterward all objects we observe are imprinted with its image and bathed in
> its brilliance? Just as the particular manner in which the universe presents
> itself to you in your intuitions and determines the uniqueness of your indi-
> vidual religion, so the strength of these feelings determines the degree of
> religiousness.[41]

Nature does not provide the warrant for God; the warrant for God is found
in the human subject, either active in its choices or passive in its immediate
experience or feeling.

So profound and pervasive is this shift to the human subject as foundational
for dealing with the reality of God that both Kant and Schleiermacher can cite
it as the lynchpin of their fundamental works. Kant's four books on religion
become the study of human nature: "In order to make apparent the relation
of religion to human nature (endowed in part with good, in part with evil pre-
dispositions), I represent, in the four following essays, the relationship of the
good and evil principles as that of the two self-subsistent active causes influencing men."[42] The purpose of the *Reden* is stated: "I wish to lead you to the
innermost depths from which religion first addresses the mind. I wish to show
you *from what capacity of humanity religion proceeds*, and *how it belongs to what
is for you the highest and dearest.*" Precisely for its engagement of the human
in such depths, this inquiry is not for all, maintains Schleiermacher, but only

for "you" who are capable of "raising yourselves above the common standpoint of humanity, you who do not shrink from the burdensome way *into the depths of human nature* in order to find the ground of its actions and thought."[43]

And how does one move "into the depths of human nature?" Through the differentiation among three disciplines and the recognition and prosecution of religion as one of them. Metaphysics finds its essence in thinking; morality, in acting and doing; but religion, in intuition and feeling. In Schleiermacher, God emerges as the active source of these feelings; God is even given a nominal definition in terms of the feeling of absolute dependence: "the *Whence* of our receptive and active existence, as *implied in this self-consciousness*, is to be designated by the word 'God,' and that this is for us the really original signification of that word."[44] The original human awareness of God is simply of that which is the co-determinant in this feeling. Thus to feel oneself absolutely dependent and to be conscious of being in relation to God is one and the same thing. In this sense, God is given to immediate human awareness, i.e., in feeling, in "an original way." Indeed, this can be recognized as "an original revelation of God to man or in man."[45]

In Kant, God became a necessity not of the physical universe, but of the moral enterprise. In Schleiermacher, God summoned human beings to religion, which introduces them into the depths of what it means to be human. In both cases, the divine took its character and its value from its enhancement of the human. What was implicitly absolute, both as warrant for belief and conferral of value, was the human person.

God as alienation

The dialectical reversal of the theistic proposition that obtained in early modernity repeated itself analogously within the changed coordinates of the subsequent century. The positive moment, in its implicit contradiction, generated its own commensurate self-negation. In the nineteenth century, philosophy and theology had moved to ground religious affirmation on the entailments of human nature; now they will be contradicted on the same ground in the struggle that Henri de Lubac so aptly called "the drama of atheistic humanism."[46]

One must begin with the originating genius of this movement, Ludwig Feuerbach – a Bavarian theological student become philosopher under the instruction of Hegel, only to become an atheist – the man whose writings were so successful, so influential that Marx saluted him as the great precursor of dialectical atheism and Freud held him as his favorite philosopher.[47] Atheism came to climax his intellectual development, and he summarized the stages of this algorithm in three moments: "God was my first thought; Reason my second; Man, my third and last thought."[48] The character of the nineteenth century's fundamental thinking dictated that Feuerbach begin the *Essence of Christianity* with an analysis of the essential nature of the human person as a thinking subject, i.e., as self-consciousness. He could deduce his conclusions about the source and object of religion from the fact that human beings have religion while brutes do not. This means that it must derive from what is uniquely human, i.e., species-consciousness.

Feuerbach did this by a very simple change. Modernity had settled upon the thinking subject as its fundamental datum. Human consciousness became in Feuerbach not only the subject or agent – as in the immediate centuries past – but its own essential object. Human consciousness was reflexive: both the *source* of consciousness and also the *term* of consciousness.[49] The crucial thesis about religion in the *Essence of Christianity*, one that the entire book is to defend, was added by Feuerbach to the third edition as summary of its basic thesis: "Das Wesen des Menschen im Unterschied vom Tiere ist nicht nur der *Grund*, sondern auch der *Gegenstand der Religion*" ("The essence of the human being [self-consciousness] in differentiation from the beasts is not only the ground [or cause] but also the object of religion").[50] The human being is alpha and omega. Just as mechanics had become reflexively autonomous in the eighteenth and nineteenth centuries, i.e., mechanics with only mechanical principles, so humanism was to become reflexively autonomous: human subjects with (ultimately) only human objects. Feuerbach's insistence upon the reflexivity of his principle, humanity, embodies the whole of his argument. He did not need any other hypothesis. Any other principle would illegitimately displace the human from the centrality that was its due.

In his various works, Feuerbach repeatedly formulates three basic arguments in which he instantiates this reflexive principle, arguments basing their evidence upon (1) human consciousness (the object of human consciousness is human nature); (2) propositional predication (the attributes of God are human); and (3) God as the hostile antagonist of the human. These arguments deal successively with thoughts, words, or things. I should like to consider here the last of these – easily the most popular and influential of the three – as it sustains one wing of Feuerbach's contribution to the advancement of atheism, i.e., God as the debasement of humanity. In the next chapter, I should like to take up the two foundational arguments that ground the argument from alienation and estrangement, i.e., God as the projection of humanity.

This third argument also proved historically to be the most telling: God is the alienation or estrangement of the human from the human. The human subject projects onto this imaginary subject what belongs properly to the human essence. The attributes ascribed to God – as a false subject – are always taken away from human beings. In this way, the human being is stripped of that which one attributes to God. God is holy, human beings are sinful; God is pure, human beings are corrupt; God is wise, human beings are foolish and ignorant. God is thus the estrangement of the human from itself, the despoiler of all that is dearest about human beings and their ideals. "Religion is the disuniting of man from himself; he sets God before him as the antithesis of himself."[51] The historic weight and force of all three of these arguments come together in this last, the state of alienation of the human and God as its estrangement. Thoughts about God are really about the defrauded human species; attributes predicated of God are really owed to human beings. Thus, everything attributed to God – whether in thought, words, or values – is really alienated from human beings. Divinity despoils human beings of what is really theirs. "To enrich God, man must become poor; that God may be all, man must be nothing."[52] In this zero-sum game, the human subject and the divine subject are antithetical. To ascribe something to one is to remove it from the other. One must perish if the other is to live and flourish.

If, then, the human is actually to be affirmed authentically, this alienation must be recognized and negated, and this can only be done by an atheism that comes to perceive the human being to be the actual secret of religion as the real absolute.[53] This contradiction between the human and the divine cannot be resolved unless God is seen to be the projected essence of the human. Thus, it is necessary to *interpret* – this word is very important in Feuerbach – to interpret religion (as one interprets dreams) in order to understand the alienated realities it symbolizes. "I, on the contrary, let religion itself speak; I constitute myself only its listener and *interpreter*, not its prompter."[54] Feuerbach's grammar of atheism will translate the symbols and creed out of the contradictions inherent in theology to the resolving discovery that what is actually worshipped is the human.[55] That a projection of the human would take place is to be understood as even a necessary stage in human self-appropriation through otherness. But if one fails to recognize what has happened and fixates at this stage, however, one formulates the defrauding illusions kept inflexible by theology.[56]

But the developments of philosophic history have reached a time of further progress. Philosophy, now the interpreter of the truth of religion, is called to restore these "divine" attributes to the human, to retrieve for human beings their grandeur. One does not negate the divine predicates, but only the imaginary divine subject of these attributes. One returns these attributes to the defrauded human being. The attributes are true, but not of this supernatural illusion; they are true of the human actuality. What is "God" in this state of illusion? The alienation of the human from itself: "a perversion, a distortion; which, however, the more perverted and false it is, all the more appears to be profound."[57]

It is common knowledge that Karl Marx moved from being an enthusiastic Feuerbachian to becoming a severe critic, but he saw his criticism as fulfilling the early but unrealized promise of Feuerbach. For this, it was necessary to correct Feuerbach in two crucial areas: that of method and of principle.

Feuerbach's method must be changed to a dialectical one, one that moved through actual history – and not just in thought – to the negations that would constitute the actual resolution of historic contradictions. The reflexivity that Feuerbach had ascribed to his principle must be translated into the dialectical method, but the negation must be social, economic, and political, not just interpretative and intellectual. For this dialectical method – this pattern of movement – will be found not simply in the way one thinks, but in the way all reality moves and develops and the way that human agents must struggle. The intellectual movement that was method must realize, recapitulate, energize, shape and be shaped by that historic movement. Dialectics is indeed embodied in thought, as Plato himself had asserted – but the dialectical is also in things, in the heart of all historical forces, in social and economic structures and mass movements, which Plato had never allowed. It is the inner life of progress. Contradictions inherent in the social and historical order are dynamic; they generate the negations of their own intrinsic oppositions and estrangements. As one realizes this, so one can instigate, enter, and facilitate this process.

Marx's second correction of Feuerbach lay with the character of his principle. Feuerbach's principle had been reflexive: "the subject has for his object the infinity of his own nature." The philosophical activity of the subject was the interpretative reappropriation of itself in consciousness, the intellectual realization of what it is. In place of this, Marx introduced a new "revolutionary principle," one that would have not itself, but another for its object. It was not a reflexive principle, but an actional principle – one that would move beyond Feuerbach's reflexive enclosure where the subject and object were one and where philosophical activity was executed in the interpretation of alienation. Revolutionary praxis would pass from the subject to alter or eliminate the object, not to contemplate or interpret it. Praxis would not simply recognize the internal contradictions it faced, but destroy whatever alienations are found in thinking, in economic structures and social oppression. Marx's famous eleventh thesis was written directly against this deficiency of Feuerbach's reflexivity of principle: "The philosophers have only *interpreted* the world in various ways [precisely what Feuerbach had claimed]: the point, however, is to *change* it."[58] It is this revolutionary principle that transforms philosophical activity into *praxis*. Marx changes the human subject from an interpreter to a practical agent whose transitive activity is not simply to size up alienation and estrangement, but to destroy it – in the social order.

Human beings are not merely thinking subjects; they are sensuous and practical. Such a sensuous, revolutionary principle was necessary if the dialectical progress of humanity was to occur. If there was movement, it would be dialectical. But there need not be movement. Whole cultures could stagnate. The function of the revolutionary principle, of the human as this revolutionary principle, was to incite the dialectic, to push the contradictions within the social order to such an extreme that the superficial stability breaks up and yields to the movement that was its negation.

For this emphasis, Marx changes the meaning of "practical," collapsing the distinction between Aristotle's πρᾶξις and ποίησις – so that "practical" now contains the "poetic" activity that creates a new world. Praxis took on a "factive" meaning. The human being is not an abstract essence, but economic and social, essentially called to a much greater "making" activity than Feuerbach had understood. The failure of Feuerbach's materialism was that it did not grasp the practical human activity, its essentially revolutionary and transitive character. To reach its effect, revolutionary praxis essentially passes into the external world, overturning its economic, political, and religious structures.

Praxis transforms the accepted conceptualization of "truth." Truth is not discovered; it is constituted by this activity. Human beings make their world true. Anything else is scholasticism! To realize this human dynamism in practice is to come into possession of one's humanity, and this realization of what it means to be human brings with it an enormous responsibility for the world and for the lot of human beings.

And God? Marx accepted Feuerbach's reading of God as projection and alienation. Indeed, Feuerbach's critique of religion served as the foundation of a later social and economic criticism. "For Germany, the *criticism of religion* is *in the main* complete, and criticism of religion is the premise of all criticism."[59] But Feuerbach's critique embodied the deficiencies of his philosophy. The truth of a situation is not something that one assimilates or judges; it is not already "there." It is something that revolutionary *praxis* produces: "The question whether objective [*gegenständliche*] truth can be attributed to human thinking is not a question of theory but a *practical* question. In practice man must prove the truth."[60] Thus, when any such alienation as religion is found, it must "be *criticized* in theory and *revolutionized* in practice."[61] "Criticized in theory:" Feuerbach had done the theoretical criticism of religion; "revolutionized in practice:" Marx would complete it with a dialectical elimination – the word is not too strong. "The *abolition* of religion as the *illusory* happiness of the people is *required* for their *real* happiness."[62] One is not simply to recognize the alienation and estrangement that is religion, but to destroy it in all social, economic, and political reality. Marx's *Contribution to the Critique of Hegel's Philosophy of Right* stated that a care for humanity demanded this abolition. The elimination of religion is the only way that human beings can be restored to their humanity: "the criticism of religion ends with the teaching that *man is the highest essence for man*, hence with the *categorical imperative to overthrow all relations* in which man is a debased, enslaved, abandoned, despicable essence."[63]

This debasement had obsessed Marx long before his involvement in economics. As a maxim for his doctoral dissertation, Marx had abbreviated and appropriated a verse from Aeschylus's Prometheus as philosophy's "motto against all gods, heavenly and earthly, who do not acknowledge the *consciousness of man* as the *supreme divinity*: ʿἁπλῷ λόγῳ, τοὺς πάντας ἐχθαίρω θεοὺςʾ" [In a simple word, I hate all gods].[64] Prometheus becomes the hero of philosophy; his defiance is truncated by Marx to become the maxim for humanity and for the mission of philosophy. Marx's call is not to reinterpretation; Feuerbach had done that. His call is even at so early a stage to the historical and social elimination of anything that by claiming superiority denigrates the human. This would come to constitute the radical nature of his humanism: "To be radical is to grasp the root of the matter. But for man the root is man himself. The *evident proof* of the radicalism of German theory, and hence of its practical energy, is that it proceeds from a *resolute, positive abolition of Religion*."[65] This humanism will lie at the heart of Marx's atheism. It alone will be the alternative to religion; it alone can displace religion: "religion is only the illusory sun which revolves round man as long as he does not revolve round himself".[66] The philosopher must not simply realize the alienation that religion entails, but destroy it in its social and economic sources and products. Grammar was not enough. If medieval grammar was the discipline most analogous to Feuerbach's project, rhetoric seems most apt for Marx's. It is critically important to see that the destruction of belief in God became for

Marx an ethical imperative – not simply a political or social strategy. As has been noted, Marx even employs Kant's vocabulary: this destruction is a "categorical imperative."[67]

Religious thinkers can never understand the character of authentic Marxism unless they understand this profoundly moral, even "religious" commitment from its beginnings. To destroy the estrangement that is God is like stamping out a virulent disease. Marx's humanism is one of the earliest expressions of this hatred for the person of God, found so early in his dissertation with its apotheosis of the person of Prometheus, the great rebel against the gods – a figure that will run emblematically through the nineteenth century.[68] What Christ is to Kant, Prometheus is to Marx: the embodiment of a morally developed humanity. With the Prometheus of Marx, humanity is now in open competition with God. God, the relentless enemy of Prometheus, is the anti-human. To destroy this God constitutes a moral claim upon human beings, just as Prometheus knew and suffered for the death of Zeus that was to come if Prometheus remained faithful – a death devoutly to be wished.

Marx's exaltation of Prometheus, "the noblest of saints and martyrs in the calendar of philosophy," indicates how far the argument has turned from Schleiermacher. Schleiermacher had censured Prometheus as an arrogant coward: "To want to have speculation and *praxis* without religion is rash arrogance. It is insolent enmity against the gods; it is the unholy sense of Prometheus, who cowardly stole what in calm certainty he would have been able to ask for and to expect."[69] But Marx did not want human beings "to ask for and to expect" anything from God. Speculation and *praxis* were not indebted to a divine gift but bespoke the powers and freedom of a human being. Claiming them was no theft, and to stigmatize it as such simply marks out how far religion had estranged human beings from their own humanity. Prometheus does not apologize to the gods.

The very first work of Friedrich Nietzsche, *The Birth of Tragedy*, also extols the rebellion of Prometheus, "the great lover of mankind."[70] In his defiance and in his resultant sufferings, Prometheus embodied the unalterable contradiction between the human and the divine: "Because of his titanic love for man, Prometheus must be torn to pieces by vultures."[71] Prometheus knows that the cultural rise of the human entails rebellion against the divine. The horrors and sufferings of life had brought the Greeks to invent their gods and to frame them within their greatest artistic achievement, Greek tragedy. "It was in order to be able to live that the Greeks had to create these gods from a most profound need."[72] But the gods, even while for a time mirroring human greatness, have come to inhibit human development. The gods had sequestered the

fire that could free human beings for limitless cultural advancement. In rebellion, Prometheus seized it for them – "without receiving it as a present from
heaven."[73] To steal fire was sacrilege and this – the first philosophical problem
– "immediately produces a *painful and irresolvable contradiction* between man
and god and moves it before the gate of every culture."[74] The phrase is crucial,
for the contradiction denotes the radical opposition that ranges through
Nietzsche's works from the beginning: God and the human are antithetical.
Humanity's advance sounds the death-knell for the gods. It is the defiance of
the divine.

Ethics and the death of God merged in Friedrich Nietzsche in two ways. The
death of God is now a cultural, even an epistemological, phenomenon: belief
in the Christian God has become unbelievable.[75] God's death is not an event
to bring about as with Marx. It is an event that has already occurred, but like
the bursting of a great star billions of light years away, its news has not yet
reached human beings – though human beings have effected this death themselves. And how have human beings accomplished this? By their own cultural
development, a development into the forms of knowledge and morality that
Die fröhliche Wissenschaft traces through the first three books that build to the
death of God. Human beings have developed from a growing set of perceptions and experiences, uncommon common sense about humanity (Bk. 1),
through advances in affectivity and art (Bk. 2), to disciplined knowledge, logic,
science, and morals (sect. 113) – all of which led inevitably to the death of God
(sect. 125) (Bk. 3). Human development entailed in its progress the death of
God. Moral courage and honesty demand that this death be acknowledged.

This death is not an ontological change, but an epistemological one – something that would touch very closely on the sociology of knowledge. Christian
faith is incapable of eliciting human faith. Locke wished to establish what
objects human understanding was capable of grasping; Nietzsche determined
what objects are capable of being believed. And the Christian faith in God is
not among them. One can no longer believe in this belief. Unlike Marx,
Nietzsche did not attempt to bring this death to pass, but to formulate a
teaching to deal with its aftermath. For it has already come to pass.

Thus *Also sprach Zarathustra* celebrates Zarathustra as a moral teacher of a
wisdom he is eager to give away. His teaching is to counter a nihilism that
could come out of the death of God. His premise is almost the exact opposite
of Kant's conclusion: the ethical enterprise emerges in its character and necessity from the cultural fact of the death of God: "I teach you the Overman
[*Übermensch*]."[76] The Overman becomes the new moral ideal. The position
Prometheus held in the admiration of Marx, the Overman holds in the moral

intentions of Nietzsche: the human must be overcome in the heroic progress to the Overman. Zarathustra takes his mission from this call to the heroic: "I shall show them the rainbow and all of the steps to the Overman."[77] His instructions stood in contrast to the lessons of the "teachers of virtue" and their securing contagious sleep for humanity.[78]

If the Overman is the great challenge to human history, the will to power is its basic moral energy: "A new will I teach men: to *will* this way which man has walked blindly, and to affirm it, and no longer to sneak away from it like the sick and decaying."[79] The heroic will constitutes the fundamental moral dynamism. "Alas, that you would understand my word: 'Do whatever you will, but first be such as are *able to will*.'"[80] The entire "On Old and New Tablets" builds in a hymn to the sovereign will: "O thou my will! Thou cessation of all need, my *own* necessity! Keep me from all small victories! Thou destination of my soul, which I call destiny! Thou in-me! Over-me! Keep me and save me for a great destiny!"[81]

But all of this is cast into ambiguity when the realization dawns that no victory, no achievement is ultimate, that there is no final overcoming. The return of all things and of all states is sempiternal. All victories are provisional. With a finite amount of matter in the universe and an eternal quantity of time, everything must reoccur endlessly – indeed had already endlessly reoccurred.[82] All of the past, even the "last man," will return, and return endlessly.[83] The hope for something beyond the provisional only comes to mirror the efforts and the history of Sisyphus. This realization works a profound change in Zarathustra. He becomes the teacher of the eternal recurrence, and this intractable return posed the fundamental challenge to the project to which he has given his life. The eternal return becomes the alternative to the creating God.

Also sprach Zarathustra must put the three together: the Overman, the will to power, and the eternal return. The human can transmogrify itself into the Overman – can realize the supreme possibilities of her or his humanity – by willing absolutely the eternal return, by loving and accepting the eternal return.[84] This radically redefines the heroic human being. He or she becomes a process of development, of advance towards the Overman. The finality of human nature is to become a bridge to the Overman, while the foundation of human nature in all its native dynamism is fundamentally the will to power. In these terms, human activity must be recognized both in its possibilities and in its glory.

Nietzsche can then move atheistic consciousness to a deeper level than Marx. What is God? The anti-human, the destruction of the entire heroic and humanistic project of Zarathustra and the progression of humanity to the Overman. God is the limit, the finitude of humanity. All of Zarathustra's doctrine pounds against God as against its absolute contradiction. "But let me reveal my heart to you entirely, my friends: *If* there were gods, how could I endure not to be a god! *Hence* there are no gods. Though I drew this conclusion, now it draws me."[85] The human being and God: one is necessarily the refusal of the other.

Lastly, Sigmund Freud would further human development in a struggle no less passionate than Friedrich Nietzsche's. Freud undertakes his critical examination of religion and religious ideas such as "God" in order to call human beings to advance into a world where affirmations are rationally grounded. His is the call to a process that was "*'education to reality.'* Need I confess to you that the sole purpose of my book is to point out the necessity for this forward step?"[86] The elimination of God will throw human beings on their own rational resources, as both Marx and Nietzsche had also argued. Only then will human beings learn to make a proper use of these rational, human abilities. Atheism emerges in Freud's writings, not as directly argued, but as he discloses that theistic ideas are groundless and inhibit human beings from growth in rationality. But for this growth "men are not entirely without assistance. Their scientific knowledge has taught them much since the days of the Deluge, and it will increase their power still further. And, as for the great necessities of Fate, against which there is no help, they will learn to endure them with resignation."[87] Like Nietzsche, Freud found the advance of science the inevitable cultural extirpation of religion – the rational at enmity with the irrational.

God does not figure neutrally in a statement leveled at humanity. Religious ideas become destructive of the human, hindering a sense of responsibility and growth. "The whole thing is so patently infantile, so foreign to reality, that to anyone with a friendly attitude to humanity, it is painful to think that the great majority of mortals will never be able to rise above this view of life."[88] So profoundly does God undermine human development that religion can be listed as the great enemy of the advance of science: "Of the three powers which may dispute the basic position of science, religion alone is to be taken seriously as an enemy."[89]

What is the future of religious ideas, of God? Marginalization and extinction. Freud does not argue the truth of atheism. He simply discounts any rational basis for religious ideas. He sees that there will be an increasing turning away from religion as human beings develop in their rationality. Rationality and religion are at war with each other. Gradually, painfully, the human intellect is coming into its own and breaking the bonds around it, bonds that have been placed and tightened by religion: "The voice of the intellect is a soft one, but it does not rest till it has gained a hearing. Finally, after a countless succession of rebuffs, it succeeds. This is one of the few points on which one may be optimistic about the future of mankind, but it is in itself a point of no small importance. . . . The primacy of the intellect lies, it is true, in a distant, distant future, but probably not in an *infinitely* distant one."[90] The contradiction between the human and the divine could not be more antagonistically drawn: rational and irrational, humane development and inhibiting illusions, knowledge and belief.

The glory of God or the glory of the human?

The apologetics of the early nineteenth century had argued to the reality of God from human nature and its entailments: God is a requirement that life be human in the fullest sense, either ethically or in humanistic self-appropriation. The rising atheism of later decades also took the human as the point of departure, as the area of evidence within which the struggle was to be conducted, and it argued exactly to the opposite conclusion: God alienates humanity from itself and from its promise. For there was contradiction at the heart of this evidence.

The atheistic exploration of human nature was conducted by philosophical anthropologies that moved through differing and at times overlapping levels in their analyses of the human being and of human development: Feuerbach saw the human being as sensuous self-consciousness, with this self-consciousness uniquely able to focus upon and project the human species; for Marx, this sensuous self-consciousness was both socially constituted in communal solidarity and called to engage in human society as revolutionary praxis; for Nietzsche, what lay beneath all praxis, however revolutionary, was the human being as the dynamism of the will to power, the bridge to the Overman and heroic human transcendence; for Freud, the human being was psychologically constituted even in the *eros* of its self-affirmation by its collective and personal history and by the massive inner struggles of the components within its psyche as also with nature, and civilization. Its cultural development identified with progress towards scientific rationality.

For all of these, God loomed as the intolerable enemy. For Feuerbach, belief in God fixed the human essence outside of itself; for Marx, it alienated the human person from the practical, revolutionary activity by which alone praxis could achieve freedom; for Nietzsche, God was the external finitude of the

Overman as something which would always transcend and so limit in frustration the Overman; for Freud, belief in God was the permanent infantilization of the human being.

Each of these formative thinkers argued that the human and the divine are antithetical, that God preys on the human, that one must die if the other is to live. Historically and psychologically, they are posed in ineluctable threat and hostility. The affirmation of one necessarily means the denial of the other. One can only choose between them.

In the early decades of that century, one argued to God because God was a necessity for human life. Now human nature evoked precisely the alternative proposition: the human was the evidence against God. But how had the human been put on the antinomic balance with God – both treated as if they were two units in a symmetrical or asymmetrical relationship, each posed in such contradiction that one must sink if the other is to rise?

Let us look once more at the career of modern philosophy. One finds both increasingly central to much of its interest and even the measure of its statements: the human person – the human being precisely as an autonomous thinking and creating subject. So much of the world of culture and intellect came to revolve and even to be defined in terms of the human person. The human gave the divine as well as the human its necessity, its meaning, and its value. And this not simply in the philosophical and theological systems so briefly registered in the previous pages, but even in the progress of language. The thinking subject had become more and more definitive of reality, i.e., implicitly absolute.

One example must suffice: our use of the word "objects" to denote things. We call things "objects" – a usage that has grown since the fourteenth century. But notice what a telling change this was. *Objectum* in the high Middle Ages did not denote a thing; it denoted that which was brought before human consciousness. Cognoscitive potencies had objects; habits had objects; purposeful activity had objects. But natural things were not objects as such, and the term was only applied to natural things in so far as they bespoke human potentialities, habits, and activities. But for the medieval mind, things were more than this. They were *things*, subjects of their own actualization in being, in attributes, in processes, and in the realizations of their potentialities. Metaphysically, things were not *objecta*; they were *res* as they were indeed beings. One could classically list six terms for things, terms that are mutually convertible, what were later called the transcendentals: *ens, res, unum, bonum, verum, aliquid.*[91] But *objectum* is not among them. To make that term convertible with "thing" demanded a very different intellectual world, one given its character by the conscious, thinking subject. Professor Kenneth Schmitz has very perceptively summarized the change that was well under way by the time of John Locke and to which Locke contributed so substantially:

> The philosophy of object which characterizes so much of seventeenth century thought is a half-conscious philosophy of subject. During the break-down of the medieval intellectual structure, the subject came to mean a subject of consciousness. Natural things came to be viewed as that which is thrown over against a subject, and their new role was to be objects.[92]

In so subtle and unrecognized a shift in the grammar of "objecta," the world indicated that it was to be gradually and increasingly denominated by reference to the human thinking subject.

But so also is God and the theological reflection that explores "what one understands as God."[93] This chapter has already argued that in some of the world of the nineteenth century, the existence of God could be established only if in some way the thinking subject provides the critical evidence for the assertion and relevance of God. Further, the existence of God must be established not because of the call to worship or to obedience or to love, but because a particular system will not work unless God does his part. Cartesian mechanics and Kantian ethics fail if God does not fulfill a particular function within it. God obtains his relevance and the warrant for his existence as a necessity for a human strategy. Even the experience of dependence in Schleiermacher becomes – in the subsequent tradition of his text, one must underline – both the evidence in which God's existence can be intuited, but, far more importantly, the radical criterion for the relevance of all doctrine or revelation about God. We can come to apprehend God only in so far as we understand God *for us*. The seeming modesty of this claim disguised the new and absolute importance of the thinking subject. Finally, the enhancement of the human person becomes the only reason ethically for introducing the existence of God; the only reason apologetically is that religion is necessary to open up the mysteries of humanity. In all of this, the human person, the thinking subject, has achieved an implicit but effective centrality; in one way or another, the divine existence is asserted and evaluated as a corollary of the human.

The internal contradiction was already present. The conclusions reached in each of these systems and habits of religious thought overtly and emphatically affirmed the absolute centrality of God, with the human being finite and created. But the drift of the philosophical arguments by which this conclusion was sustained depended increasingly, though covertly, upon the absolute centrality of the human being, conferring on God a useful function or allotting his value from the manner in which he touched human life. But this is implicitly to make the human being absolute while explicitly arguing the presence and absoluteness of God, who is engaged in so far as he is usefully at the service of human life and system. This is not a God to whom one is drawn in adoration. The internal incoherence between these two absolutes must inevitably generate their resolution by negation. Each can ultimately only threaten the other.

What is contradictory in these systems or habits of mind must pass over to its resolution. There cannot be two absolutes. It was only a question of time until the centrality of the human saw itself threatened by the very God whose *ex professo* existence it was explicitly to sustain. Each of these systematic affirmations of God may well have been unaware how deeply it was at war with itself. But Feuerbach, Marx, Nietzsche, Freud were not. The *ex professo* God was actually defrauding human beings of their centrality.

God and the human being had in this way been placed initially in an unrecognized struggle for primacy. In this unspoken polar opposition, one must perish that the other may live as absolute and central. This could and did happen in many ways, but what marks each of their careers was that the implicitly absolute character of the human was simply to be explicitly recognized and accepted. The contradiction disclosed in the hermeneutics of suspicion could only be resolved by eliminating God. The inherently vicious antinomy between the divine and the human led inexorably to the elimination of the divine.

In so many ways, the first moment, the contradictory affirmation of the reality of God, immanently generated what Hegel called "its own Other." Contradiction is the soul, the internal moving principle of this historic process, and in this development atheism emerges as a negation that is both analysis and synthesis of what went before: analysis, because the negation of God develops immanently from within the previous moment of affirmation; synthesis, because this development shows itself to be other than this affirmation, but implicitly present of what was previously affirmed.[94]

But it is not simply nineteenth-century culture that has formulated this contradiction and brought it to issue. One can point to a much longer theological tradition that posed this antithetical relationship, this contradiction, between God and human beings. Feuerbach stated it: "Man thanks God for those benefits which have been rendered to him even at the cost of sacrifice by his fellow men. . . . He is thankful, grateful to God, but unthankful to man."[95] Human beings give to God what they take from humanity itself. This could have been disclosed in a thousand lesser authors influenced by the giants of the Christian tradition. In a great variety of modalities, the question has been posed: "aut gloria Dei aut gloria hominis?" "The glory of God or the glory of the human being?" Choose. "What is truly negative," argued Feuerbach, "is theism, the belief in God; it negates nature, the world and mankind; *in the face of God, the world and man are nothing.* God was before the world and man were; he *can exist without them.* He is the nothingness of the world and of man; at least according to strict orthodox belief."[96] Feuerbach cited both Augustine and Luther as evidence that a "believer in God takes everything away from man and from nature in order to adorn and glorify his God. 'Only God alone is to be loved,' says St. Augustine, for example, 'this world (i.e., all sensuous things) is to be dispised.' 'God,' says Luther in a Latin letter, 'wishes either to be the only friend or no friend at all.' "[97] For Feuerbach, "Luther has only brought to light again the doctrinal system of Augustine, the most influential of the Catholic Church Fathers."[98]

For centuries, preachers, spiritual authors, and theologians influenced in various ways by this tradition had posed the issue, railed against pride, and advocated the glory of God, while insisting that to give glory to human beings would be to take it away from God. Feuerbach had explicitly claimed that Pelagius and Augustine, in setting the antinomy between God and the Human, were actually denying the distinction.[99] In the nineteenth century, buoyed by the growing centrality of the human person, the same issue was joined; but this time the alternative choice was made, the choice for the glory of the human rather than God. God was necessarily adversary.

This sense of threat and contradiction has not died in our own century. A few years ago, the distinguished American philosopher Thomas Nagel wrote of God and religion as menace, granting that it is "just as irrational to be influenced in one's beliefs by the hope that God does not exist as by the hope that God does exist."[100] Nevertheless, he writes:

> I am talking about something much deeper – namely, the fear of religion itself. I speak from experience, being strongly subject to this fear myself. I want atheism to be true and am made uneasy by the fact that some of the most intelligent and well-informed people I know are religious believers. It isn't that I don't believe in God and, naturally, hope that I'm right in my belief. It's that I hope there is no God. I don't want there to be a God; I don't want the universe to be like that.[101]

One can easily see that to pose God and the human being in antithesis or competition is a ruinous endeavor. It is a contradiction whose resolution has but one possibility out of the two. Once that contradiction has been drawn –

whether explicitly in the history of theology or implicitly in the history of philosophy – there is no consistent way to obviate disaster.

One must recognize that there is something profoundly religious here, something that may well explain so much of the intensity and zeal that unbelief came to possess in the nineteenth century. In this fundamental contradiction, what the nineteenth century eventually came to was God as "the enemy of human nature." Those with a background in spiritual literature know that phrase. It is the name for Satan. *The Spiritual Exercises* of Ignatius Loyola, for example, never used the word Satan and rarely Lucifer. The common and frequent term for Satan is "the enemy of human nature." It is the name, but it is also the definition of the Satanic. The anti-human is the diabolical.

What the dialectical movement of the nineteenth century had come to assert over the earlier theism was actually a Satanic understanding of God, the enemy of the human. God was understood – deconstructed, if you will – as Satan. Christianity was revealed as a destructively parasitic and decadent hostility to human life. To understand the passion, the urgency, and even the hatred of the anti-theism that emerged from within that century, it is imperative to understand that – without ever naming it as such – atheistic humanism thought itself in a struggle to eliminate the satanic in human history, the alienation and destruction of the human.

5

The Radical Finitude of Religious Ideas: Atheism and Contemplation

Prologue

At this juncture, it seems appropriate to join to the exploration of nineteenth-century atheism the consideration of another, seemingly radically different, religious critique, the mystical or the contemplative. Professors James Faulconer and Kevin Hart have already drawn attention to the remarkable similarities between deconstruction and negative theology and, "after some initial hesitation, Derrida has himself made the comparison, though it would be a mistake to say that his work constitutes a negative theology."[1] Their judgment suggests a line of inquiry into the understanding and evaluation of the religious implications of modern atheism. It is not simply that these two religious movements, atheism and contemplation – let us call them this – affect in some general way the theological character of the twentieth century, having obtained such a presence in contemporary culture that they provide a context in which much serious religious reflection is to be done. More than context, they pose or specify directly many of the actual issues that lie at the heart of contemporary religious judgments and capacities, even the ability to believe or not to believe. Atheism and contemplation, in very different ways, specify presuppositions today according to which theological inquiry itself is judged critically valuable or culturally peripheral.

Our considerations, however, will – as they must – limit themselves severely to a single aspect of these great movements. Much that is crucial to their comprehensive definitions, descriptions, and evaluation – their profound social implications, their historical development, their economic and social bases, the great varieties assumed in their modern embodiment and grammars – must be omitted. What I wish to argue is that these two movements are not simply to be juxtaposed; that they do more than tender two divergent preoccupations and positions within contemporary theological awareness; that both of them treat either the phenomenon of religious experience and its commitments or the religious dimensions of experience and its conceptualizations; and that both of them intersect at the single hermeneutical issue raised already in the last chapter: the self-projection inescapably present in religious ideas. In their insistence upon the presence of projection, atheism and contemplation, either in their practice or in the critical theories by which they are described and defended, both raise the question: What is the actual content of religious awareness and of its engagements?

If the previous chapter, then, explored the divine as the antithesis of the human in the nineteenth century, this one will take up the foundations for that antithetical relationship: the divine as projection, the unacknowledged but influential presence of the human in the words and the thoughts about God. This means that we must take another look at Feuerbach and Freud, for projection lies at the basis of their analyses of religion, the projection of self-consciousness, the projection of the human imagination and will.

Atheism

Much of the philosophy of the nineteenth century was in one way or another an attempt to give content to terms and concepts about God. The interpretation of religious belief, the actual subject of religious predication, the implications of religious practice, the disclosure given by religious objects, their relationship with history and with philosophy, engaged men of critical reflective authority. Hegel saw this as "that which is in general at the present moment the first concern of philosophy, namely to place God once again absolutely right in front at the head of philosophy."[2] The place would be kept by Hegel's followers, but the one who occupied the place would by some be radically transformed.

Pivotal to this history of interpretation, perhaps the central figure to alter the flow of Western religious philosophy into radically new channels, was someone whose significance has been noted previously, Ludwig Feuerbach. It is almost impossible to exaggerate his importance here. Feuerbach insisted upon a new hermeneutic of religion and its divinity as they actually existed, reaching their real meaning – as Freud would later interpret dreams – by moving through symbolic structures into their hidden content. It was

Feuerbach, maintains Sidney Hook, who began the Marxist revolution. His critique of religion was the beginning of all critiques – not just for Marx but for all the young Hegelians.[3] But it is critical to emphasize that Feuerbach saw himself simply as a translator, and his work only a hermeneutic of religious belief – the religious faith actually proclaimed by the Christian Church to men and women in the marketplace.

What was the truth of this belief? It was and always had been the self-projection of the human. Human beings worshiped – all unknowingly – what they had found as essence within themselves and had objectified; what they believed is what their fears and loves projected into objectivity, ultimately, that is, the human species, giving the human essence an imaginative existence over and against their own: "Thus man transforms his feelings, desires, imaginings, and thoughts into beings; though what he wishes, thinks or imagines has no other existence than in his mind, it takes an objective existence for him."[4] The cumulative critique of religious belief in the nineteenth century and the judgment which has lain upon it throughout the twentieth was succinctly summarized in Feuerbach's synthesis of his own work in a sentence: "This is why I wrote in the *Essence of Christianity* that man's belief in God is nothing other than his belief in himself, that in his God he reveres and loves nothing else than his own being."[5] The source of belief had become utterly reflexive: the subject and object were the same.

Periodically, this assertion had found its voice in the history of Western philosophy, perhaps for the first time in Xenophanes's attack on Homeric theology and his caustic statement about the projectional nature of popular religion: "If cattle and horses or lions had hands or were able to draw with their hands and do the work that men can do, horses would draw the forms of the gods like horses, and cattle like cattle, and they would make their bodies such as they each had themselves."[6] This theme would move in its variations to David Hume: "The Idea of God, as meaning an infinitely intelligent, wise, and good Being, arises from reflection on the Operations of our own Mind and augmenting those qualities of Goodness and Wisdom, without Bound or Limit."[7] But Xenophanes professed a commitment to the God who was above the gods of Homer: "One God, greatest among the gods and men, in no way similar to mortals either in body or in thought."[8] Hume – without considering why human beings are driven to the infinite, i.e., to "augmenting without Bound or Limit" – while he came to dismiss institutional religion as the "established superstition," countenanced "one simple, though somewhat ambiguous, at least undefined proposition, *that the cause or causes of order in the universe probably bear some remote analogy to human intelligence.*"[9]

The lengthy history of religious criticism has repeatedly registered human self-projection in religious beliefs and practices. But God simply-as-projection comes to an irreversible emergence in the work and influence of Ludwig Feuerbach. Indeed, Eugene Kamenka maintains that the "psychological use of the word 'projection,' so pervasive in contemporary English, originates with George Eliot's translation of Feuerbach's *The Essence of Christianity*." Eliot employed this term to translate two German ones which Feuerbach had taken from Hegel: *Vergegenständlichung*, "objectification," and *Entäusserung*, "alienation."[10] Perhaps one should modify Kamenka's judgment slightly. Ralph Waldo Emerson some ten years before Eliot's translation applied this creative, conscious activity to God and made the world itself "a projection of God in the unconscious," and consequently the world is "to us, the present expositor of the divine mind."[11] In Feuerbach, this interpretation of all religious belief is given a definitive importance and moves out under his influence into such diverse fields as the revolutionary philosophy of Marx, the psychology of Freud, and the sociology of Durkheim. The conviction of the man or woman in Nietzsche's marketplace that religious belief is no longer possible – a conviction that for Marx becomes more atmosphere than argument, much more part of the air Europe is to breathe than a conclusion seriously demonstrated by him – must be engaged in Feuerbach as it is mediated into our culture through Feuerbach. In his own words and in contrast with the speculative idealism of Hegel:

> I, on the contrary, let religion itself speak; I constitute myself only its listener and interpreter, not its prompter. Not to invent, but to discover, "to unveil existence," has been my sole object; to see correctly, my sole endeavour. It is not I, but religion that worships man, although religion, or rather theology, denies this; it is not I, an insignificant individual, but religion itself that says: God is man, man is God. . . . If therefore my work is negative, irreligious, atheistic, let it be remembered that atheism – at least in the sense of this work – is the secret of religion itself.[12]

Feuerbach takes from Hegel not the dialectical method but the reflexivity of the dialectical method. His own method is operational, elaborating general matrices that he brings to bear upon religious phenomena or arguing through a series of self-substantiating aphorisms. What becomes reflexive in his method, i.e., in his "historical-philosophical analysis," is a new principle, the real and complete nature of the human person.[13] What constitute this human person, this *ens realissimum*, are reason, will, and affection, and in Feuerbach's reflexivity each of these has itself for its own object. The agent and the object are ultimately the same:

Reason, Will, and Love are not powers which a man possesses, for he is nothing without them, he is what he is only by them; they are the constituent elements of his nature, which he neither has nor makes, the animating, determining, governing powers – divine absolute powers – to which he can oppose no resistance. . . . In the object which he contemplates, therefore, a man becomes acquainted with himself; consciousness of the objective is the self-consciousness of man. We know the man by the object, by his conception of what is external to himself; in it his nature becomes evident; this object is his manifested nature, his true objective ego. . . . The *absolute* to man is his own nature. The power [*Macht*] of the object over him is therefore the power of his own nature. Thus the power of the object of feeling is the power of feeling itself; the power of the object of the intellect is the power of the intellect itself; the power of the object of will is the power of the will itself.[14]

Out of this strong reflexivity of principle come the three arguments that disclose the secret of religion as atheistic anthropology: the argument from consciousness, the argument from language, and the argument from the historical experience of alienation. We have considered the last; now let us look at the first two which are actually foundational to this last.

(1) Thinking is essentially reflexive. The truth of the subject is found in its essential *objects*. Unless an object is given in sense perception, the unique and characteristic object of any form of consciousness is nothing more than the essential nature of the conscious subject. What one thinks about uniquely discloses what one is. Here, in the reflexivity of human consciousness, the subject gives and is given by the object. Thus the major premise: the object to which a being necessarily and essentially relates is nothing else than its own revealed essence, its objectified nature. But God uniquely and characteristically in religion, then, is an object of human consciousness, but not an object of sense perception. Religion purports an object far removed from sense experience, and only human beings have religion. Only human beings have that object which they worship as God, while brute animals have neither religion nor God. Thus God – the unique object – is nothing else than the human subject. The subject is actually projecting itself into objectivity. The truth about the "divine" object lies in the human subject. "Man – this is the mystery of religion – projects his being into objectivity, and then again makes himself an object to this projected image of himself thus converted into a subject."[15] What is projected is not the individual, but the essence of the individual – the complete, perfect essence that is the human.

(2) Language is essentially reflexive. The truth of the subject is found in its *predicates.* "When it is shown that what the subject is lies entirely in the attributes of the subject; that is, that the predicate is the true subject; it is also proved that if the divine predicates are attributes of human nature, the subject of those predicates is also human nature."[16] But the attributes classically predicated of God, such as thinking, loving, wise, and so on, can, upon examination, be seen to be validly predicated only in the world of human experience and of human nature as such. For these predicates about God are stamped with the human referent from their inception, and they can never lose this essential mark. This language and its grammar come from human experience and human interchange and so patently belong to a human reality. The human predicates are the truth about the divine subject. Thus, linguistically, God is revealed as human. The truth of the human subject lies in these "divine" predicates.

Human consciousness, then, discloses the actual humanity of God; religious grammar discloses the humanity of God; the practices and claims of religion instantiate these projections. Feuerbach has often been countered by a philosophical psychology that distinguishes a modification of consciousness from a creation *ex nihilo,* by an analysis of predication which insists upon analogical attribution of human and divine predication, and by apologetic critiques that point to the human, enhancing qualities within the religious traditions. These ripostes have themselves been deflected by asserting that they miss something of the point, that Feuerbach did not claim to interpret what religious consciousness should be doing, but what it is doing. But this return itself does not recognize that Feuerbach claimed to disclose the secret of all religious consciousness and predication and to deal with religion in its essence. It was obvious to him from both the nature of human awareness and the history of religion, even of the Judeo-Christian tradition, that human beings have tended essentially and inescapably to (a) create the divine in their own image and according to their own needs, (b) reduce transcendence to human managements, and (c) destroy human values in the name of religion as if one had to choose between the glory of God and the glory of humanity. And is not each of these a form of projection and consequently an estrangement of the human?

Projection was not confined in modernity to religious criticism. As a characteristic of human consciousness and practice, it was a discovery and a revolution against the objectivity-claims of the eighteenth-century Enlightenment. It has come to influence almost all of the sciences and their concomitant philosophies. Émile Durkheim argued that in religious practice human society was worshiping itself writ large. History has moved from the objectivity and clean-slate theories of Leopold von Ranke to recognize that human interest and preconceptions are always involved in the selection of facts and in the evaluation of data.

Perhaps the most startling and recent change in this direction has occurred in what was once considered paradigmatically objective, i.e., physics. John von Neumann's discussion of observation and measurement climaxes in questions and reconsiderations about the "objectivity" of contemporary physics. In classical mechanics the contribution of the observer to the content of what he studied was regarded as negligible, since the measurement process was fully analyzable in terms of the equations of motion alone. Von Neumann, following a paper of Neils Bohr of 1929, postulated that the intervention of the observer through the process of measurement introduces into the causal propagation of the wave function an instantaneous change that is discontinuous and non-causal.[17]

This means that, in sharp contrast to the universal hopes of the Newtonian physics "to derive the rest of the phenomena of Nature by the same kind of reasoning from mechanical principles" and the centuries of mechanics which followed, "it is not possible to formulate the laws of quantum mechanics in a complete and consistent way without a reference to human consciousness."[18] The postulation of projection within particle movement changed radically the statements that this science would support: "Experience only makes statements of this type: an observer has made a certain (subjective) observation; and never any like this: a physical quantity has a certain value."[19] Despite serious and rigorous attempts to unseat this projection-postulate, it has won many physicists who would agree with Heisenberg that the "laws of nature which we formulate mathematically in quantum theory deal no longer with the particles themselves, but with our knowledge of the elementary particles."[20]

The atheistic tradition, then, was not alone in its discovery of projection, but it assimilated this discovery as a strategic device to discount any independent reality to the object of belief. The divine subject was purely imaginary, was simply human projection. One more example might underscore the fundamental nature of this modern critique in its religious employment. Let us consider once more Sigmund Freud.

In 1907 Freud published his hypothesis that obsessional neuroses and religious practices are parallel. Both are defense mechanisms against instinctual satisfaction and against future punishment, linked with an inner sense of guilt. The essential resemblance between religious practice and obsessional neurosis lies with the renunciation of the satisfaction of inherent instincts, and the chief difference between them is that neurosis is predominantly sexual, but religious practices are egoistic in origin. The parallel is so close that one could define obsessional neurosis as a private religious system or describe religion as a universal obsessional neurosis. What is interesting here is that these patterns of religion come out of psychic displacement to the eternal or ceremonial, a displacement that allows a person to express unconscious motivations through symbolic activity, warding off pervasive anxiety, guilt, and danger.[21]

By *The Future of an Illusion* (1927), Freud had worked out a much more complicated structure of religious belief, one which corresponded to the two aspects of culture or civilization, i.e., knowledge (*Wissen und Können*) and regulations (*Einrichtungen*). Every civilization depends upon these two components of social life. Consequently, civilization has to compensate its members for the instinctual sacrifices enacted from them in the form of work and renunciation of destructive antisocial drives. Religious ideas become for Freud "what is perhaps the most important item in the psychical inventory of a civilization" – the means by which the masses could be coerced or reconciled or recompensed for these needed renunciations.[22] Religion transmogrified the two components that civilization necessarily possessed: what is knowledge in civilization becomes belief in religion; what are regulations within a civilization, become the practices and observances alluded to above. The structure of religion mirrors in its anatomy the structure of all civilized life.

Through a consideration of the origins and path of development, one can offer an assessment of the past and trace the emergence of "God" and religion as a mental asset for the self-protection of civilization. The basic force or drive behind every human development, even that of religious ideas, is the same: "The libido follows the paths of narcissistic needs and attaches itself to the objects which ensure the satisfaction of those needs."[23] To understand the needs out of which religion has come, it is essential to recognize that the components of the total human personality, the superego, the ego and the id, parallel the massive cultural triad that comprises civilization, the human person, and nature. Each of these components is lodged in continual struggle against the other.

Within this structure of endless conflict emerges the psychological significance of religious ideas. They are technically illusions, i.e., beliefs grounded not in evidence but in wish-fulfillment. They are crafted or projected to handle the threats delivered against human beings by nature and by civilization.[24] Seemingly promising, these illusions are ultimately destructive of human growth. For religion apes, as well as supports, civilization. As civilization is constituted by knowledge and regulations, and religion corresponds by beliefs and practices, so religion also mirrors, as well as suggests, psychopathologies. As belief or illusion, religion resembles Meynert's amentia, a "state of acute hallucinatory confusion;" as practice, it resembles a universal obsessive neu-rosis – issuing out of the Oedipus complex.[25] Religion is really ersatz civiliza-tion, substituting for the knowledge and rational conduct of culture irrational beliefs and obsessive practices.

When civilization falters, religion subsumes the three tasks of civilization against nature: human "self-regard, seriously menaced, calls for consolation; life and the universe must be robbed of their terrors; moreover, human curios-ity, moved it is true by the strongest practical interest, demands an answer."[26] On the other hand, the beliefs and practices of religion can reconcile the human person to the instinctual renunciations demanded by civilization.

The lengthy genesis of the projection of God can be traced from preanimistic or magical stages, animistic stages, through totemism and polytheism to monotheism. For Freud also, the "death of God" occurs, but not as the Marxist project for the future or Nietzsche's epistemological fact in the recent past. This death occurs rather at the origins of religion – as the his-torical event of the killing and eating of the primeval father by the sons, the regret and fear that followed this event, and the rules of totemism that arose as an attempt to ease the guilt and to appease the murdered father. God emerges out of human history, rather than out of ethics (as with Kant) or out of human religious experience (as with Schleiermacher). The death of God is not the terminus of belief, as with Nietzsche, but its origin. And Freud's history is both of the human race and of the individual.

Belief can be followed in its history as a series of projections: first in the humanization of nature, i.e., animism, through the projection of psychic forces into natural events and things; then in a polytheism in which the gods with-draw from nature; and finally in a monotheism where the gods of antiquity are condensed into one projected father figure. Animism does not equal reli-gion for Freud, but it is the foundation of religion.[27] The causal factors which effect the various stages of religious belief are (a) desire, the human need to make its helplessness before nature and civilization bearable, and (b) infantile prototypes which govern the features and path of development of the pro-jected objects of belief. It is the identification of this latter which Freud considered his chief contribution to the analysis of religion. As he wrote in his study of Leonardo da Vinci: "Psycho-analysis has made us aware of the intimate connection between the father-complex and belief in God, and has taught us that the personal God is psychologically nothing other than a magnified father."[28]

Freud continued the tradition that God is projection, but there are signifi-cant differences between his position and that of Feuerbach. In Feuerbach, what was projected was the perfect essence of the human; in Freud what was finally projected was a protecting-and-threatening father figure. In Feuerbach, the human person was essentially reflexive and infinite, the mind and the will and the feelings had themselves for their own objects, and consequently they could in their farthest reaches only be conscious of themselves. In Freud, the human person is essentially finite and threatened; out of the need for narcissistic satisfaction before the demands of civilization and for physical security before the threats of nature and death, he or she projects a God who will minister to a sense of worth and provide protection from the horrors of the future. The shape of Freud's God is not the projected perfection of the human; it is the Oedipal Father figure, projected by human energies. For in the final analysis, Freud's principle is actional: "libido follows the path of narcissistic need."[29] For Freud, God emerges either out of the needs for satisfaction or behind those demands of the superego to "do it right." As Paul Ricoeur has indicated, in Freud

> the mechanism of "projection" explains the appearance of transcendence connected with the religious source of the forbidden and the feared; the mechanism of introjection, by which a source of authority is set up within the ego, is thus complicated by the mechanism of projection by which the omnipotence of thought is projected into real powers – demons, spirits, gods. Projection is not meant to account for institutions as such, but for the illusion of transcendence, attaching to the belief in spirits and gods, that is, in the real existence of powers higher than man.[30]

But whatever the difference between Feuerbach and Freud, they agree that what is believed in religion is a projection of the human, that the divine must be "deconstructed" and disclosed as the human. The difference between them only underlines their agreement; whatever variances they exhibit lie with their understanding of the human. In fact, as Eugene Kamenka maintains, "The modern social theorist is not so much inclined to choose between theories like Feuerbach's, Freud's, and Durkheim's, as to combine them."[31]

Contemplation

It is paradoxical perhaps that the advance of contemporary atheism intersects in this critique with another great religious movement in the twentieth century: the developing interest in contemplation and in the mystical life together with the retrieval within this movement of negative theology. This contemporary interest in religious experience cannot be reduced to religious enthusiasms nor a sweeping call to revival nor some form of spiritual narcissism. The call to a contemplative life entails in its own authenticity both a serious engagement with God and so with the "passive" experience of God and the ascetical and psychic disciplines prerequisite for this self-transcendence, sensibility, and engagement. This contemplative growth within American culture has encouraged a rising interest in the literature of spirituality and mysticism and is reinforced by a strong influence from Eastern religious practices. It is here, it seems to me, in the richness of the contemplative tradition, that the conviction argued by atheists of the nineteenth and twentieth centuries becomes co-ordinate with a movement equally aware of the proclivity of religion to become projection.

What has been somewhat neglected in much of the popular renditions of the contemplative life in all its forms, however, is the dialectical correction of concept and experience that the contemplative tradition insists upon, that "God" always contradicts "god," that the vectors of finite experience point beyond experience, that knowing must yield to unknowing, a knowing unknowing. Contemplative authors and mystical theology at its finest have insisted that human experience is always and everywhere a finite modification of a finite subject, no matter what its intensity and extension, and that if it does not point beyond itself such an apotheosis of experience becomes idolatrous in any claim to represent the divine adequately. Mysticism and contemplation are informed by a radical self-transcendence, a self-transcendence that is the polar opposite of self-preoccupation and narcissism, a transcendence that insists upon God as mystery above conceptualization. In the Christian Neo-Platonic tradition, the purification from these projections develops beyond the negation of one's concepts and experiences as projection to the further negation of the negation itself in the affirmation of the Trinity, whose mystery transcends all being, gods, and even the good "in the brilliant darkness of a hidden silence" [κατὰ τὸν ὑπέρφοτον ἐγκεκάλυπται τῆς κρυφιομύστου σιγῆς γνόφον].[32]

That is why the ascent of Moses became so paradigmatic in this mystical theology. Moses moves on from purification to the encounter with God upon Sinai, "into the darkness of unknowing. Here renouncing all that the mind may conceive, wrapped entirely in the intangible and the invisible, he belongs completely to the One who is beyond everything. Here, being neither oneself nor someone else, one is supremely united by a completely unknowing inactivity of all knowledge, and knows beyond the mind by knowing nothing."[33] This is not anti-intellectualism. It is to come to the awareness of God as incomprehensible. Gregory of Nyssa in his *Life of Moses* had formulated that same corrective of concept, language, and experience, arguing their infinite inadequacy: "This is the true knowledge of what is sought; this is the seeing that consists in not seeing because that which is sought transcends all knowledge, being separated on all sides by incomprehensibility as by a kind of darkness. Wherefore John the sublime, who penetrated into the luminous darkness, says 'No one has ever seen God' [Jn 1:18], thus asserting that knowledge of the divine essence is unattainable not only by men, but also by every intelligent creature."[34] Moses had come to see "that what is divine is beyond all knowledge and comprehension."[35] "Mystery" does not point to an insolvable problem or an enigma; it points to that which is inexhaustible in its fullness, and consequently cannot be comprehended, i.e., is incomprehensible. This is what is meant by a "brilliant darkness." To insist upon the adequacy or to entertain such expectations of human concepts, feelings, and experience is simply to make a finite, human reality divine, for "creatures of heaven and earth are nothing when compared to God."[36]

Perhaps no one continues to represent this sensitivity more artistically and at the same time more analytically for the contemporary world than the sixteenth-century Spanish Carmelite John of the Cross. For the question posed by the nineteenth and twentieth centuries is critical. If one admits that religious belief – to be authentic – must recognize its own set of projections, whether psychologically individual or social, and if one admits this not as a metaphysics but as a phenomenology of belief and of a particular cultivation of religious experience, does this admission not indicate a destruction that constitutes the rejection of all divinity, the death of God, and the end of religion? Or can it equally indicate that this engagement with God must move dialectically into the stern demands of a life of contemplation, one moment of which is apophatic?

The vitality of this second option figures continually in the theological literature of today. For at least thirty years, issues of the *Journal of Religion* and *Theological Studies* have carried articles on negative or apophatic theology, and the writings of John of the Cross are found importantly within each.[37] But what is crucial to underscore is that apophatic theology is not primarily one that does or does not make statements about God. It is not a theology about conclusions or statements. It is primarily an experiential process and a development of a faith that points beyond experience and concepts, a process through negation into the infinite mystery that is God, a reality that beggars language. Gradually one is transformed by the self-communication of God, as this grace moves one through the intense experiences of darkness into union

with the incomprehensible God. Apophatic theology involves both interpretation and criticism, conceptualization and theological argument. But all of
these point – as descriptive or explanatory – to the process in which one is
engaged, a process in which one must be engaged, in order to grasp its interpretation in any depth – or, better, to be grasped by its unyielding, but drawing,
intimations and promise. The metaphor often used for this is that of blinding
light.

John of the Cross, perhaps the most influential of the apophatic doctors,
did not write works of scriptural commentary, but he does share with Gregory
of Nyssa the emphasis upon *praxis*. The *Ascent of Mount Carmel* is "el modo
de subir hasta la cumbre del monte," "the way that leads to the summit of the
mountain, that sublime state of perfection we here call the union of a soul
with God."[38] In John of the Cross, finally, it is not theology speculatively interested in God or in human beings, but theology descriptive of this process by
which God "takes His abode in a human being by making him (her) live the
life of God."[39] In a word, it is theology not about process, but theology which
is essentially an experiential process with its description, its negative analyses,
its stages of development, and its prescriptive counsels. In this, John is much
more like Freud than like Feuerbach.

Interestingly enough, the hearty figures of the nineteenth century were not
wild in their admiration for John of the Cross. When William James wanted
a passage which would exhibit "the passion of self-contempt wreaking itself
on the poor flesh, the divine irrationality of devotion making a sacrificial gift
of all it has (its sensibilities, namely) to the object of its adoration," he selected
the celebrated chapter 13 of the first book of the *Ascent of Mount Carmel.* He
chose John of the Cross, whom he described as a "Spanish mystic who flour-
ished – or rather existed, for there was little that suggested flourishing about
him."[40] James's judgment becomes somewhat more mild as the *Varieties of Religious Experience* develops, but his voice parallels other religious writers of the
nineteenth century. R. A. Vaughan, in his *Hours with the Mystics* (1856), finds
John's mysticism "miserably mistaken . . . a dark negation, permeated with a
fantastic gloom and a passionate severity." Dean Inge, in *Christian Mysticism*
(1899), dismissed John of the Cross as one who "carried self-abnegation to a
fanatical extreme and presents the life of holiness in a grim and repellent
aspect."[41]I think it is fair to say that none of the three understood John of the
Cross.

There is no doubt that in John of the Cross there is the denial both of
pleasure as the final motive for choice and of the adequacy of any human
concepts before the activity of God within the soul. There is the negation that

constitutes the nights in which no satisfaction is found in God and in which there is no experience of religious reassurance. There is a resoluteness of longing in which one desires nothing together with God, but all things only in God, a starkness of faith which moves beyond finite images and concepts as final guides into a surrender to a God whose infinite light is blinding. There is no question that there is suffering and abnegation in the doctrine of John of the Cross and the contradiction of religious expectations. He warns away from his works "the kind of spiritual people who like to approach God along sweet and satisfying paths."[42] Written both in his theology and at the base of his sketch of Mount Carmel are the almost Zen-like verses in which he summarized the movement of a human being into the contemplative possession of God:

> To reach satisfaction in all
> desire its possession in nothing.
> To come to possess all
> desire the possession of nothing.
> To arrive at being all
> desire to be nothing.
> To come to the knowledge of all
> desire the knowledge of nothing.
>
> To come to the pleasure you have not
> you must go by a way in which you enjoy not.
> To come to the knowledge you have not
> you must go by a way in which you know not.
> To come to the possession you have not
> you must go by a way in which you possess not.
> To come to be what you are not
> you must go by a way in which you are not.
>
> When you turn towards something
> you cease to cast yourself upon the all.
> For to go from all to the all
> you must deny yourself of all in all.
> And when you come to the possession of the all
> you must possess it without wanting anything.
> Because if you desire to have something in all
> your treasure in God is not purely your all.[43]

These aphorisms are particularly difficult to understand; they are the very ones which roiled the exuberance of William James. The poetry and the hundreds of prose pages of John of the Cross are little more than a very nuanced theological reflection upon their meaning and the directions they offer. But neither the poetry nor the prose mitigates the starkness of the demand within this process and the moments of renunciation that are essentially part of the contemplative maturation of the soul. It is an evolution in which the experience of the desert is the essential preparation for contemplation and in which the reality of the cross with its experience of abandonment figures critically as the final movement into union with God, in a love that is beyond human language and concepts. One moves through contradiction into a love "in which the will of the soul, united with that flame [Spirit of God], loves most sublimely."[44]

The obvious question is: why? "Since the things of God in themselves produce good in the soul, are beneficial, and give assurance, why does God in this night darken the appetites and faculties so that they derive no satisfaction in such good things and find it difficult to be occupied with them?"[45] The question appears over and over again throughout the progress of his writing. And in his answer John sounds very much like Feuerbach and Freud. What Feuerbach and Freud cited as projection, John of the Cross subsumed under this more general scholastic maxim: "Quidquid recipitur secundum modum recipientis recipitur [Whatever is received is received according to one receiving]."[46]

Andrew of the Incarnation credits Aquinas with the origin of this statement in John of the Cross, but the proposition was common coin in the scholastic theology of the Middle Ages, taking on different meanings as it was thematically embodied in different systems.[47] St. Thomas himself attributes the doctrine, or at least the insight, to Plato: "Plato saw that each thing is received in something else according to the measure of the recipient."[48] The Quaracchi editors of St. Bonaventure attribute it to the *Liber de causis*, where it stands as the ninth proposition: "Aliqua ex rebus non recipit quod est supra eam nisi per modum secundum quem potest recipere ipsum" ("No thing receives what is above it unless in the manner according to which it is able to receive it").[49] This formulation both suggests Neo-Platonic origins and embodies the concern it will carry for John of the Cross. For the problem is this: "that in the initial stages of the spiritual life, and even in more advanced ones, the sensory part of the soul is imperfect, it frequently receives God's Spirit with this very imperfection."[50] It would reconfigure God according to its own consciousness and desires.

John argues that even if God were miraculously to impart himself directly to the persons seeking him, they would be unable to receive the divine communication, except in their own human way. They would reduce God to their god, to the finite capacity of their own feelings, thoughts, and expectations. Normally, this is called an idol. "Since these natural faculties do not have the purity, strength, or capacity to receive and taste supernatural things in a super-natural or divine mode, but only according to their own mode, which is human and lowly, as we said, these faculties must be also darkened regarding the divine so that weaned, purified and annihilated in their natural way, they might lose that lowly and human mode of receiving and working."[51] Without that purification and transformation, human beings would always understand God with what Hegel called "a contracted religiosity," reducing God to the human.[52]

What John of the Cross is stating is the radical inadequacy of religious expe-rience, of religious consciousness. Our inadequate understanding and loves are limited by what we are. What we grasp and what we long for is very much shaped and determined by our own preconceptions, appetites, concepts, and personality-set. If these are not disclosed and gradually transformed by grace and by its progressive affirmation within religious faith, working its way into the everyday of human history and choices, then there is no possibility of contemplation of anything but our own projections. The human person would receive the divine not "spiritually, but rather humanly and naturally, no matter how much his faculties are employed in God and no matter how much satis-faction he derives from this."[53] With Feuerbach, John is sensitive to the human-ization which consciousness works upon its God; with Freud, he is acutely aware that the religious movement towards God can emerge either from the desire for satisfaction or from the drive to be morally reassured. In contrast to both, what he elaborates is not a process of assimilation or of psychotherapy, but of the purification and transformation of the person by grace, the gradual "becoming God by participation" in the joy and the love that is the union with the divine nature towards which this process moves.[54]

The nights of John of the Cross constitute this process of negation and purification. A human being can come to God initially for the same reason that instinctual energies move towards any pleasure fulfillment. "The love of pleasure and attachment to it usually fires the will towards the enjoyment of things that give pleasure."[55] Until the person has broken the automatic con-junction between instinctual satisfaction and the motivation of his choices, he will "be incapable of the enlightenment and the dominating fullness of God's pure and simple light."[56] In the night of the senses, motivation is gradually purified: actively through an immersion in the life of Jesus, so that the moti-vation of Christ's life gradually becomes one's own; and passively through the aridity, sometimes protracted over many years, when there is no experience of felt satisfaction either from the things of God or from other elements within one's life. On the contrary, there is often a distaste or disgust, coupled with a painful sense that one is not integrally serving God and that one can no longer pray discursively, making use of protracted insights and imaginations. This night of aridity gradually interiorizes a new love of God and a deeper joy, not dictated by the human needs for immediate religious satisfaction but brought to birth by the infusion of purgative contemplation: "For contemplation is nothing else than a secret and peaceful and loving inflow of God, which, if not hampered, inflames the soul in the spirit of love."[57] What the night of the senses brings about is the development beyond the pleasure principle in religion of a contemplative love – either actively through choices made under the guidance and motivation of Christ, or passively when satisfaction is gone and one continues to follow the directions of grace even though there seems to be no recompense. Gradually out of this night arises a surrender to One whose incomprehensibility defies the immediate demands for conceptualization and satisfaction, and whose influence brings the person to a new kind of prayer that is peaceful, deeply loving, and without images. What is critical to see here is that this takes place through a love that is gradually being infused and which serves as the basis of contemplation.

The second night, maintains John of the Cross, is far more terrible and demanding than the first. It is the night of the spirit, the night of faith. Here it is not so much a question of motivation as of support systems and security: the concepts, the systems of meaning, the symbolic structures by which reassurance is forthcoming. In the movement towards deeper union with God, faith alone becomes the ultimate guide – a faith which puts us into mystery because it both transvaluates all that we have known and "informs us of matters we have never seen or known, either in themselves or in their likeness."[58] What functions critically here for John is the infinite distance between human concepts or experiences and the divine, and it is this gap that will suggest religious development: "Like the blind, they must lean on dark faith, accept it for their guide and light and rest on nothing of what they understand, taste, feel, and imagine. All these perceptions are darkness that will lead them astray. Faith lies beyond all this understanding, taste, feeling and imagining."[59] All of the projections of need or will or concept are attacked as inadequate and misleading. The god they embodied dies in human awareness. Through faith one moves into utter mystery, what is incomprehensible and unimaginable; "for however impressive may be one's knowledge or feeling of God, that knowledge or feeling will have no resemblance to God and amount to very little."[60]

This night also has its active and passive aspects: active, in that a human being takes faith profoundly as the guide of his or her life, a faith which both opens a contact with what "transcends every natural light and infinitely exceeds all human understanding" and relocates everything known within a new horizon in which it is radically reinterpreted and transvaluated; passive, when all the supports drop away from one's consciousness and there is only the experience of emptiness, impurity, weakness, abandonment, and death. It is the experience of the cross, for John, and what the "soul feels most is that God has rejected it and with an abhorrence of it casts it into darkness."[61] Paradoxically, it is precisely within this experience of the cross – when images, concepts, symbols, and experiences provide nothing but their own emptiness – that the final union between God and the person is being effected. It is through the experience of this abandonment that God is transforming a human being in love, a possession that is not understood at the time and whose symbolic expression during this period of purification is dispossession and death.

In either night, if one insists upon the god projected by the apotheosis of the human or by the need for security and pleasure or by expectations generated "by my own experience," the working of God cannot proceed. There is really only one night in John of the Cross: the progressive purification and transformation of the person in what he cherishes and understands and in what gives him security and support. This continual contemplative purification of the human person is a progressive hermeneutic of the nature of God, the gradual disclosure of the One who in his love infinitely "transcends the intellect and is incomprehensible to it." The darkness is an event of the disclosure, and contemplation becomes much more the reception of a reality which is beyond grasp, of the bringing into awareness of what is inexhaustibly mysterious. Whatever knowledge one has does not move into the objectification of God but passes through objectifications, contradicts their adequacy, and in faith "reaches God more by not understanding than by understanding."[62]

This dark disclosure of God – dark because it gradually introduces a surrender to the unconcealment of infinite Mystery – is not anti-intellectual or antihuman. John has both a quality of poetry and a profundity of theology of rare achievement. It is rather that clear knowledge gives way before the incomprehensible, that there is a *docta ignorantia*, a recognition that whatever is grasped is not the ultimate mystery by which one's own self is grasped, that everything we can conceive or feel points beyond itself into this Mystery that is infinite and hence incomprehensible love.

Nor is John's mystical theology antidogmatic. The articles of faith are the rungs of the ladder by which the person moves into the Mystery.[63] The doctrine of John coincides here with much of the theology of Karl Rahner. For both, God is the infinite, the incomprehensible, the holy Mystery; for both, the individual dogmatic statement possesses a "represented conceptual content" which is "merely the means of experiencing a being referred beyond itself and everything imaginable."[64] "A being referred": The function of dogmatic stability is not to explain the mystery of God, but to lead into it and to safeguard its incomprehensibility. Dogma is to secure the inviolability of the mystery of the incomprehensible God.

The self-disclosure of God, of One so infinitely Other, is finally only possible within the disclosure of the contradiction within finite concepts and human expectations that touch upon God. The darkness and its pain are here, but they are finally dialectical movements in which the human is purified from projection by a "no" which is most radically a "yes," a "no" that is generated by the initial "yes." The disclosures of God contradict the programs and expectations of human beings in order to fulfil human desire and human freedom at a much deeper level of love than subjectivity would have measured out in its projections.

A final word

The point here is not to persuade anyone that the theogenesis, the "becoming God by participation," is correctly schematized by John of the Cross, a schema that is finally no schema. The point is that the foundational persuasion of the need for this kind of purification coincides with the radical criticism of religious belief in our own day. Ludwig Feuerbach and Sigmund Freud on one side and John of the Cross on the other are persuaded that much projection lies at the heart of our relationship with and conceptualization of God. For the former, the response is to deny the reality of God; for John, it is to insist that the evolution or personal development of faith must pass through the contradictions that are the desert and the cross.

In this purification of desire and of awareness, the critical influence for John is Christ. The active night of the senses begins with immersion into the Jesus of the Gospels.[65] The intelligibility of the night of the spirit is essentially found in him: "Because I have said that Christ is the way [*el camino*] and that this way is a death to our natural selves in the sensory and spiritual parts of the soul, I would like to demonstrate how this death is patterned on Christ's. For he is our model and light."[66] And the completion of the mystical union is achieved through being touched by him and absorbed into him: "You subtly penetrate the substance of my soul, and, lightly touching it all, absorb it entirely into Yourself."[67]

It is the Spirit of Christ that is the agent of this passive transformation of the person, gradually permeating individual experiences and influencing the patterns of direction and growth – the Spirit which John of the Cross calls fire and whose progress he repeatedly compares to "the fire that penetrates a log of wood . . . that first makes an assault upon it, wounding it with its flame, drying it out, and stripping it of its unsightly qualities until it is so disposed that it can be penetrated and transformed into the fire."[68] The contemplative evolution is an assimilation into the love of God through the progressive possession by the Spirit that configures the soul to Christ.

It is in this deeply mysterious assimilation to Christ, this gradual movement from the initial stages of purification from expectations and conceptual clarity until the final moments of union, that John throws into bold relief what is the experience, in various degrees and infinite varieties, of many deeply good people. What appears at first sight as a rare or highly specialized experience of mystical development "writes large" the outline by which the surrender that is faith evolves into its own fullness in many lives. Any serious following of Christ leads by way of the reversals of concepts or the disappointments of expectations, the sacrifice or the suffering – by way of the deconstruction of an initial understanding of God – into the loving awareness that God is beyond concept, beyond management, and beyond form. There is in Christian living an abiding purification from expectations and projections that social workers or mothers of families or dedicated teachers undergo – must undergo if they are to continue faithful to the God who dwells in light inaccessible, whose incalculable reality is embodied in Jesus, and whose draw they feel within their own spirits.

Aquinas maintains that this progression in purification of concepts is the dynamic intrinsic to the gifts of the Spirit which are native to the life of faith, specifically to the gift of understanding which "de auditis mentem illustrat."[69] Understanding involves a *depurgatio*, the purifying of images, experiences, and concepts within all of those graced by the indwelling Spirit, by which a person comes to see that what he believes transcends everything he grasps. The gift of understanding is that through which, "while we do not see what God is, we do see what he is not. And we know God in this life so much more perfectly as we understand that he transcends [*excedere*] whatever is comprehended by our intellect." The gift of understanding is the opposite of projection. It is this influence of the Spirit, gracefully present in the mystery of lives that look externally so ordinary, that grounds Aquinas's contention: "The contemplative life is begun here and reaches its completion in a future existence."[70]

René Voillaume makes a similar point as he introduces the *Journal* of one of the major disciples of John of the Cross in the twentieth century, Raïssa Maritain:

> The contemplative prayer of Raïssa, whose life was above all dedicated to intellectual work, and who was called on to testify mainly in the world of thought and of art, is but one with the experience of a factory girl or a woman wholly occupied in domestic tasks in a poor neighbourhood. I have known some such, who by these paths in appearance very different have found the same simplicity of gaze on God and endured the same acute ordeals of purification, to achieve a more complete union with the supreme object of their love.[71]

This contemplative purification, which in one way or another catches up the lives of those who move within grace, is delineated in its progressive moments and in its fullest completion by the mystical theology of John of the Cross.

Not all atheism comes out of Feuerbach and Freud; not all contemplatives are influenced by John of the Cross. But there is an intersection here of religious criticism that seems to me highly significant. If it is correct, then the concern of a theology that sees development somewhat dialectically should be less to refute Feuerbachian and Freudian analysis than to learn from them what they have to teach about the relentless remolding of the image of God by religious consciousness and to suggest alternative stages to the processes they elaborate of anthropological recognition and reduction. The model for such an alternative may well lie with the patterns within the theology of John of the Cross or with the mystagogical theology of Karl Rahner. What I am suggesting is that the contemporary interest in spirituality may well not be of incidental importance or of accidental occurrence, that for the reflective and sensitive mind – one which grasps the conditionality of imaginative and cultural structures, the necessities which issue from a background of which one can only be half aware, the profound limitations of one's knowledge and social situation – for such a person, the alternative may well lie between atheism and contemplation.

6

The Negation of Atheism

Religion and the retrieval of the religious

Present in many variations, contradiction has run like a theme through the past five chapters. Attempting to probe certain initial – let us call them 'theistic' – conceptions, arguments or positions, whether philosophical, humanistic, or ethical, these chapters have explored each for an internal incoherence, either of concept or of argument. Negation revealed the contradiction latent in precisely what the theistic advocacy was explicitly asserting or defending. The two variables whose values constituted the parameters of these contradictions were content and the form of thought. Nature (as content) with its purportedly contrived designs and mechanics (as its appropriate form of thought) yielded to dynamic matter and to a universal mechanics with only mechanical principles. Human nature considered with certain epistemological, ethical, and humanistic preoccupations yielded a primacy to the human that the divine threatened; so god was recognized not as the enhancement but the enemy of the human to be countered and extirpated. Finally, one could have remarked the same transposition in the understanding of the scientific study of "religion" itself. Over the centuries "religion" shifted from the medievals' virtue that dictated the ways in which human beings worship and interrelate with God to denote particular beliefs, myths, practices, and symbols indicative of the character of a human culture. Both religion and God became a subset of human culture as well as its symptomatic product. The appropriate form of inquiry into religion was increasingly found in anthropology, ethnology, psychology, or sociology.[1] "Religion" became another way of bracketing the religious.[2]

Nature and human nature had over recent centuries been made foundational for the affirmation of the existence of God. They had been pursued for theistic evidence from which one could infer the divine existence in such disciplines as metaphysics and mechanics, ethics and anthropology, ethnology and sociology. But each of these projects, in omitting or bracketing the religious, had brought to the surface in the second moment of its career a fundamental incoherence, one disclosing its own prior inadequacy that passed over into negation.

This remarkable self-contradiction of concept and argument was noted not just by the "cultured despisers of religion," but by extraordinary contemplative and mystical theologies within Christianity. The very finitude and human origin of the terms designating belief and disbelief necessarily entailed their own inadequacy, and this, in turn, dictated their negation. It seems paradoxical to find that the secret revealed by nineteenth-century atheism had been recognized for centuries by a tradition of radical spirituality, that the students of Derrida, and the Master himself, could compare the pursuit of their own enterprise with the project of negative theology. But the career of the atheistic tradition and that of negative theology developed into profoundly different propositions. The history of each tradition eventuated in the difference between atheism as a final moment in the negation of theism and negation as an indispensable stage in an ongoing religious dialectics. But in both, one was dealing with the self-negations of language and method. Let me explain.

To recognize such internal incoherence in concept and argument, the overthrow in primacy of the binary terms "theism" and "atheism" might constitute a project of contemporary atheism, but this recognition of itself does not move beyond the discovered antinomies to reach the dynamism of the dialectical. To settle upon this contradiction as final would be to fixate it irretrievably at this second stage of judgment, i.e., at the moment of the disclosure of self-contradiction or of irreducible opposition. If this discovered negation is not allowed to generate its own further negation, the negation of the negation, there is no dialectic, only static antinomies.

The inner life of any reality or the thought that follows it, however, may continue to pursue its own truth through the further development of negation. No one maintained more firmly the inadequacy of human concepts in the apperception of the divine reality than the Pseudo-Dionysius; but it is the same author who insisted upon the still further negation, the career of the dialectical: "What has actually to be said about the Cause of everything is this. Since it is the Cause of all beings, [1] we should posit and ascribe to it all the affirmations we make in regard to beings, and, [2] more appropriately, we should negate all these affirmations, since it surpasses all being. Now we should not conclude that the negations are simply the opposites of affirmations, but rather [3] that the Cause of all is considerably prior to this, beyond privations, beyond every denial, beyond every assertion."³

This triadic progress of a history or of an idea or of an argument, produced by the negation of this first negation, constitutes its dialectical development, although – very importantly – not as a fixed schema superimposed upon thought or reality, but as the secret of their own life, a progression or a career revealed to be within it. Hegel praised Kant and Fichte for having perceived that the structure of true method comprised a triplicity, but he censured their failure to see that one cannot simply impose operationally a triadic form on any subject matter.⁴ The dialectic must proceed not from the external application of determinations from a schema, but as the inner – even organic – progress of the subject under study. Dialectical negation and the negation of the negation must be seen to emerge as the immanent life of the subject reflected in thought. One need not be a Hegelian, an Absolute Idealist, or a Marxist, a dialectical materialist – as indeed I am neither – to recognize that such a dialectic can be the development both of the things studied and the process of inquiry into them, that even organic development is into otherness – from the bud to the flower to the fruit.⁵ This evolving pattern, in which one stage supplants another as mutually incompatible while keeping an organic unity, is made possible, even necessary, by inner incoherence. As early as Aristotle, Western philosophy recognized that contradiction – here, between privation and form – lay at the heart of movement.⁶

This is not to assert, however, a result removed from further development. As long as the product is finite, it will carry the seeds of its own inadequacy and contradiction within it. Nor is it to assert the universality of the dialectical structure, but only that it did obtain in the genesis of atheism.

As we have seen, a dialectical contradiction may occur either within the components of the content or between the form of thought appropriate to that content and the form of thought in use.⁷ In content, to take another example, one recalls in Islam the attacks upon Alfarabi and Avicenna (Ibn Sina) for being self-contradictory and metaphysically false to the nature of God, an attack mounted by the greatest of medieval Moslem theologians, Abú Hamíd Al-Ghazáli, in a work engagingly entitled "The Incoherence of the Philosophers" (*Tahafut al-Falasifah*).⁸ When Averroës (Ibn Rochd) countered with his defence of philosophical teachings, he proposed it as the negation of the negation, "The Incoherence of the Incoherence" (*Tahafut al-Tahafut*), entering into Al-Ghazáli's negation to disclose its own fundamental self-contradiction, its "infelicitous mingling of faith and reason."⁹ Or the internal contradiction may lie between the form of thought appropriate to the content and the form of apprehension or cognition *de facto* in use. Thus Absolute Spirit in Hegel must continue to develop through art and religion to philosophy because these prior forms of apprehension – sensuous presentation in art and imaginative representation (*Vorstellung*) in religion – stand in some contradiction to this Absolute Content. The contradiction is not resolved until the content of the thought and the form of thought coincide, when one is appropriately within the other or even identified with the other.[10] And because there will always be the semantic slippage that prevents this sign from ever "coinciding with itself in a moment of perfect, remainderless grasp," the internal contradiction will always generate the recognition of inadequacy and of contradiction, continuing to generate a dialectic that is endless.[11]

Over the past five chapters we have seen these inner incoherences, these contradictions emerge into light either between content and content – as between impersonal evidence and personal conclusion – or between form in use and the form appropriate to content – as between scientific inference and religious disclosure. There is no need to rehearse them here. Wittgenstein made a similar point in his conversations with Maurice Drury: "If you and I are to live religious lives, it mustn't be that we talk a lot about religion, but that our manner of life is different. It is my belief that only if you try to be helpful to other people will you in the end find your way to God."[12] What was pervasively absent in the systems that were to entail theism was the intellectual assimilation of the religious, of its own proper practices and manifestations or symbols, for example, in the practices of holiness or in the mystery present as a horizon of life, or in that galaxy of fundamental religious experiences, whether personal or communal, represented in popular religiosity or in that mysticism which Henri Bergson maintained "must furnish us with the means of approaching, as it were experimentally, the problem of the existence and the nature of God. Indeed we fail to see how philosophy could approach the problem in any other way."[13]

More astonishing in their absence – within a Christian Europe – were the two trinitarian modes of divine self-disclosure and communication: the self-expression of God become an incarnate component within human history or the Spirit transforming human subjectivity in its awareness, affectivity, and experience. These did not figure at all. It is astonishing to record this absence, but it is not extraordinary. We are coming upon a game whose rules – as we have seen – were set at the dawn of modernity.

This game and its rules provoked Wittgenstein to link Bertrand Russell paradoxically with Christian theologians, Christian "parsons." In his daybook for 1929, Maurice Drury recorded the statement of Wittgenstein that "Russell and the parsons between them have done infinite harm, infinite harm." Drury was puzzled by Wittgenstein's coupling of a pair not often associated with one another. What did they share in common? Both attempted to "give some sort of philosophical justification for Christian beliefs, as if some sort of proof was needed."[14] For Wittgenstein, the question about the existence of God constitutes a problem very different from that of the existence of any finite person or object. Evidence and inquiry, consequently, function in a very different way in religious reflection from the way they do in any other form of discourse, for God is not another thing in the universe, only bigger.

It is not that one form of discourse and evidence is rational and the other irrational. To restrict or confine religious inquiry to the lines indicated by scientific method or even common-sense procedure is to violate the logical syntax appropriate to the question, i.e., its grammar, thereby making any appropriate answer impossible.[15] "If we make religious belief a matter of evidence in the way that science is a matter of evidence, says Wittgenstein, then 'this would in fact destroy the whole business.'"[16] It would project God as another thing in the universe. Indeed, there is a remarkable statement of Wittgenstein's in which he recapitulates so much of the spirit of nineteenth-century atheism, no matter how far he is mistaken about the First Vatican Council: "It is a dogma of the Roman Church that the existence of God can be proved by natural reason. Now this dogma would make it impossible for me to be a Roman Catholic. [Now notice *why* and *what* he thinks this kind of demonstration bespeaks.] If I thought of *God as another being like myself, outside myself, only infinitely more powerful*, then I would regard it as my duty to defy him."[17] The argument would, in other words, generate its denial. The evolution of modern atheism would appear to lend weight to his reserve.

Wittgenstein did not move to defiance. He insisted upon the "enormous gulf" between the grammar appropriate to religious language and that appropriate to any other. The former was "on an entirely different plane."[18] These chapters have been driven to this same conclusion by the analysis of the theistic "experiments" of hundreds of years and by the sympathy and protests of the mystics. If the denials of the atheists and the darkness of the apophatic tradition have disclosed the inadequacies of previous linguistic and conceptual settlements, is the religious progression to halt here with the negation they have worked or is it to move to further negation? What would be the negation of the character of the evidence as well as of the forms of thought that were present in both the theistic systems and their atheistic denial? What would be a negation of that negation that was atheism, a negation that would allow for a positive affirmation of the reality of God? The issue now confronts us: what would constitute a specifically religious evidence and an appropriate mode of thought?

Such a negation would have to be the retrieval of religious disclosure, of the experiences and practices of the holy and the symbols in which the sacred is manifest and effective. The negation of the atheistic negation of the conclusions of theism would consist in the recognition of the substantially religious. The restoration of the religious as of crucial cognitive importance – i.e., the religious experience both as evidence and as form of thought – would be such a negation.

I wonder again if Wittgenstein does not give us something of a hint when he stated so emphatically to Drury that "the symbolism of Christianity is wonderful beyond words, but when people try to make a philosophical system out of it I find it disgusting."[19] What does it mean to say that symbols are "wonderful?" That they evoke wonder. And how? In and through the reality they embody and manifest. Wittgenstein also acknowledged this religious cogency in such works as Augustine's *Confessions*, Dostoyevski's *The Brothers Karamazov*, Tolstoy's short stories, and William James's *Varieties of Religious Experience*. It is not that these narratives or reflections upon narratives argued a case, but rather that they made *manifest*, they *disclosed*, the reality they *embodied*. They offered a manifestation rather then an inference – quite literally a presentation, an emergence into presence – quite different from scientific argument, but not anti-intellectual.

Here Wittgenstein's statement from the *Tractatus* is profoundly apposite: "There are, indeed, things that cannot be put into words. They make themselves manifest [*Dies zeigt sich*]. They are what is mystical."[20] "They make themselves manifest." This is the crucial fact. Must this not obtain above all in the mystery we call "God?" But does God make *himself/herself* manifest in a way to which the religious is the appropriate response? In inference, something else makes God manifest. Can the religious claim of an actual self-manifestation of God be substantiated?

It was precisely such a self-manifestation – a disclosure and a recognition, that are two aspects of the same religious experience – that had been bracketed or negated by so much of the theistic argumentation through the centuries as irrelevant before the disciplined and philosophical assertion of the existence of God. Disclosure and recognition do not so much *entail* as *manifest* and *accept* the reality of God. Dialectically, such experience would negate as inadequate for the vital assertion of God both the form of thought that is inference or entailment and the scientific, humanistic, and anthropological evidence that offers such an illation. And it can do this because, as John Dewey wrote: experience is a double-barreled word. It means both content and process. To understand the grammar of experience that Dewey offers to our reflections, let me first contrast it with its usage in Aristotle and Kant.

The concept of experience

The term "experience" is a notoriously ambiguous one in the history of Western thought. Alfred North Whitehead has written that "the word 'experience' is one of the most deceitful in philosophy," while Hans-Georg Gadamer judged that "the concept of experience seems to me one of the most obscure we have."[21] The late George Schner urged a very careful set of precisions on its meanings and use.[22] There are few concepts in contemporary religious discourse that seem more abused. Contemporary appeals to religious experience often have an emotional intensity that is in direct correlation to their vagueness and imprecision, leaving one with the unhappy alternatives either of being swept away by the fervor of enthusiasms without commensurate serious thought, or of insisting upon criticisms and careful reflection that ring inappropriate and pedestrian among such exalted emotions. This conundrum might seem to justify the strategies of many theologians at the dawn of modernity to bracket religious experience, but I think not. There is no question that the word is often equivocal, but I should like to confront this equivocation in the hope of isolating one meaning I think particularly promising. Allow me to follow Richard P. McKeon and make three brief sorties into the history of ideas that range over two thousand five hundred years.[23]

In Aristotle, "experience" indicates a pattern of memories from the past that allows someone to gauge something particular about the present or the future. Some animals, he maintained, have only perception – present sensations; higher forms of animal life can retain these perceptions over time and hence remember past events. This means that they have memory. Still others have connected these memories of past events into a pattern: they remember that such a sound was associated with such a pain or that a liquid like this is associated with such a cure or that such a personality was associated with such an action. Coleridge wrote his histories with this understanding of experience, and Agatha Christie's Miss Marple uses it to solve village crimes. Experience in Aristotle is an acquired skill. Memories so synthesized allow for a recognition of likeness, and this awareness of similarity allows for connections to be acknowledged that are the necessary preparation for theoretical and practical knowledge.[24]

In Kant, experience is not such an acquired skill; it is the empirical dimension of all theoretical knowledge. For knowledge to occur, the onrush of the manifold of sensation must become synthesized through the forms of intuition and the categories of understanding. This anchoring of thought in sensation is knowledge. There can be no theoretical knowledge, except of objects of possible experience, since the synthesis of concepts with the intuited sensible manifold actually constitutes theoretic knowledge. Knowledge, then, must always have its empirical dimension, that is, it must contain a synthesis of thought with sensible intuition. All knowledge in this sense is empirical knowledge, and "empirical knowledge is experience."[25] Without experience one may think an object, but not know it. Without experience given through sensible intuition, concepts are empty; without concepts given through thought, experience is blind. This is underlined by the famous maxim of Kant: "Without sensibility, no object would be given to us; without understanding, no object would be thought. Thoughts without content are empty; intuitions without concepts are blind. It is, therefore, just as necessary to make our concepts sensible, that is, to add the object to them in intuition, as to make our intuitions intelligible, that is, to bring them under concepts. These two powers or capacities cannot exchange their functions. The understanding can intuit nothing, the senses can think nothing. Only through their union can knowledge arise."[26] Knowledge looked upon as concepts made sensible is experience.

In the twentieth century, "experience" took on a still more comprehensive character in such American philosophers as John Dewey and William James. With them, experience is not an acquired skill preparatory to theoretical or practical knowledge nor does it name the empirical character of all theoretical knowledge. Rather, everything that a human being knows or does is not only in some sense derived from experience, but is experience itself. John Dewey agreed with William James that "experience" indicates – importantly for our purposes – both content and the process by which the content is acquired and possessed. Experience "includes [both] – *what* men do and suffer, *what* they strive for, love, believe and endure, and also *how* men act and are acted upon, the ways in which they do and suffer, desire and enjoy, see, believe, imagine – in short, the process of *experiencing*." And "experience" is "double-barreled," maintains Dewey, because "it recognizes in its primary integrity no division between act and material, subject and object, but contains them both in an unanalyzed totality."[27]

Dewey's comprehensive understanding of experience has an advantage over that of Kant and the British empiricists, namely, it does not focus upon a passive undergoing. Experience is an interaction, an organic exchange between the experiencing organism and its environment. This fundamentally different understanding of experience makes possible a very different location of religious experience as an object of reflection:

> Experience becomes an affair primarily of doing. The organism does not stand about, Micawberlike, waiting for something to turn up. It does not wait passive and inert for something to impress itself upon it from without. The organism acts in accordance with its own structure, simple or complex, upon its surroundings. As a consequence the changes produced in the environment react upon the organism and its activities. The living creature undergoes, suffers, the consequences of its own behavior. This close connection between doing and suffering or undergoing forms what we call experience.[28]

Dewey's formulation of experience – especially his insistence upon a vital interaction as constitutive of its unity – offers a heuristic device of some importance. Perhaps the failure to appreciate the interaction that constitutes experience permitted the bracketing of those very events that in the actual history of religious commitments and faith have proved most cogent. If one can credit personal testimonies of highly sensitive thinkers upon the radiance from symbols, practices, personal testimonies and narratives, it is in such an interaction that the manifestation of the holiness of God occurs – in any of the mediated or disguised manners in which the abyss of God opens before the human person as absolute or commanding or attracting the totality of her longing and commitment to a surrender that the Christian calls "faith." It is *de facto* in this interaction that the average Christian assents or comes to assert the reality of God.

Taking a distinction from the pages of Karl Rahner, let us examine the two constituents of religious experience as it issues in the assertion of the existence of God. Let us examine it first in its categorical or historical dimension, i.e., as a concrete unit within time and space; and then in its transcendental dimension, as a permanent and comprehensive orientation or alignment of the human mind.

Christian religious experience: the categorical dimension

The lives of very ordinary people contain events that they assessed as marked by the influence or the presence of God. These could be moments or episodes or steady dimensions of life in which the truth or the reality of God emerged into human awareness and evoked an unsuspected depth of desires from within a person or a community. The person is drawn by some recognition to the disclosure of holiness, and such an encounter enables or draws a human being to assent to the reality of God. But I don't want to argue this point in the abstract. Experience is concrete, and both James and Wittgenstein point to the concrete in narrative and symbols. Let me, then, try to be very concrete. Let me give two examples from reflective thinkers of the twentieth century.

Edith Stein had gradually moved from a positive atheism to a greater sympathy for Christianity. She was a woman whose entire and rigorous academic formation lay with Husserl's phenomenological method, the descriptive analysis of the phenomena of consciousness. It explored that of which the subject is aware within lived experience as she moves to grasp the essence or *eidos* of that which is given in this experience. Edith Stein's coming to God emerged from her ability to read personal and intersubjective experience. To take only the final act of that history: In the summer of 1921, on a visit to the philosopher Hedwig Conrad-Martius, she chanced to be left to herself one evening. She picked up the *Autobiography of Teresa of Avila* and read it through the night. As dawn was breaking, she closed the book, saying to herself: "This is the truth."[29] This is not the chance reading of a pious tale by a religious enthusiast. It is the disclosure of the divine within a very complex human history to one who was able to interpret it as such. I will come back to this in a moment.

A second example, not to prove my point but to illustrate it, could be taken from the lives of Jacques and Raïssa Maritain as found in the autobiographical writings of Raïssa. She recalls the influence of Léon Bloy upon Jacques Maritain and herself in their coming to belief: "Months were to pass, and we might have been permanently halted by these insurmountable [intellectual] difficulties if Léon Bloy had sought to use with us an apologetic of demonstration. On what bases? Our reason was equipped to destroy, not to construct, and our confidence in reason, as well as in historical criticism, was very much shaken. But he did not even think of such a thing. He placed before us the fact of sanctity. Simply, and because he loved them, because their experience was near his own – so much so that he could not read them without weeping – he brought us to know the saints and mystics."[30] Previously the Maritains had studied Plotinus and Blaise Pascal, had attended the lectures of Henri Bergson and engaged in lengthy conversations with Charles Péguy. Now Léon Bloy brought this history to its completion. He introduced this young couple not to argument and inference, but to narrative, to the lives and the writings, i.e., to the experience and the holiness, of the saints. So Raïssa

Maritain could place the story of their baptism in the chapter entitled "The Call of the Saints."

For John Henry Newman, an encounter with the saints or with the reports of their lives could work such a disclosure as it did for Augustine: "They enlarge the mind with ideas it had not before, and they show to the multitude what God can do, and what man can be. . . . They are raised up to be monuments and lessons, they remind us of God, they introduce us into the unseen world. . . ."[31] If I may be allowed only to cite but not detail the analogous experience of another extraordinarily gifted woman, I would call to mind the fourth letter of Simone Weil to Henri Perrin: "The greatest blessing you have brought me is of another order. In gaining my friendship by your charity (which I have never met anything to equal), you have provided me with a source of the most compelling and pure inspiration that is to be found among human things. For nothing among human things has such power to keep our gaze fixed ever more intensely upon God, than friendship for the friends of God."[32]

These examples are cited from the Christian religious tradition – a tradition with which I am somewhat better acquainted – but one can find similar narratives of being brought before the reality of God by the witness of holiness in the deeply religious traditions of Judaism and Islam. I recall these examples to illustrate a single point: among the highest categorical disclosures of God are the lives of holiness, that they are among the surest historical warrants for the reality of God. Sanctity manifests rather than entails the reality of God as a living presence in the interaction and struggles in which human beings act and are drawn, in which they move towards God in accord with their longings and the structures of their consciousness, and then undergo a response that they may not realize as divine. One thinks of the effect worked upon Wittgenstein by Tolstoy's *Gospel in Brief,* Anzengruber's *Die Kreuzelschreiber,* and James's *Varieties of Religious Experience.*[33]

If what these histories point to is true, is it not extraordinary that so much Christian formal theology for centuries has bracketed this actual witness as of no intellectual weight – aside from polemic defenses of the holiness of the Church? Is it not a lacuna in the standard theology, even of our day, that theology neither has nor has striven to forge the intellectual devices to probe in these concrete experiences the disclosure they offer of the reality of God and so render them available for so universal a discipline? It would be a difficult and complex task.

One of the few exceptions to this general judgment would be John of the Cross. His explicit methodology constitutes an interplay between four factors: Experience, expression, theological hermeneutics, and communication. John appropriates the religious experiences of his life by embodying them and expressing them within an art-object – in this case, his poetry. From there, he moves to a theological hermeneutics of the art-object, bringing to bear as interpretative instruments the resources of scripture, the doctrine of the Church, and the experience of the reader. These are the devices by which one can learn to read accurately the art-object and the experience it embodies. Again the influence flows both ways. The art-object is the embodiment of experience, and his hermeneutic of this art object constitutes his theology. Finally all three of these moments – experience, expression, and interpretation – serve the communication to others of what has been experienced and disclosed in this circular inquiry. His methodology unites both the expressive-experiential model with the cultural-linguistic model in a dynamic circular relationship.

But it is necessary to remark that he remains very much an exception from the religious *epoché* (suspension, bracketing) that characterized so much of the theistic arguments in modernity. Nevertheless, the point must be made that the negation of religious concepts and terms cannot itself be negated as final without such constituents of Christian life as the lives of the saints, the life of prayer, the abiding call to holiness, the committed practices of justice and compassion, the interaction and effective love within the community, the beauty and symbolic world of liturgy, and so on – in short by all of the categorical manifestations of the holy in the interchanges that constitute personal histories and experience.

Christian religious experience: the transcendental dimension

There is still another dimension of this matter that must be explored. Dewey maintains that the origins of experience lie with the initial movement or action of the subject: "the organism acts in accordance with its own structure, simple or complex, upon its surroundings." This raises a further and perhaps even more pertinent consideration about the constitution or the character of the subject, according to which it acts. It raises the question of interiority. This requires one to move to the transcendental dimension of experience. If the categorical presence of the sacred (as in various concrete experiences of holiness in time and place) is a revelation of the reality of God, to whom is such a religious disclosure possible? Who has the capacity to read it? In other words, what is the transcendentality or the conditions of human subjectivity that allow one to recognize the holy and the divine in the particular events of life?

Here the Thomistic inquiry into the formal object of faith seems of immense suggestive importance. We shall mention this later, but now – to continue to try to avoid abstractions – let us return to the histories from which we previously drew: What is the human concentration or the focus of the subjectivity of Edith Stein and the Maritains and Simone Weil? What constitutes the prior centering and integrity of their persons that allowed for what I am calling "disclosure" and its commensurate "recognition?" I suggest that it was the acknowledgment of or the surrender to the absolute claim of truth in their lives, realized in their undeviating commitment to its discovery and service – however truth would emerge. This concentration of their persons and alignment of their desires would be called in a different tradition "purity of heart." It lay as the headwater of the reverence that flowed through their lives. It energized the inquiry that engaged them intractably. It made such categorical disclosures possible.

The unremitting absoluteness of this commitment explains Edith Stein's engagement with phenomenology, from her initial eagerness for Husserl's *Logische Untersuchungen* and its promised return to things themselves to her translation of Aquinas's *De veritate*. Jan Nolta recalled her refusal to "allow herself any illusions" about her approaching death at the hand of the Nazis. He then commented on the concurrence of this with her entire life: "Edith Stein's concern for the truth extended beyond its application to herself to a concern for the truth *in se*."[34] But even in her early days as a student at the University of Göttingen her classmate Rose Bluhm-Guttmann noted: "Edith had a deep love for the truth," while Professor Gertrud Koebner recalled her tutoring him in the phenomenological method as a student in Breslau and her remark that "she would have to live and act according to whatever she discovered in them, out of obedience to the Eternal Truth."[35]

Raïssa Maritain is quite explicit about the engagement that dominated their life through those years of anguish and preparation: "Despite all that might have turned us from it, we persisted in *seeking the truth – what truth? –* in continuing to bear within ourselves the hope of the possibility of a full adherence to a fullness of being."[36] Or Simone Weil: "It seemed to me certain, and I still think so today, that one can never wrestle enough with God if one does so out of pure regard for the truth. Christ likes us to prefer truth to him because, before being Christ, he is truth. If one turns aside from him to go toward the truth, one will not go far before falling into his arms."[37]

Why is it that this commitment to truth, as a primary and absolute consecration within human life, could become the transcendental condition for the possibility of recognizing the holy as revelatory? Not because this same absolute claim upon human choice and life cannot be found also in the experience of the good, in the practices of and self-sacrificing commitments of justice, or the apperception of the beautiful. One thinks here of the experience of Paul Claudel. It can be found, indeed, wherever an engagement with the absolute authentically obtains. These classical transcendentals permeate one another in a perichoresis, a mutual involvement and compenetration that bespeaks what Raïssa Maritain called "the fullness of being." In experiencing the claim of truth, one must experience its unsurpassed goodness, and in experiencing the claim of goodness or beauty, one must experience its truth and the duty to which it summons one – as in "true beauty" or "real goodness." This chapter casts the experience of absolute claim in terms of truth, but it could in a somewhat different way speak of beauty or goodness or justice or compassion or beauty or of any of the aspects under which absolute being makes it claim upon human life. As absolute, these are classically called "the attributes of God", and each of these attributes is the very being of God. It is in the experience of these attributes that one is drawn to the knowledge of God. In the experience of something finite that mediates any of these as absolute – of having its value and making its claim simply by what it is – one is brought before the Mystery that is God, inexhaustible in truth, goodness, justice, and beauty.

In the commitment to truth in any of its realizations, no matter how minor, there is an implicit, mediated commitment to truth as such, in its highest and primordial form. There is a surrender to what is alone absolute, to its unconditioned lordship, to a summons to obedience and a love that takes priority over any conflicting claim. May I underline this assertion: The claim of truth to be acknowledged and obeyed not only takes priority over all other contingent claims, but these latter depend for their validity upon their participation in this primordial claim of truth.

I would maintain, then, that the experience of the mediated, but absolute claim of truth is the experience of the claim of God. There is no claim that is more absolute; there is no claim that is more pervasive. And the surrender to this claim – long before it has reached adequate categorical embodiment – is *de facto* a surrender to God, the only absolute. Were it otherwise, then one would experience a claim that would be morally stronger than that of God, a claim upon oneself that would take obvious precedence over any positive religious precept or assertion or revelation. If God were not the primordial claim of truth upon our lives, God would not be God. Something else would be supreme.

For the first thing to be noted about this claim is that it is absolute. It is neither negotiable nor is it justified by something other than itself: One acknowledges, accepts and follows the claim of truth simply because it is true, not because it is popular or pragmatically useful or comfortable. It may be none of these things; it may even contradict them. The draw or imperative of the truth is to be admitted and obeyed simply because of what it is – irrespective of the cost or of other considerations. We may not always do this, but when we do not, we know that we have seriously failed. For this claim carries with it the sense of unconditional lordship to which obedience is due. Note also that one does not infer or prove or justify this claim of truth to be acknowledged and obeyed. The claim is prior to all inference. The sovereignty is given, and given as absolute. It provides the context in which we inquire and argue, while one does not argue to establish the truth of this claim. It has no need to be argued; argument presupposes it. It demands only that it be accepted and obeyed.

Secondly, one finds this claim mediated in everything that one confronts, in every demand for acknowledgement, judgment and agreement that one encounters. The claim is pervasive, omnipresent.

Notice, then, that in this experience one accepts a mediated claim that is pervasive in all things and that is supreme above all things in its summons. If one probes the transcendental dimensions of this experience of the claim of truth, one will see immediately many of the attributes that are classically predicated of God. And, in contrast, without this unconditioned commitment to truth, there is no possibility of a good-faith affirmation of the reality of God. It is here that Aquinas's tractate on faith makes major contributions.[38]

For Aquinas, that which makes faith possible is a prior commitment to the truth, the truth that is ultimate and definitive, the only truth that can be called "divine." This he calls *veritas prima*, first or primordial truth, and he argues that it is the "formal object" of Christian faith, the condition under which it is possible to believe.

When Aquinas uses "truth" in this context, it is not the truth of a proposition or of a judgment. It is the "ontological truth" that identifies with the real. It is by this truth that statements and judgments are evaluated. It is the truth that is convertible with "being." When Aquinas couples this with "first," he points to the truth that is ultimate, that is fundamental and absolute, that is the source of the truth of all other things. This first truth *de facto* is convertible with the reality that is God, though this may not be known. What must be the case for the disclosure of God is the human commitment to the truth, a commitment to the truth that is unlimited. Otherwise there is only "bad faith." The primordial truth that is the "formal object" of faith makes it possible for one to assent to God authentically. The absolutely fundamental religious choice is whether to surrender oneself to primordial truth as the medium – the unique medium or formal object – by which one comes to affirm religiously the reality of God.

Whether one refers to the formal object of faith with Thomas or to the purity of heart in the Beatitudes, Christianity insists that it marks those who will see God. For there is present within the experience of this claim already an intentional experience of God in God's attributes that enables a person to recognize by a kind of connaturality the presence of God in the disclosures of the holy – however these appear.

Perhaps the position I am advancing will enable us to understand something more of Ludwig Wittgenstein. He insisted that one cannot treat the existence of God as if its determination did not bear profoundly upon the character of the religious subject, as if it were parallel to issues in thermodynamics or non-Euclidian geometry. He gave his emphasis to the radical need for a change in the human subject asking this question, rather than to the intuition of or inference to the divine existence. As Ray Monk writes: "Wittgenstein did not wish to see God or to find reasons for His existence. He thought that if he could overcome *himself* – if a day came when his whole nature 'bowed down in humble resignation in the dust' – then God would, as it were, come to him; he would then be saved."[39] The issue of the divine existence can only be resolved if there is a profound integrity in those who ask the question – if there is purity of heart. One cannot act as if the questioner himself/herself were not totally engaged by this question. One cannot bracket oneself. To live by the light that one has is not the only condition for addressing this question; but it is an utterly indispensable condition.

This interior acceptance of an absolute claim whether of truth or love or justice can occur or be realized in so many categorical encounters, all of which bespeak a radical attention in life. One finds it embodied and mediated, for example, in a self-sacrificing commitment to social justice and life-long compassion for the exploited and the marginalized, a commitment to the alleviation of human misery that is non-negotiable and continued even in a context in which these efforts are ridiculed, misunderstood, or repudiated. One finds it mediated in a commitment to the integrity of an art-object when that focus embodies an utter reverence and even total submission before the beautiful and the true so that one hears with Rilke the claim: "You must change your life."[40] One finds it in an interpersonal self-transcendence to the love of another human being when the love that summons can even claim the sacrifice of one's own life. One experiences this haunting presence of God – so hidden and so pervasive – wherever a human being encounters what is and should be recognized as the absolute, the non-negotiable. One recognizes that sacred presence within this sovereign claim as it pervades all things and is utterly uncompromising in its demands for surrender or obedience or love or acceptance.

This is *de facto* to encounter God mediated in unsurpassable closeness. God is close not by geography or physical nearness. The closeness of persons to each other bespeaks a qualitative likeness, a sympathetic configuration by which each friend is able to know connaturally how the other thinks or feels or loves. One is "close" to such a friend. Personal closeness is an affinity which makes interpersonal communication possible and to which it ministers.[41] Christian theology has for two thousand years insisted that this closeness of God, this radical change in human transcendentality, is worked through the Spirit of God, configuring the person to Christ. The mission of the Spirit is to work this change within human affectivity and awareness, to effect a divine likeness that allows one to recognize connaturally the presence of God when its expression is categorical and historical.

This categorical expression of God is not only in the lives of the holy. It pervades history as it pervades the human subjectivity that confronts history and is the condition for its possibility. It is in the sacraments of the Church and in the concrete structures of social justice for which the Christian must struggle; it is in the solemn event that is liturgy and also in the popular religiosity in which so much symbol and affective weight is carried in a density that defies propositional adequacy. And for those who, like the tall nun in Hopkins's "The Wreck of the Deutschland," know how to see, the categorical disclosure of Christ can also be in what passes for ruin, destruction, and death. Hopkins saluted this woman with rare praise:

> Ah! there was a heart right!
> There was single eye!
> Read the unshapeable shock night
> And knew the who and the why;
> Wording it how but by him that present and past,
> Heaven and earth are word of, worded by?[42]

She "read the unshapeable shock night:" For the Christian understanding and imagination, the categorical speaks out God, discloses the One through whom and for whom it is made, the One in whom all things hold together: Christ, the image of the unseen God.[43] As a human being is configured or conformed subjectively to the mystery that is God through acceptance of the divinizing Spirit – however anonymously this acceptance takes place – so one connaturally comes to recognize the expressions of this God which words and interprets transcendental experience and gives it full contour and definitive historical meaning.

Religious experience, if it is to be human experience, has both its transcendental and categorical dimensions. The categorical is known only through the transcendental; the transcendental is known only through the categorical. But in themselves, they constitute that complex interchange between the organism and the environment or between the subject and her context that Dewey called experience. Understood in this way, the self-disclosure of God is always trinitarian. For all the manifestations of holiness within the externalities of history in some way participate in or approach that supreme holiness or union of the finite with God that is the hypostatic union; and the movements of holiness within the interiority of human subjects and communities in some way participate in or approach the transforming outpouring of the Spirit that is Christ's greatest gift.

The testimony of concrete experience, so trinitarianly understood, seems to be precisely what had been bracketed so ruinously in the rise of a putative atheism in the West, in a strategy of religious *epoché* that was dialectically to generate what it was constructed to destroy. This bracketing of religious experience or of the religious dimensions of experience set a style for the consideration of this issue which has lasted up until our own time. I think that, in their different ways, many philosophers and theologians on both sides of this divide are themselves heirs to this tradition, one that prescinds from anything innately religious, let alone explicitly or implicitly trinitarian, in order to justify or attack religion's principal assertion – the existence of God – by a line of inference.

A last word

What, then, can we determine from these six considerations of one thread of the complex history of religious disbelief? This book began with an examination of the purported enmity between science and religion. This turned out to be false. Are we to end with an enmity between philosophy become natural theology and religious faith? This would be equally false – both to the history of philosophy and to its native dynamism. Sartre remarked with a sigh that all of the great philosophers up until his time had been believers in one way or another![44] However one evaluates that comment, it does point out some historical congeniality between the genius of philosophy and the assertion of the reality of God. At its best the natural theology that emerges in so many different ways from metaphysics indicates the human spirit's essential openness to God as the final truth of all things, that God is implied in what things are and, even more perhaps, by the fact they are, that there is something rather than nothing.

There are many aspects of postmodernity, of course, that are coordinate with what I am urging: the reverence for the Absolute of transcendence; the suspicion both of the liability of formulae and rituals to idolatry and of the identification of the divine with concrete institutions; the inclination to the mystical and apophatic; and the openness of all creation before religious intuition, and so on. But if this is prolonged into a rejection of inference, critical reasoning, institutions, science and philosophy in favor of sentiment, emotions, autonomous "emotional communities" and mystified vagueness, it would become as destructive as its contrary. Institutions and traditions, inference, philosophy and speculation are also components or demands of authentic religion, indeed, of authentic religious experience brought to its completion.[45] It is not by accident that so many of the greatest philosophers of the Middle Ages were theologians. Philosophy or metaphysics does not betray the genius of religion. Religion can only betray itself.

Perhaps above all we must realize that one cannot excise, cannot bracket the religious, in order to come to the existence of God, that one must bring to experience and reflection the manifold of the religious itself in order to justify the assertions of religion. One must include all of the components that constitute religion in its fullness, as, for example, one finds outlined in the great treatise of Baron von Hügel: the intuitional, emotional and volitional; the speculative and rational; the institutional, historical and traditional.[46] None of these can be finally omitted without being false to the authenticity of the religious. If this book has emphasized one set of these components, it is because it has been historically neglected in scientific theology; but none of them can be finally bracketed without grave harm done to the genius of religion in general and to Christianity in particular.

But if one ignores or brackets as cognitively unimportant this religious manifold and turns to other disciplines to give basic substance to its claims that God exists, one has implicitly admitted that religion – or that reflection upon religion for its evidence that we have been calling theology – possesses an inner cognitive insubstantiality. This can only be negated in the insistence upon the interpersonal interchange that is the life of religion.

Further, this book argues that inference simply cannot substitute for experience. One will not long believe in a personal God with whom there is no personal communication, and the most compelling evidence of a personal God must itself be personal. To attempt something else as foundation or as substitute, as has been done so often in an effort to shore up the assertion of God, is to move into a process of internal contradictions of which the ultimate resolution must be atheism.

Abbreviations

K.C.	Isaac Newton, *Philosophiae naturalis principia mathematica*, ed. Alexandre Koyré and I. Bernard Cohen, with the assistance of Anne Whitman (Cambridge, Mass.: Harvard University Press, 1972).
KGW	Johannes Kepler, *Gesammelte Werke*, ed. Walther von Dyck, Max Caspar, Franz Hammer, and Martha List (München: C. H. Beck'sche Verlagsbuchhandlung, 1937–).
MC	Johannes Kepler, *Mysterium Cosmographicum: The Secret of the Universe*, trans. A. M. Duncan, introduction and commentary by E. J. Aiton, with a preface by I. Bernard Cohen (New York: Abaris Books, 1981).
PG	*Patrologia Graeca*, ed. J. P. Migne, 162 vols (Paris, 1857–66).
RG	*Rawleigh His Ghost* (English translation of Leonard Lessius, S.J., *De providentia numinis et animi immortalitate*), trans. A. B. (1631), in vol. 349 of *English Recusant Literature, 1558–1640*, ed. D. M. Rogers (London: Scolar Press, 1977).
TCWS	Galileo Galilei, *Dialogue Concerning the Two Chief World Systems – Ptolemaic and Copernican*, trans. Stillman Drake, 2d ed. (Berkeley: University of California Press, 1967).
TNS	Galileo Galilei, *Dialogues Concerning Two New Sciences*, trans. Henry Crew and Alfonso de Salvio (New York: Dover Publications, 1914).

Notes

Preface

1. Editors, "Editorial Statement," in "Religion and the Intellectuals," *Partisan Review* 17, no. 2 (February 1950), 97–105.
2. Hannah Arendt, "Religion and the Intellectuals," 115–116.
3. Friedrich Nietzsche, *The Gay Science*, trans. Walter Kaufmann (New York: Random House, 1974), bk. 3, sect. 125, p. 181.
4. Ibid.
5. G. W. F. Hegel, *Lectures on the History of Philosophy*, trans. E. S. Haldane and Frances H. Simson (New Jersey: Humanities Press, 1968), 3:393.
6. Ibid., 387. This caution was also cited in Michael J. Buckley, S.J., *At the Origins of Modern Atheism* (New Haven: Yale University Press, 1987), 27.
7. The phrase is that of the theologian Samuel Clarke, building upon the universal mechanics of Isaac Newton. See Buckley, *At the Origins of Modern Atheism*, 193.
8. Paul Tillich, "The Two Types of Philosophy of Religion," *Union Seminary Quarterly Review* 1, no. 4 (1946): 4.
9. James Turner, *Without God, Without Creed: The Origins of Unbelief in America* (Baltimore: The Johns Hopkins University Press, 1985).
10. Alan Charles Kors, *Atheism in France, 1650–1729*, vol. 1, *The Orthodox Sources of Disbelief* (Princeton: Princeton University Press, 1990), 379.
11. Charles Taylor, *Hegel* (Cambridge: Cambridge University Press, 1975), 129.
12. James Collins, *God in Modern Philosophy* (Chicago: Henry Regnery, 1959), 56.
13. John of the Cross, *The Dark Night of the Soul*, in *The Collected Works of Saint John of the Cross*, trans. Kieran Kavanaugh and Otilio Rodriguez, with revisions and introductions by Kieran Kavanaugh, rev. ed. (Washington, D.C.: Institute of Carmelite Studies, 1991), bk. 2, ch. 16, no. 4, p. 431; bk. 1, ch. 4, no. 2, p. 368, etc.
14. Pseudo-Dionysius, *The Mystical Theology*, in *Pseudo-Dionysius: The Complete Works*, trans. Colm Luibheid and Paul Rorem, Classics of Western Spirituality (New York: Paulist Press, 1987), 135. For Greek text, see *PG* 3:998.
15. Baron Friedrich von Hügel, *The Mystical Element of Religion as studied in Saint Catherine of Genoa and Her Friends* (London: J. M. Dent & Co., 1909), 50–82.

Acknowledgments

1. John Adam Moehler, *Symbolism: Or Exposition of the Doctrinal Differences Between Catholics and Protestants as Evidenced by their symbolical writings*, trans. James Burton Robertson (New York: Edward Dunigan, 1844), "Preface to the First Edition," ix.

Chapter 1. The New Science and Ancient Faith

1. Herbert Butterfield, *The Origins of Modern Science, 1300–1800*, rev. ed. (New York: Free Press, 1965), 7, 191, 202.
2. John William Draper, *History of the Conflict Between Religion and Science* (New York: Appleton and Company, 1897), 364.
3. Steven Weinberg, "A Designer Universe?" *New York Review of Books* 46, no. 16 (1999): 48.
4. I. Bernard Cohen, *The Birth of the New Physics* (London: Penguin, 1992), 88–89, see 196–204.
5. Galileo Galilei a Elia Diodati in Parigi, 25 July 1634, *Galileo e gli scienziati del seicento*, tomo 1 of *Opere di Galileo Galilei*, ed. Ferdinando Flora (Milano: Riccardo Ricardi, 1953), 1071. For an English translation, see Antonio Favaro, ed., introduction to *Dialogues Concerning Two New Sciences*, trans. Henry Crew and Alfonso de Salvio with an introduction by Antonio Favaro (New York: Dover Publications, 1914), ix (this book is henceforth cited as *TNS*). The Latin and Italian original of this work, with its Latin preface to the "Third Day," can be found in Antonio Favaro, ed., *Le opere di Galileo Galilei*, vol. 8, nuova ristampa della edizione nazionale (Firenze: Barbera, 1968). The dialogue is in Italian, but the preface, definitions, axioms, theorems, and extensive explanations are in Latin. Since the English translation includes references to the pagination in this Italian edition, these references will not be supplied independently here.
6. Favaro, introduction to *TNS*, ix–x. See Stillman Drake, *Galileo at Work: His Scientific Biography* (Chicago: University of Chicago Press, 1978), 314–318, 335–336, 353–356, 358–359.
7. Drake, *Galileo at Work*, 362, 365.
8. Louis Elzevin, "The Publisher to the Reader," in *TNS*, xx. See Drake, *Galileo at Work*, 374–375, 381–387.
9. For the much controverted relationship between Galileo's inquiries into resistance and the Newtonian concept of inertial mass, see Edwin Arthur Burtt, *The Metaphysical Foundations of Modern Physical Science* (London: Routledge and Kegan Paul, 1967), 88–89.
10. Galileo, "Third Day," in *TNS*, 153–154. Translation modified by the author (henceforth such a modification or a complete translation by the author will be indicated by (m)). I. Bernard Cohen points out that the standard English translation by Henry Crew and Alfonso de Salvio added the words "by experiment" to this preface to the "Third Day" (*Birth of the New Physics*, 201 n).
11. See, for example, Galileo, "Third Day," 178. For the much disputed use of experiment in Galileo, see Cohen, *Birth of the New Physics*, 196–204.
12. Galileo, *The Assayer*, in *Discoveries and Opinions of Galileo*, translated and with introduction and notes by Stillman Drake (New York: Anchor, 1957), 237–238, cited in

Annibale Fantoli, *Galileo: For Copernicanism and for the Church*, trans. George Coyne, 2d ed. (Vatican City: Vatican Observatory Press, 1996), 290.

13. Galileo, *Assayer*, 276–277, cited in Fantoli, *Galileo*, 292.
14. Galileo, "Third Day," 152. This analysis of Galileo is pervasively influenced by and indebted to the courses offered in the Committee for the Analysis of Ideas and the Study of Methods under the influence of Richard P. McKeon. For a detailed transcription of such a course, see Richard McKeon, *On Knowing – The Natural Sciences*, comp. David B. Owen and ed. David B. Owen and Zahava K. McKeon (Chicago: University of Chicago Press, 1994). The author's own examination of Galileo began under the tutelage of Professor Herbert Lamb, one of the professors attached to the Committee, and it is to him and to Professor McKeon that he must express both his great indebtedness and his gratitude.
15. Cohen, *Birth of the New Physics*, 100.
16. Galileo, "Third Day," 167 (m).
17. See Michael Sharratt, *Galileo: Decisive Innovator* (Cambridge: Cambridge University Press, 1996), 191.
18. Galileo, "Fourth Day," in *TNS*, 276. For the coining of the term "operational" and its meaning, see Percy Williams Bridgman, *The Logic of Modern Physics* (New York: Macmillan, 1927), 3–32. For the meaning and use of this term by Richard P. McKeon and its application to Galileo, see *On Knowing – The Natural Sciences*, passim.
19. Galileo, "Third Day," 160–161.
20. Ibid., 161 (emphasis in italics and comments underlined, both added).
21. Ibid., 164.
22. For the identification of the interlocutors of the Galilean dialogues, see Fantoli, *Galileo*, 85–86, 156, 156 n. 26, 348. One should note that "Simplicio" here "represents the predominant science and philosophy in the universities of Galileo's time" (ibid., 348).
23. Galileo, "Third Day," 194.
24. Galileo Galilei, "Letter to the Grand Duchess Christina (1615)," in *The Galileo Affair: A Documentary History*, ed. and trans. Maurice A. Finocchiaro (Berkeley: University of California Press, 1989), 90–91 (the English translation is taken from this compilation, denoted henceforth as *Letter*).
25. Galileo, "Third Day," 165–166.
26. Ibid., 166–167.
27. See Ernan McMullin, ed., introduction to *Galileo, Man of Science* (New York: Basic Books, 1968), 13.
28. Galileo, "Third Day," 166; "Fourth Day," in *TNS*, 271. On both occasions Sagredo raises the question about physical cause, on the "Fourth Day" called *energia e forza* – and Salviati fends him off, representing Galileo explicitly in calling them "fantasies, or if you please, vagaries, as far as I can recall them from the words of our Academician" (ibid., 271–272).
29. Galileo Galilei, "The Author's Dedication to the Grand Duke of Tuscany," in *Dialogue Concerning the Two Chief World Systems – Ptolemaic and Copernican*, trans. Stillman Drake, foreword by Albert Einstein, 2d ed. (Berkeley: University of California Press, 1967), 3 (henceforth cited as *TCWS*).
30. Ernan McMullin, "The Conception of Science in Galileo's Work," in *New Perspectives on Galileo: Papers deriving from and related to a workshop on Galileo held at Virginia Polytechnic Institute and State University, 1975*, ed. Robert E. Butts and Joseph C. Pitt (Dordrecht and Boston: D. Reidel, 1978), 238, 240–252.
31. Ibid., 227.

32. Galileo, "The Fourth Day," in *TCWS*, 462–463.
33. See Galileo, *TCWS*, 14, 21, 29, 57, 101–105, 122–123, 240, 357–358, 367–370, etc.
34. Galileo, *Letter*, 96; for the original see Galileo Galilei, "Lettera a Madama Cristina di Lorena, Granduchessa di Toscana [1615]," in *Le opere di Galileo Galilei*, ed. Favaro, 5:319.
35. Galileo, *Letter*, 90.
36. See, for example, ibid., 90–91, 96, 101.
37. Ibid., 96.
38. Ibid., 92–93.
39. Galileo, "Lettera a Madama Cristina di Lorena," 5:319. See *Letter*, 101–104.
40. Benedictus Pererius [Benito Pereira] deserves at least a footnote! He was an early instructor in physics or natural philosophy in the Roman College and published his *De communibus omnium rerum naturalium principiis et affectionibus* in 1576. Wallace speaks of this work as exerting considerable influence and subscribing "to a number of Averroist theses, among which was a strongly expressed opposition to the use of mathematics in the study of nature. His Averroism plus differences of opinion with Christoph Clavius, the mathematics professor at the Collegio ["the modern Euclid"] who urged the use of mathematics in physics, may explain his later 'promotion' to the Scripture faculty of that institution – *promoveatur ut amoveatur*, as the Romans would say" (W. A. Wallace, "Galileo's Concept of Science: Recent Manuscript Evidence," in *The Galileo Affair*, 16–17). Wallace maintains that Pererius's attitude was typical of that period in the Italian universities (24). This changed radically with Pererius's successors in the Roman College, Antonius Menu and, then, Paulus Valla. Valla's notes, through the plagiarism of Ludivico Carbone, became the unacknowledged source of Galileo's early lectures in logic and natural philosophy. It is ironic that Pererius takes his principal place in astronomy through his scriptural hermeneutics.
41. Fantoli, *Galileo*, 23–25, 182–189.
42. Ernan McMullin, "Galileo on Science and Scripture," in *The Cambridge Companion to Galileo*, ed. Peter Machamer (Cambridge: Cambridge University Press, 1998), 285.
43. Ibid., 317.
44. Galileo, *Letter*, 104 (emphasis added).
45. Gerald Holton, *Thematic Origins of Scientific Thought: Kepler to Einstein* (Cambridge, Mass.: Harvard University Press, 1988), 53.
46. I. Bernard Cohen, preface to *Mysterium Cosmographicum: The Secret of the Universe*, by Johannes Kepler, trans. A. M. Duncan, introduction and commentary by E. J. Aiton, with a preface by I. Bernard Cohen (New York: Abaris Books, 1981), 9 (henceforth cited as *MC*). Cohen cites with approval the judgment of Eric Aiton that "almost all 'the astronomical books written by Kepler (notably the *Astronomia nova* and the *Harmonice mundi*) are concerned with the further development and completion of themes that were introduced in the *Mysterium cogmographicum.*'"
47. Cohen, *The Birth of a New Physics*, 147.
48. Kepler, "Original Preface to the Reader," in *MC*, 63. For this text, as for an entertaining and insightful introduction to Kepler, see Arthur Koestler, *The Sleepwalkers: A History of Man's Changing Vision of the Universe*, with an introduction by Herbert Butterfield (New York: Grosset and Dunlap, 1963), 248–249. Koestler's work must be checked against the primary sources he cites, but despite this necessary reserve, the author is indebted throughout this section both to Koestler and also to Max Caspar, *Kepler*, trans. and ed. C. Doris Hellman (London: Abelard–Schuman, 1959), as well as to Carola Baumgardt, *Johannes Kepler: Life and Letters* (New York: Philosophy Library, 1951), especially for calling one's attention to texts of central importance. At times, the

author has retranslated these texts from the Latin or the German and this has been indicated by (m). The Latin and German original texts have been taken from Johannes Kepler, *Gesammelte Werke*, ed. Walther von Dyck, Max Caspar, Franz Hammer, and Martha List (München: C. H. Beck'sche Verlagsbuchhandlung, 1937–), and is henceforth cited as *KGW*. For Kepler, see also the important essay by Richard S. Westfall, "The Rise of Science and the Decline of Orthodox Christianity: A Study of Kepler, Descartes, and Newton," in *God and Nature: Historical Essays on the Encounter between Christianity and Science*, ed. David C. Lindberg and Ronald L. Numbers (Berkeley: University of California Press, 1986), 218–237. The author learned of the existence of Westfall's essay only after he had composed the second draft of this chapter and found it somewhat parallel to his own interests, complementary rather than repetitive.

49. Cohen, preface to *MC*, 7–8.
50. Kepler, *MC*, 92.
51. For a summary statement of this conviction, see Frederick Copleston, *Greece and Rome*, vol. 1 of *A History of Philosophy* (Garden City, N.Y.: Doubleday, 1962), pt. 1, pp. 289–290.
52. Kepler, *MC*, 96 (m). The expression Θεόν αἰεὶ γεωμετρεῖν is attributed to Plato by Plutarch, *Questionum Convivalium*, Lib. VIII, and furnishes the second question of that book with its query: "Why did Plato say that God always geometrizes?" See Plutarchi, *Scripta Moralia*, ed. Fredericus Dübner (Paris: Firmin–Didot et Sociis, 1890), 2:875ff.
53. Thomas L. Heath, ed., *The Thirteen Books of Euclid's Elements*, translated from the text of Heiberg with introduction and commentary by Thomas L. Heath, 2d ed. (New York: Dover Publications, 1956), bk. 13, prop. 18, p. 507.
54. Kepler, *MC*, 97; see 69.
55. Ibid., 97 (emphasis added).
56. Ibid., 99.
57. Ibid., 92.
58. Ibid., 107 (m).
59. Ibid., 107 (m).
60. Kepler, "Original Preface to the Reader," in *MC*, 63.
61. Kepler, *MC*, 71 n. 4.
62. Kepler to Michael Mästlin in Tübingen, 3 October 1595, *KGW*, 13:35. For citation and translation of part of this text, see Koestler, *Sleepwalkers*, 261–262 (m).
63. Baumgardt, *Johannes Kepler: Life and Letters*, 31.
64. Kepler, *MC*, 149 (m).
65. Plato, *Timaeus*, in *The Dialogues of Plato*, trans. B. Jowett (1892; reprint, New York: Random House, 1937), 2:29d: "τὸν εἰκότα μῦθον." The reason for this in Plato is important to note, namely that "the accounts given will themselves be akin to the diverse objects which they serve to explain" (ibid., 29b–c).
66. Kepler, *MC*, 149. Aiton comments: "Here Kepler expresses quite clearly that his *a priori* reasons were only probable and needed to be tested against the empirical data" (ibid., 243 n. 1).
67. Johannes Kepler, *Harmonice Mundi*, bk. 4, ch. 1, in *KGW*, 6:223 (m); for the translation, see Koestler, *Sleepwalkers*, 262 (m).
68. Kepler to Herwart, 9–10 April 1599, *Johannes Kepler: Life and Letters*, 50.
69. Johannes Kepler, *Astronomiae pars optica*, in *KGW*, 2:10 (m).
70. Kepler could put his position quite emphatically: "Atque haec de sacrarum literarum authoritate. Ad placita vero Sanctorum de his Naturalibus, uno verbo respondeo. In Theologia quidem authoritatum, in Philosophia vero rationum esse momenta

poneranda. Sanctus igitur Lactantius, qui Terram negavit esse rotundam: Sanctus Augustinus, qui rotunditate concessa, negavit tamen Antipodas; Sanctum Officium hodiernorum, qui exilitate Terrae concessa, negant tamen ejus motum: At magis mihi sancta veritas, qui Terram et rotundam, et Antipodibus circumhabitatam, et contemptissimae parvitatis esse, et denique per sidera ferri, salvo Doctorum Ecclesiae respectu, ex Philosophia demonstro" (Johannes Kepler, introduction to *Astronomia nova*, in *KGW*, 3:33–34).

71. Kepler, "Author's Notes on Chapter One," in *MC*, 85 (m).
72. Koestler, *Sleepwalkers*, 253.
73. Ibid., 313; see 277.
74. Ibid., 338; see 328–339.
75. Ibid., 258, 313–336, 394–398.
76. Ibid., 314.
77. J. L. Heibron, *The Sun in the Church: Cathedrals as Solar Observatories* (Cambridge, Mass.: Harvard University Press, 1999), 10.
78. Ronald W. Clark, *Einstein: The Life and Times* (New York: World Publishing Company, 1971), 340–343. For the "EPR Paper," see A. Einstein, B. Podolsky, and N. Rosen, "Can Quantum–Mechanical Description of Reality Be Considered Complete?" *The Physical Review* 47 (1935): 777–780.
79. Werner Heisenberg, "Science and Religion (1927)," in *Physics and Beyond: Encounters and Conversations*, Harper Torchbook (New York: Harper and Row, 1971), 82–83.
80. See Max Jammer, *Einstein and Religion: Physics and Theology* (Princeton: Princeton University Press, 1999), 85, 223, 230.
81. See Ian Barbour, *Religion in an Age of Science* (San Francisco: Harper, 1990), 129.
82. Sir Isaac Newton, *Mathematical Principles of Natural Philosophy and His System of the World*, trans. Andrew Motte in 1729, revised and supplied with historical and explanatory appendix by Florian Cajori (Berkeley: University of California Press, 1962), xvii. This English translation, henceforth cited as *Principia*, has been used with modifications, indicated by (m). For the Latin original, see Isaac Newton, *Philosophiae naturalis principia mathematica*, ed. Alexandre Koyré and I. Bernard Cohen, with the assistance of Anne Whitman (Cambridge, Mass.: Harvard University Press, 1972), 15 (henceforth cited as *K.C.*). For an extensive consideration of Newtonian universal mechanics, see Buckley, *At the Origins of Modern Atheism*, 99–144.
83. Newton, *Principia*, xvii; Newton, *K.C.*, 15 (emphasis added).
84. Newton, "Preface to the First Edition," in *Principia*, xviii.
85. Newton, *Principia*, def. 3 and 8, pp. 2 and 8; *K.C.*, 40–41, 44–46.
86. Newton, "Preface to the First Edition," in *Principia*, xvii–xviii; *K.C.*, 16.
87. For Newtonian analysis and synthesis as well as for the universality of mechanics, see Buckley, *At the Origins of Modern Atheism*, 120–128.
88. Newton, "General Scholium," in *Principia*, 543; *K.C.*, 760.
89. Newton, *K.C.*, 760; see "General Scholium," 544 (m).
90. Newton, "General Scholium," 544.
91. See Edward Strong, "Newton and God," *Journal of the History of Ideas* 13, no. 2 (1952): 167. This analysis of phenomena back to "a first cause which is certainly not mechanical" should not be confused with Newton's repeated attempts to account for gravitation or for force. For an extensive treatment of this question, see Ernan McMullin, *Newton on Matter and Activity* (Notre Dame: University of Notre Dame Press, 1978), 75–109. For a discussion of the interrelationship between Newtonian mechanics and theological inquiry, see Michael J. Buckley, "The Newtonian Settlement and the Origins of Atheism," in *Physics, Philosophy, and Theology: A Common Quest for*

Understanding, ed. Robert John Russell, William R. Stoeger, S.J., and George V. Coyne, S.J. (Vatican City State: Vatican Observatory, 1988), 81–102.

92. Newton, "General Scholium," 544–546; *K.C.*, 760–761.

93. Newton, "General Scholium," 546; *K.C.*, 762.

94. Newton, "General Scholium," 546; *K.C.*, 763.

95. Newton, "General Scholium," 546; *K.C.*, 764.

96. Isaac Newton, *Opticks: or, A treatise of the reflections, refractions, inflections & colours of light*, based on the 4th ed., London, 1730, with a foreword by Albert Einstein, an introduction by Sir Edmund Whittaker, a preface by I. Bernard Cohen, and an analytical table of contents prepared by Duane H. D. Roller (New York: Dover, 1952), bk. 3, query 28, p. 369.

97. Isaac Newton to Richard Bentley, 10 December 1692, *Correspondence*, 7 vols., ed. H. W. Turnbull (Cambridge: Cambridge University Press, 1959–1977), 3:233.

98. Newton, "General Scholium," 546; *K.C.*, 763. See Buckley, *At the Origins of Modern Atheism*, 138.

99. Isaac Newton, "A Short Scheme of the True Religion," in *Sir Isaac Newton: Theological Manuscripts*, selected and edited with an introduction by H. McLachlan (Liverpool: At the University Press, 1950), 48: "Religion is partly fundamental and immutable, partly circumstantial and mutable. The first was the religion of Adam, Enoch, Noah, Abraham, Moses, Christ and all the saints and consists of two parts, our duty towards God and our duty towards man, or piety and righteousness, which I will here call Godliness and Humanity."

100. Newton, *Opticks*, bk. 3, query 31, pp. 405–406.

101. Newton, "A Short Scheme of the True Religion," 48.

102. Heisenberg, "Science and Religion," 85. Dirac goes on to say that "if religion is still being taught, it is by no means because its ideas still convince us, but simply because some of us want to keep the lower classes quiet. Quiet people are much easier to govern than clamorous and dissatisfied."

103. Barbour, *Religion in an Age of Science*, 6–7.

104. Alfred North Whitehead, *Science and the Modern World* (New York: The Macmillan Company, 1925), 173–174.

105. Dan Wakefield, "And Now, a Word from Our Creator," *New York Times Book Review*, 12 February 1989, 1, 28–29.

106. Paul Davies, *God and the New Physics*, a Touchstone Book (New York: Simon and Schuster, 1983), ix. For an extended consideration of this work, see Michael J. Buckley, S.J., "Religion and Science: Paul Davies and John Paul II," *Theological Studies* 51, no. 2 (1990): 310–324.

107. Aristotle, *Physics*, Loeb Classical Library (1929), 2.7.198a16–18.

108. Aristotle *Physics* 2.9.199b34–200b11.

109. Nietzsche, *The Gay Science*, bk. 3, sect. 125, p. 181. For the German text: *Die fröhliche Wissenschaft*, in Nietzsche, *Werke*, ed. Giorgio Colli and Mazzino Montinari, Kritische Gesamtausgabe (Berlin: de Gruyter, 1973), Abteilung 5, Band 2, pp. 158–160.

Chapter 2. A Dialectical Pattern in the Emergence of Atheism

1. Michel de Certeau, *The Writing of History*, trans. Tom Conley (New York: Columbia University Press, 1988), 74.

2. For the differentiation of the kinds of history, see Richard P. McKeon, "Has History a

Direction?" in *Freedom and History and Other Essays* (Chicago: University of Chicago Press, 1990), 126–159.

3. Jacques Barzun, *From Dawn to Decadence: Fifty Years of Western Cultural Life* (New York: HarperCollins, 2000), xviii.

4. Thucydides, *History of the Peloponnesian War*, in *Landmark Thucydides: A Comprehensive Guide to the Peloponnesian War*, ed. Robert B. Strassler (New York: Free Press, 1996), 1.22.4, p. 16.

5. Aristotle, *Politics* 1.2.1252a24, in *The Basic Works of Aristotle*, ed. Richard McKeon (New York: Random House, 1941).

6. Etienne Gilson, *The Unity of Philosophical Experience* (New York: Charles Scribner's Sons, 1937), vii–viii.

7. Jacques Derrida, *Positions*, trans. A. Bass (Chicago: University of Chicago Press, 1981), 6 (emphasis added).

8. Joyce Appleby, Lynn Hunt, and Margaret Jacob, *Telling the Truth About History* (New York: W. W. Norton, 1994), 290.

9. T. S. Eliot, "The Dry Salvages," in *Collected Poems, 1909–1962* (Franklin Center, Pa.: The Franklin Library, 1979), II, 195.

10. Arthur M. Schlesinger, Jr., *A Life in the 20th Century*, vol. 1, *Innocent Beginnings, 1917–1950* (Boston: Houghton Mifflin Company, 2000), 45.

11. Henry F. May, *The Divided Heart: Essays on Protestantism and the Enlightenment in America* (New York: Oxford University Press, 1991), 14.

12. John Dewey, *Logic: A Theory of Inquiry* (New York: Holt, Rinehard and Winston, 1938), 104–105.

13. John Milbank, review of *At the Origins of Modern Atheism*, by Michael J. Buckley, S.J., *Modern Theology* 8, no. 1 (January 1992): 90.

14. Lord Burleigh in 1572 said that the English "realm is divided into three parties, the Papists, the Atheists, and the Protestants. All three are alike favoured: the first and the second because, being many, we dare not displease them; the third, because having religion, we fear to displease God in them." Four years later, Walter, Earl of Essex, died seeing only religious ruin: "There is nothing but infidelity, infidelity, infidelity, atheism, atheism, atheism, no religion, no religion." Twenty years later, Thomas Nashe was to warn that there was no "Sect now in England so scattered about as Atheisme." Cheke, Rastell, Hutchinson, and Latimer were to write against it, with John Veron's book bearing the remarkable title: *Fruitfull Treatise of Predestination and Providence . . . against the Swynishe Gruntings of the Epicures and Atheystes of Oure Time.* See Buckley, *At the Origins of Modern Atheism*, 10. This book contains a much more detailed exploration of the history and the argument in the initial section of this chapter.

15. Leonard Lessius, S.J., *De providentia numinis et animi immortalitate: Libri duo adversus atheos et Politicos*, in *Opuscula Leon. Lesii, S.J.* (Paris: P. Lethielleus, 1880), 1.1.10, p. 323. An English translation of this work is *Rawleigh His Ghost. Or, A Feigned Apparition of Syr Walter Rawleigh, to a friend of his, for the translating into English, the Booke of Leonard Lessius (that most learned man) entituled, De providentia Numinis, et Animi immortalitate: written against Atheists, Polititians of these dayes*, trans. A. B. (1631), in vol. 349 of *English Recusant Literature, 1558–1640*, ed. D. M. Rogers (London: Scolar Press, 1977) (henceforth cited as *RG*). For the history of this text, see Buckley, *At the Origins of Modern Atheism*, 42.

16. Lessius, *RG*, 1.3, pp. 19–20 (m).

17. Francis Bacon, "On Atheism," in *The Essays* (New York: A. L. Burt, 1883), 103.

18. Kors, *Atheism in France, 1650–1729*, 1:26. Guy le Fevre de la Boderie, whom Professor

Kors is citing, was the translator in 1578 of Marcelo Ficino's *De la religion chrestienne.*

19. For an exposition and analysis of the Stoic topics as classification of arguments for the existence of God, see Michael J. Buckley, S.J., *Motion and Motion's God: Thematic Variations in Aristotle, Cicero, Newton, and Hegel* (Princeton: Princeton University Press, 1971), 110–117.

20. Lessius, *RG*, 1.3, pp. 13–15.

21. Lessius, *De providentia numinis*, 1.2.16–19, pp. 325–328. See *RG*, 1.3, pp. 19–26. The telescope was invented many times over the centuries, finally to be made and sold by Hans Lippershey in the Netherlands in 1608, an achievement Galileo heard of and tried to pass off as his own in Italy. For the history of the telescope, known to Galileo as the *perspicillum*, see *New Encyclopedia Britannica*, 15th ed., s.v. "Measurement and Observation: Telescopes." See also Alexandre Koyré, *From the Closed World to the Infinite Universe* (New York: Harper and Brothers, 1957), 90–94. See Buckley, *At the Origins of Modern Atheism*, 379 n. 53.

22. For "Marin Mersenne and the Platonizing of Epicurus," see Buckley, *At the Origins of Modern Atheism*, 56–64.

23. René Descartes, "Epistola," in *Meditationes de prima philosophia*, in *Oeuvres de Descartes*, ed. Charles Adam and Paul Tannery (Paris: Léopold Cerf, 1887–1909), 7:2–3 (m).

24. In a letter to his mistress, Sophie Volland, Denis Diderot described a hilarious evening in which the great English philosopher David Hume was given his French come-uppance on this issue:

> Hume was attending his first dinner at the Rue Royale. In his conversation with the Baron Paul d'Holbach, "the English philosopher took it into his head to remark that he did not believe in atheists, that he had never seen any. The Baron said to him, 'Count how many we are here.' 'We are eighteen.' The Baron added: 'That isn't too bad a showing to be able to show you fifteen at once; the others haven't made up their minds.'"

The story is too French to gain unsuspicious acceptance, but . . . (Ernest Campbell Mossner, *The Life of David Hume*, 2d ed. [Oxford: Clarendon Press, 1980], 483).

25. Arthur M. Wilson, *Diderot: The Testing Years, 1713–1759* (New York: Oxford University Press, 1957), 194.

26. Mircea Eliade, "Cosmogonic Myth and 'Sacred History,'" in *The Quest: History and Meaning in Religion* (Chicago: University of Chicago Press, 1969), 45.

27. Ibid., 47.

28. Ibid., 82–83.

29. Robert Lowell, "Watchmaker God," in *The Harvard Book of Contemporary American Poetry*, ed. Helen Vendler (Cambridge, Mass.: Harvard University Press, Belknap Press, 1985), 108. "Newton" has been substituted for "Paley."

30. John Henry Newman, *An Essay in Aid of A Grammar of Assent*, ed. I. T. Ker (Oxford: Clarendon Press, 1985), ch. 6, pp. 105ff.

31. Ibid., 181.

32. Gilbert Murray, "The Stoic Philosophy," in *Essays and Addresses* (London: George Allen and Unwin, 1921), 103. Murray attributes this phrase to Mr. Bevan. He alludes to it again in his essay, "What is Permanent in Positivism," in *Humanist Essays* (London: Unwin Books, 1964), 177–178.

33. Turner, *Without God, Without Creed.* This section of the present chapter is very much in debt to this study by Professor Turner.

34. Cotton Mather, preface to *The Christian Philosopher: A Collection of the Best*

Discoveries in Nature, with Religious Improvements, A facsimile Reproduction with an Introduction by Josephine K. Piercy (1721; reprint, Gainesville, Fla.: Scholars' Facsimiles and Reprints, 1968), 8.

35. Kenneth Silverman, *The Life and Times of Cotton Mather* (New York: Harper and Row, 1984), 249.

36. Mather, introduction to *The Christian Philosopher,* 3.

37. Ibid., 1.

38. Ibid., 2–3.

39. Ibid., 2.

40. Ibid., 6. In a *coda* as remarkable in its contents as in its rhetoric, Cotton Mather warns his fellow Christians: "*Audite Ciceronem, quem Natura docuit* [listen to Cicero, whom Nature taught]. However, this I may say, *God has thus far taught a* Mahometan! And this I will say, *Christian,* beware lest a *Mahometan* be called in for thy *Condemnation!*"

41. Mather, "Essay I: *Of the* Light," in *The Christian Philosopher,* 9–16 (underlining added).

42. Mather, "Man," in *The Christian Philosopher,* 294.

43. Ibid., 295.

44. Mather, introduction to *The Christian Philosopher,* 5.

45. Turner, *Without God, Without Creed,* 52–53.

46. Ibid., 78–79.

47. Ibid., 78.

48. Silverman, *Cotton Mather,* 250.

49. Ibid., 78–79, 81, 96, 103, 182.

50. This listings comes from Turner, "Christianity Confused, 1840–1870," in *Without God, Without Creed,* 141–167.

51. Turner, *Without God, Without Creed,* 96–97.

52. Ibid., 179.

53. Ibid., 179–184.

54. Ibid., 191.

55. Ibid., xiii (emphasis added).

56. James Turner, email to author, 14 May 2000.

57. Kors, *Atheism in France,* 1:xiii.

58. Kors, *Atheism in France,* 1:292.

59. See Buckley, *At the Origins of Modern Atheism,* 77–85.

60. Kors, *Atheism in France,* 1:293. The summary here is Kors's, who also records the agreement of the Benedictine Robert Desgabets and the Jesuits' *Journal de Trévoux.*

61. Ibid., 58–59.

62. Ibid., 79–80 (emphasis added).

63. Ibid., 379 (emphasis added).

64. Georg Wilhelm Friedrich Hegel, *The Science of Logic,* 2 vols., trans. W. H. Johnson and L. G. Struthers (1929; reprint, London: Allen and Unwin, 1961), 2:472. For a discussion of the dialectical method as found in the Absolute Idealism of Hegel, see Buckley, *Motion and Motion's God,* 207–225.

65. S. Thomae Aquinatis, *Summa theologiae,* ed. Petri Caramello (Romae: Taurini Marietti, 1956), 1.2.3.

Chapter 3. Thomas Aquinas and the Rise of Modern Atheism

1. See chapter 2, n. 29.

2. Tillich, "The Two Types of Philosophy of Religion," 3ff.

3. Ibid., 4.
4. Ibid., 5.
5. Ibid., 6–7 (emphasis added).
6. Ibid., 9.
7. Ibid., 11.
8. Paul Tillich, *Systematic Theology*, vol. 1 (Chicago: University of Chicago Press, 1951), 205.
9. Tillich, "Two Types," 6–7.
10. *Summa theologiae* 1.2.prol. The purpose of *sacra doctrina* – the teaching by God about God – is understood as "to communicate/give a knowledge of *God* [*Dei cognitionem tradere*]"and so the First Part of the theology that pertains to sacred doctrine will treat of God. Theology is seen as an *expositio* or *consideratio* of what is given in *sacra doctrina.* Aquinas divided this First Part into three sections: "Consideratio autem de Deo tripartita erit: primo, namque considerabimus ea quae pertinent ad essentiam divinam; secundo, ea quae pertinent ad distinctionem personarum; tertio, ea quae pertinent ad processum creaturarum ab ipso." The first of these subsections of the First Part, the one *ex professo* dealing with the divine essence, Aquinas divided into a threefold *consideratio*: "Circa essentiam vero divinam: primo, considerandum est an Deus sit; secundo, quomodo sit vel potius quomodo non sit; tertio, considerandum erit de his quae ad operationem ipsius pertinent, scilicet de scientia et voluntate et potentia" (punctuation supplied here and in other Latin citations).
11. *Summa theologiae* 1.2.1.obj. 1: "Illa enim nobis dicuntur per se nota, quorum cognitio nobis naturaliter inest, sicut patet de primis principiis. Sed, sicut dicit Damascenus in principio libri sui, 'omnibus cognitio existendi Deum naturaliter est inserta.' Ergo Deum esse est per se notum" (the reference is to John Damascene, *De fide orthodoxa* I. 3. Patrologia Graeca 94:793 C).
12. See Buckley, *Motion and Motion's God*, 108–109. It is interesting to note that Domingo Bañes, O.P. equates this position of John Damascene with that of Epicurus, the πρόληψις, being translated as "*anticipatio naturae*" (Dominico [*sic*] Bañes, *Scholastica commentaria: Summae theologicae in primam partem S. Thomae Aquinatis*, ed. Luis Urbano [Valencia: Editorial F.E.D.A, 1934], 1.2.1, p. 104).
13. *Summa theologiae* 1.2.1.ad 1: "Ad primum ergo dicendum quod cognoscere Deum esse in aliquo communi, sub quadam confusione, est nobis naturaliter insertum, inquantum scilicet Deus est hominis beatitudo: homo enim naturaliter desiderat beatitudinem, et quod naturaliter desideratur ab homine, naturaliter cognoscitur ab eodem. Sed hoc non est simpliciter cognoscere Deum esse; sicut cognoscere venientem, non est cognoscere Petrum, quamvis sit Petrus veniens: multi enim perfectum hominis bonum, quod est beatitudo, existimant divitias; quidam vero voluptates; quidam autem aliquid aliud."
14. The translator in the Blackfriars edition of the *Summa theologiae* would seem to have changed Aquinas's emphasis. For whereas Aquinas presents a positive affirmation that such knowledge does exist and is of the character described, the translator turns the emphasis into a denial: "The awareness that God exists is not implanted in us by nature in any clear or specific way," he writes, and opens the second part of the arguments concessively, "admittedly, man is by nature aware of what by nature he desires"(*Summa theologiae*, vol. 2, *Existence and Nature of God (1a.2–11)*, ed., trans. and notes by Timothy McDermott, O.P. [London: Blackfriars, 1964], 7). But that is not the thrust or the tone of Aquinas's remarks. The grammar of his reply is not so much to deny any

specific knowledge as to affirm a vague knowledge, and this makes greater sense of what is to follow.

15. *Summa theologiae* 1.2.1.ad 1.

16. Bañes, *Scholastica commentaria*, 1.2.1, "tertio," 105b, and "ad sextum" and "ad ultimum," 107a. For Gilson's evaluation of Bañes, see Etienne Gilson, *The Christian Philosophy of St. Thomas Aquinas*, trans. L. K. Shook (New York: Random House, 1956), vii.

17. Etienne Gilson, *Elements of Christian Philosophy* (Garden City, NY: Doubleday, 1960), 46 (emphasis added).

18. For the distinction between the *medium in quo* and the *medium sub quo*, see *Summa theologiae* 1.12.5.ad 2.

19. *Summa theologiae* 1–2.2.7.

20. *Summa theologiae* 1–2.2.7. For this distinction between the *finis cujus* (res ipsa in qua ratio boni invenitur) and the *finis quo* (usus vel adeptio illius rei), see *Summa theologiae* 1–2.1.8.

21. In his introductory lectures to the text of the Prologue and First Question of *Prima Secundae*, the Dominican scholar Ignatius Theodore Eschmann calls attention to the "somewhat misleading" notion of "parallel texts" in St. Thomas. "Often (this ought to be understood) the various expressions of one and the same thought in different works are not, in St. Thomas, simply variations of one theme, equivalent and interchangeable one with the other, differing only verbally and in no way substantially. On the contrary, very often they are moments, or parts, of an intellectual development, a movement that grew constantly in volume as well as in depth" (Ignatius Theodore Eschmann, O.P., *The Ethics of Saint Thomas Aquinas: Two Courses*, ed. Edward A. Synan [Toronto: Pontifical Institute of Medieval Studies, 1997], 10). Thomas could revisit a previous treatment, the same point or teaching, to deepen or even correct an argument or a conclusion. Revision need not mean contradiction, but it does indicate alteration and betterment, made possible by factors such as the passage of time and the contribution of critics.

22. *In 1 Sent.* 3.1.2.ad 1: "Auctoritas Damasceni intelligenda est de divina cognitione nobis insita, secundum ipsius similitudinem et non secundum quod est in sua natura; sicut etiam dicitur, quod omnia appetunt Deum: non quidem ipsum prout consideratur in sua natura, sed in sui similitudine; quia nihil desideratur, nisi inquantum habet similitudinem ipsius, et etiam nihil cognoscitur" (*Scripta super libros Sententiarum*, in *S. Thomae Aquinatis Opera omnia*, vol. 6 [Parma: Tipis Petri Fiaccadori, 1856]). Whenever it is adequate or necessary to refer to the collected works of Aquinas rather than to a more recent critical edition, the Parma edition will be used and abbreviated as *Parma*.

23. *Summa theologiae* 1.4.3.

24. See *De veritate* (*Parma*, vol. 9) 22.2.ad 1: "Omnia cognoscentia cognoscunt implicite Deum in quolibet cognito. Sicut enim nihil habet rationem appetibilis nisi per similitudinem primae bonitatis; ita nihil est cognoscibile nisi per similitudinem primae veritatis." It is this implicit knowledge that the direction of desire communicates: "Ipsum esse est similitudo divinae bonitatis; unde inquantum aliqua desiderant esse, desiderant Dei similitudinem et Deum implicite" (*De veritate* 22.2.ad 2).

25. *In 1 Sent.* 3.1.2: "Sed visis sensibilibus, non devenimus in Deum nisi procedendo, secundum quod ista causata sunt et quod omne causatum est ab aliqua causa agente et quod primum agens non potest esse corpus, et ita in Deum non devenimus nisi arguendo; et nullum tale est per se notum."

26. *De veritate* 10.12.ad 1: "Cognitio existendi Deum dicitur omnibus naturaliter inserta,

quia omnibus naturaliter insertum est aliquid unde potest pervenire ad cognoscendum Deum esse."

27. *De veritate* 10.12.ad 5.
28. *Summa contra Gentiles* (*Parma*, vol. 5) 1.11.ad 4.
29. *Summa theologiae* 1.1.6.ad 3.
30. *Summa theologiae* 1.12.4.
31. *Summa theologiae* 1–2.89.6.
32. *Summa theologiae* 1–2.89.6.
33. *Summa theologiae* 1–2.89.6: "The ultimate end of the human being is the uncreated good, namely God, who alone by reason of his infinite goodness is able to fill completely the will of the human being."
34. *Summa theologiae* 1.85.3.
35. *Summa theologiae* 1.85.3. ". . . Intellectus noster de potentia in actum procedit. Omne autem quod procedit de potentia in actum, prius pervenit ad actum incompletum, qui est medius inter potentiam et actum, quam ad actum perfectum. Actus autem perfectus ad quem pervenit intellectus, est scientia completa, per quam distincte et determinate res cognoscuntur. Actus autem incompletus est scientia imperfecta, per quam sciuntur res indistincte *sub quadam confusione*" (emphasis added).
36. *Summa theologiae* 1.85.3.
37. Aristotle *Physics* 1.1.184a22–26 (m), in *The Basic Works of Aristotle*, ed. Richard McKeon (New York: Random House, 1941).
38. *Summa theologiae* 1.85.3: "Et quia sensus exit de potentia in actum sicut et intellectus, idem etiam ordo cognitionis apparet in sensu. Nam prius secundum sensum diiudicamus magis commune quam minus commune, et secundum locum et secundum tempus. Secundum locum quidem, sicut, cum aliquid videtur a remotis, prius deprehenditur esse corpus, quam deprehendatur esse animal; et prius deprehenditur esse animal, quam deprehendatur esse homo; et prius homo, quam Socrates vel Plato."
39. Sancti Thomae de Aquino, *Expositio super librum Boethii de Trinitate*, ed. Bruno Decker (Leiden: Brill, 1959), q. 6, a. 3, pp. 220–223 (emphasis added). An English translation of this work is in St. Thomas Aquinas, *The Division and Method of the Sciences: Questions V and VI of his Commentary on the "De Trinitate" of Boethius*, trans. and ed. Armand Maurer (Toronto: Pontifical Institute of Mediaeval Studies, 1963), 74–79. Thomas's commentary on Boethius's *De Trinitate* dates from his first teaching period in Paris, 1257–1258 or early 1259. The *Summa theologiae*, in contrast, occupied the last seven years of his life. The *Prima Pars* was written during his Roman period, 1265–1268. See Jean–Pierre Torrell, *St. Thomas Aquinas* (Washington, D.C.: Catholic University of America Press, 1996), 345, 333. It is interesting to record that St. Thomas gives his most extensive treatment of the division of the sciences in the *In Boeth. de Trinitate*, where he also presents one of his most complete treatments of the difference between perfect and confused knowledge.
40. This is the imperfect knowledge also instantiated for Aquinas in the knowledge that separated souls have of all the things of nature: "anima separata intelligit per species quas recipit ex influentia divini luminis, sicut et angeli: sed tamen, quia natura animae est infra naturam angeli, cui iste modus cognoscendi est connaturalis, anima separata per huiusmodi species non accipit perfectam rerum cognitionem, sed quasi *in communi et confusam.*" Aquinas in this same Article calls this kind of knowledge "imperfectam et confusam" (*Summa theologiae* 1.89.3 [emphasis added]). The answer to the second objection states that a separated soul "nec omnia naturalia perfecte cognoscit, sed *sub quadam confusione*" (emphasis added). The similarities between this

vocabulary and 1.2.1.ad 1 are remarkable. Neither of which is dealing with the knowledge that comes from inference. See also *Quaestio disputata de Anima* (*Parma*, vol. 8), art. 15 and art. 18. For the process of inquiry as moving from confused and imperfect knowledge to more complete and distinct, see *In octo libros Physicorum expositio* (*Parma*, vol. 18), liber 1, lectio 1, pp. 226–228.

41. Col. 1:15–16 RSV (m): "He is the visible image of the invisible God, the first–born of all creation. For in him all things were created, in heaven and on earth, the visible and invisible, whether thrones or dominions or principalities or authorities – all were created through him and for him [τὰ πάντα δι'αὐτοῦ καὶ εἰς αὐτόν ἔκτισται]." The Latin text that Aquinas commented on translated this last sentence as "omnia per ipsum et *in ipso* creata sunt," and St. Thomas takes εἰς αὐτόν ἔκτισται as exemplary cause rather than as final cause or purpose. See S. Thomae Aquinatis, *Super epistolam ad Colossenses lectura*, 1.4.42, in *Super Epistolas S. Pauli lectura*, ed. Raphaelis Cai, O.P. (Taurini: Marietti, 1953), 2:134. This opens the question of how much this reading of Colossians determined his judgment that it was "convenientius" to say that if there had been no sin, there would have been no incarnation. See *Summa theologiae* 3.1.3.

42. Anton C. Pegis, *Basic Writings of Saint Thomas Aquinas* (New York: Random House, 1945).

43. M. D. Chenu, O.P., *Toward Understanding Saint Thomas*, translated with authorized corrections and bibliographical additions by A. M. Landry, O.P., and D. Hughes, O.P. (Chicago: Henry Regnery, 1964), 310 (emphasis added).

44. Ibid., 315.

45. Ibid., 315.

46. Eschmann, *Ethics of Saint Thomas Aquinas*, 23. The line–up of these texts is in debt to this section of Eschmann's book.

47. Thomas O'Meara, O.P., "Grace as a Theological Structure in the *Summa Theologiae* of Thomas Aquinas," *Recherches de théolgie ancienne et médiévale* 55 (1988): 130–153.

48. I am grateful to the Reverend Brian Davies, O.P., for calling my attention to these points, especially that "Aquinas takes *sacra doctrina* to be, effectively, the teaching of the Bible, especially the New Testament" (Davies, private correspondence, 30 April 2000).

49. *Summa theologiae* 1–2.prol.

50. *Summa theologiae* 3.prol.

51. Aristotle *Politics* 1.2.1252b32–33.

52. *Summa theologiae* 1.12.1: "In ipso enim est ultima perfectio rationalis creaturae, quod est ei principium essendi – intantum enim unumquodque perfectum est, intantum ad suum principium attingit."

53. *Compendium theologiae* (*Parma* vol. 16), no. 201 (emphasis added). See Torrell, *St. Thomas Aquinas*, 155.

54. *In 3 Sent.* (*Parma* vol. 7) 2.1.1.sol.

55. *Summa theologiae* 3.prol.

56. *Summa theologiae* 1.6.1; 1.6.3.163 ad 2, ad.3.

57. *Summa theologiae* 3.1.1. For an earlier application in the *Summa theologiae* of this understanding of the diffusive or communicating character of the good, see 1–2.1.4.ad 1; 1–2.2.3.obj 2.

58. *Summa theologiae* 1.12.1.

59. *Summa theologiae* 3.1.1.sed contra (translation from Blackfriars with modification).

60. *Summa theologiae* 3.prol: "Salvator noster Dominus Iesus Christus, teste angelo,

'populum suum salvum faciens a peccatis eorum,' *viam veritatis nobis in seipso demon-stravit, per quam ad beatitudinem immortalis vitae resurgendo pervenire possimus"* (emphasis added).

Chapter 4. *God as the Anti-human*

1. For an earlier exploration of this issue, see Michael J. Buckley, S.J., "Modernity and the Satanic Face of God," in *Christian Spirituality and the Culture of Modernity: The Thought of Louis Dupré*, ed. Peter J. Casarella and George P. Schner, S.J. (Grand Rapids, Mich.: William B. Eerdmans Publishing Company, 1998), 100–122. This chapter uti-lizes and builds upon much in this previous article. The author would like to express his gratitude to Eerdmans for their gracious permission to use this work.
2. Henri de Lubac, *The Drama of Atheistic Humanism*, trans. Edith M. Riley (New York: Sheed and Ward, 1950), v.
3. This is the basic thesis of de Lubac's *Drama of Atheistic Humanism* and these figure as some of its major *dramatis personae*.
4. See Michael J. Buckley, "Atheism and Contemplation," *Theological Studies* 40, no. 4 (1979): 680–699.
5. Derrida, *Positions*, 4.
6. The concept of "fundamental thinking" is derivative from and responds to Richard P. McKeon's formulation and use of "general selection characteristic of the philosophic communication of a period" as well as the distinctions that he drew within general selection and brought to bear so perceptively upon the history of thought. See Richard P. McKeon, "Philosophic Semantics and Philosophic Inquiry," in *Freedom and History and Other Essays: An Introduction to the Thought of Richard McKeon*, ed. Zahava K. McKeon (Chicago: University of Chicago, 1990), 251–252.
7. Thomas Hobbes, *Concerning Body*, 1:6 in *The Collected Works of Thomas Hobbes*, 11 vols., collected and edited by Sir William Molesworth (London: Routledge/Thoemmes Press, 1952), 1:70–90 (emphasis added). "The First Grounds of Philosophy" is the title that Hobbes gave to Part 2 of this work. See 1:91.
8. John Locke, "The Epistle to the Reader," in *An Essay Concerning Human Under-standing*, edited, with an introduction, critical apparatus and glossary, by Peter H. Nidditch (Oxford: Clarendon Press, 1975), 7 (henceforth cited as *Essay*) (emphasis added). For the subject matter of the discussion as well as the dating and location of these conversations, see Maurice Cranston, *John Locke: A Biography* (New York: Macmillan, 1957), 140–14.
9. Sextus Empiricus, *Against the Logicians* i. 22–23 [*Adversus Dogmaticos* i; *Adversus Mathematicos* vii], trans. R. G. Bury, Loeb Classical Library (Cambridge, Mass.: Harvard University Press, 1933), 12–13. For the epistemological shift in the Hellenistic period, see Richard P. McKeon, introduction to *Brutus, On the Nature of the Gods, On Divination, On Duties*, by Marcus Tullius Cicero, trans. Hubert M. Poteat (Chicago: University of Chicago Press, 1950), 30–38. This understanding of the epistemological revolution of the Hellenistic period and of the shifts in fundamental thinking through-out the history of philosophy is very much indebted to the writings and lectures of Professor McKeon.
10. Sextus Empiricus, *Against the Logicians* i. 22–23, pp. 10–12. Diogenes Laertius, *Lives of Eminent Philosophers*, x. 29–31, trans. R. D. Hicks, Loeb Classical Library (London: William Heinemann, 1925), 2:558–561.

11. Theophrastus, *Metaphysics*, Greek text with facing English translation, commentary and introduction by W. D. Ross and F. H. Fobes (Chicago: Ares Publishers, Inc., 1978), 4a7, 20; 4b19; 6b8; 7b15; 9b3; 11b18; 4a7, 11, 19; 6b8; 9a12; 9b4; 5a2.

12. The difference between the Second and the Third Academies lay with the comprehensive claim of the Second not only not to be certain of anything, but not to be certain that one was not certain. The Third Academy relaxed this stricture through its doctrine of probabilities. See Copleston, *Greece and Rome*, 414–417.

13. Diogenes Laertius, *Lives of Eminent Philosophers*, ix. 61–108. In the prologue to this work, Diogenes Laertius gives the basic epistemological criterion for the division of all philosophers into dogmatists and skeptics (ibid., i. 16). For the inclusion here of Pyrrho, see Copleston, *Greece and Rome*, 413. This paragraph is heavily indebted to Copleston's treatment of the Hellenistic period. See also Sextus Empiricus *Outlines of Pyrrhonism* 1.1.xiv–xvi.36–179, vol. 1 of *Sextus Empiricus*, trans. R. G. Bury, Loeb Classical Library (London: W. Heinemann, 1933), pp. 24–103.

14. Buckley, *Motion and Motion's God*, 207. For instantiations of each of these moments in fundamental thinking, see pp. 85, 164, 147–148, and 207.

15. Etienne Gilson and Thomas Langan, "John Locke," ch. 13 in *Modern Philosophy: Descartes to Kant*, vol. 3 of *History of Philosophy*, ed. Etienne Gilson (New York: Random House, 1963), 193.

16. Locke, "The Epistle to the Reader," in *Essay*, 16. In his Journal of 29 March 1677, during the years devoted to the composition of the *Essay*, Locke wrote: "Heaven being our great business and interest, the knowledge which may direct us thither is certainly so too; so that this . . . ought to take up the first and chiefest place in our thoughts." See Richard Ashcraft, "Faith and Knowledge in Locke's Philosophy," in *John Locke: Problems and Perspectives*, ed. John W. Yolton (Cambridge: Cambridge University Press, 1969), 197 n. 3. The grounds that would give solidity to this "business and interest" were the appropriation of the self in its "abilities" and "objects."

17. Ashcraft gives a helpful catena of Locke's use of and appeal to design to ground the inference to the existence of God; see "Faith and Knowledge," 203ff.

18. Locke, *Essay*, bk. 4, ch. 10, no. 1, p. 619.

19. Locke, *Essay*, bk. 4, ch. 10, no. 2–3, pp. 619–620; see bk. 4, ch. 11, no. 3, pp. 631–632.

20. Locke, *Essay*, bk. 4, ch. 10, no. 4, p. 620 (emphasis his).

21. Locke, *Essay*, bk. 4, ch. 10, no. 5–6, pp. 620–621 (emphasis his).

22. Locke, *Essay*, bk. 4, ch. 10, no. 1, p. 619.

23. Isaac Newton to Richard Bentley, 3:235–236.

24. David Hume, introduction to *A Treatise on Human Nature*, ed. L. A. Selby-Biggs (Oxford: Clarendon Press, 1888), xvi–xvii.

25. Hume, *A Treatise on Human Nature*, xvi.

26. Hume, *A Treatise on Human Nature*, xix (emphasis added).

27. Collins, *God in Modern Philosophy*, 56.

28. Buckley, *At the Origins of Modern Atheism*, 92.

29. Collins, *God in Modern Philosophy*, 56.

30. Immanuel Kant, "Preface to First Edition," in *Critique of Pure Reason*, trans. and ed. Norman Kemp Smith (London: Macmillan, 1963), 9.

31. Fred Lawrence, "The Fragility of Consciousness: Lonergan and the Postmodern Concern for the Other," *Theological Studies* 54 (1993): 58–62.

32. Immanuel Kant, "The Existence of God as a Postulate of Pure Practical Reason," bk. 2, ch. 2, sect. 5 in *Critique of Practical Reason*, ed. Lewis White Beck (Indianapolis: Bobbs–Merrill, 1956), 130.

33. Kant, "Preface to the First Edition," in *Religion within the Limits of Reason Alone*, trans. Theodore M. Greene and Hoyt H. Hudson (New York: Harper and Row, 1960), 4–5.

34. Kant, *Religion*, "Preface," 5–6. The classic treatment of the existence of God as a postulate of pure practical reason is, of course, in Book 2 of Kant's *Critique of Practical Reason*, ch. 2, sect. 5, "The Existence of God as a Postulate of Pure Practical Reason," pp. 128–136.

35. Friedrich Schleiermacher, *The Christian Faith*, ed. H. R. MacIntosh and J. S. Stewart (Edinburgh: T. & T. Clark, 1928), sect. 4, p. 68.

36. The battle against the irreligious would be waged on these grounds. (1) Fundamental thinking, what Hobbes had called "the first grounds of philosophy", had shifted its concentration from nature to human nature, and (2) the affirmation of the reality of God had established its new grounds here. God was an entailment and an enhancement of human nature (Thomas Hobbes, *Concerning Body*, in *The English Works of Thomas Hobbes of Malmesbury*, ed. Sir William Molesworth [1839; reprint, Germany: Scientia Verlag Allen, 1966], 1:91ff).

37. Kant, *Religion*, 11. This translation has been modified since the German reads: ". . . von aller Erfahrung abstrahieren muß. . . ." Immanuel Kant, *Die Religion innerhalb der Grenzen der bloßen Vernunft*, ed. Karl Vorländer (Hamburg: Felix Meiner Verlag, 1990), 13.

38. Schleiermacher, *Christian Faith*, "Introduction," sect. 4, p. 17 (emphasis added).

39. Alfred Lord Tennyson, *Tennyson: In Memoriam*, ed. Susan Shatto and Marian Shaw (Oxford: Clarendon Press, 1982), sect. 56, ll. 15–16, 25, p. 80.

40. This remark is cited by his son and introduced with the remark: "After one of these moods in the summer of 1892, he [Tennyson] exclaimed . . ." (Hallam, Lord Tennyson, *Alfred Lord Tennyson: A Memoir* [New York: Macmillan, 1897], cited in *Alfred, Lord Tennyson, In Memoriam*, ed. Robert H. Ross [New York: W. W. Norton, 1973], 119) (emphasis added). For the influence of Charles Lyell's *Principles of Geology* (1830–1833) and its demonstrations of the great age of the earth and the successive extinction of species, see Eleanor D. Mattes, *In Memoriam: The Way of a Soul* (New York: Exposition Press, 1951), 55–61, 73–86, 111–125, excerpted in Ross, *Alfred Lord Tennyson*, 120 ff.

41. Friedrich Schleiermacher, *On Religion: Speeches to its Cultured Despisers*, trans. with introduction and notes by Richard Crouter (Cambridge: Cambridge University Press, 1988), Speech 2, pp. 109–110 (emphasis added).

42. Kant, *Religion*, 10.

43. Schleiermacher, *On Religion*, 87 (emphasis added).

44. Schleiermacher, *Christian Faith*, 16 (emphasis added).

45. Schleiermacher, *Christian Faith*, 17–18.

46. Henri de Lubac, *The Drama of Atheistic Humanism*.

47. See Eugene Kamenka, *The Philosophy of Ludwig Feuerbach* (London: Routledge & Kegan Paul, 1970), vii–viii, 16, 27, 117–118; Peter Gay, *Freud: A Life for Our Time* (New York: W. W. Norton, 1988), 28–29, 532. On 7 March 1875, Freud wrote to Edward Silverstein: "Among all philosophers, I worship and admire this man (Feuerbach) the most" (Gay, *Freud*, 28).

48. Cited from Ludwig Feuerbach's *Philosophical Fragments* in Eugene Kamenka, *The Philosophy of Ludwig Feuerbach*, 39.

49. For an analysis of the nature of reflexive principles, see Buckley, *Motion and Motion's God*, 30–38.

50. Ludwig Feuerbach, *Das Wesen des Christentums*, ed. Werner Schuffenhauer, 3d ed. (Berlin: Akademie–Verlag, 1973), p. 29, no. 3. This sentence appeared for the first time

in this third edition (1849), while Feuerbach was still alive. The celebrated English translation by George Eliot was done from the second edition of 1843 and published in 1854, and hence it is omitted from that translation. See Feuerbach, *The Essence of Christianity*, trans. George Eliot (New York: Harper, 1957).

51. Feuerbach, *Essence of Christianity*, 33.
52. Feuerbach, *Essence of Christianity*, 26 ff.
53. Feuerbach, *Essence of Christianity*, 231, xxxvi.
54. Feuerbach, "Preface to the Second Edition," in *Essence of Christianity*, xxxvi (emphasis added).
55. Feuerbach, "Preface to the Second Edition," xxxvi.
56. Feuerbach, "Preface to the Second Edition," xxxvi–xl; *Essence of Christianity*, 213–214, 230–231. That is why the *Essence of Christianity* comprises two parts: "the true or anthropological essence of religion," and "the false or theological essence of religion." For the importance of the religious phase: "Religion is the first form of self–consciousness," ibid., 270. See Feuerbach, *Lectures on the Essence of Religion*, trans. Ralph Manheim (New York: Harper and Row, 1967), 33–35.
57. Feuerbach, *Essence of Christianity*, 231.
58. Karl Marx, "Theses on Feuerbach," in *On Religion*, by Karl Marx and Friedrich Engels, introduction by Reinhold Niebuhr (New York: Schocken Books, 1964), no. 11, p. 72.
59. Marx, "Contribution to the Critique of Hegel's Philosophy of Right", in *On Religion*, 41.
60. Marx, "Theses on Feuerbach," no. 2, p. 69 (emphasis added).
61. Marx, "Theses on Feuerbach," no. 4, p. 70
62. Marx, "Contribution to the Critique," 42.
63. Marx, "Contribution to the Critique," 50 (m).
64. Marx, "Forward to Thesis: The Difference Between the Natural Philosophy of Democritus and the Natural Philosophy of Epicurus," in *On Religion*, 15 (emphasis added). The citation is from Aeschylus, *Prometheus Bound*, l. 975. Marx omits the completion of the sentence: ". . . who received good at my hand and with ill requite me wrongfully," as in the translation of Herbert Weir Smyth, *Aeschylus*, Loeb Classical Library (Cambridge, Mass.: Harvard, 1973), 305.
65. Marx, "Contribution to the Critique," 50 (emphasis added).
66. Marx, "Contribution to the Critique," 41. "The abolition of religion as the *illusory* happiness of the people is required for their *real* happiness. The demand to give up the illusions about its condition is the *demand to give up a condition which needs illusion*. The criticism of religion is therefore *in embryo the criticism of the vale of woe*, the *halo* of which is religion" (42).
67. Marx, "Contribution to the Critique," 42.
68. For an illuminating development of this theme, see Joseph C. McLelland, *Prometheus Rebound: The Irony of Atheism* (Waterloo, Ont.: Wilfrid Laurier University Press, 1988).
69. Schleiermacher, *On Religion*, 102.
70. Friedrich Nietzsche, *The Birth of Tragedy*, trans. Walter Kaufmann (New York: Random House, 1967), sect. 3, p. 42. This is Nietzsche's first book.
71. Nietzsche, *The Birth of Tragedy*, sect. 4, p. 46.
72. Nietzsche, *The Birth of Tragedy*, sect. 3, p. 42
73. Nietzsche, *The Birth of Tragedy*, sect. 9, p. 71.
74. Nietzsche, *The Birth of Tragedy*, sect. 9, p. 71.
75. Nietzsche's specification of the death of God is precise and nuanced and deserves to be cited as a corrective to its misunderstanding in popular usages: "Das größte neuere Ereigniss, – daß 'Gott todt ist,' daß der Glaube an den christlichen Gott unglaubwürdig

ist – beginnt bereits seine ersten Schatten über Europa zu werfen" (Nietzsche, *Die Fröhliche Wissenschaft* V. sect. 343, in Giorgio Colli und Massino Montinari, ed., *Nietzsche Werke*, Fünfte Abteilung, Zweiter Band, p. 255).

76. Friedrich Nietzsche, *Thus Spoke Zarathustra*, trans. Walter Kaufmann (New York: The Viking Press, 1968), Prologue, sect. 3, p. 12 (punctuation slightly altered).
77. Nietzsche, *Thus Spoke Zarathustra*, Prologue, sect. 9, p. 24; see sect. 3, p. 12.
78. Nietzsche, *Thus Spoke Zarathustra*, pt. 1, sect. 2, "On the Teachers of Virtue," pp. 28–30.
79. Nietzsche, *Thus Spoke Zarathustra*, pt. 1, sect. 3, "On the Afterworldly," p. 32.
80. Nietzsche, *Thus Spoke Zarathustra*, pt. 3, sect. 5, "On Virtue That Makes Small," p. 172.
81. Nietzsche, *Thus Spoke Zarathustra*, pt. 3, sect. 12, "On Old and New Tablets," p. 214.
82. Nietzsche, *Thus Spoke Zarathustra*, pt. 3, sect. 2, "On the Vision and the Riddle," pp. 155–154.
83. Nietzsche, *Thus Spoke Zarathustra*, pt. 3, sect. 13, "The Convalescent," pp. 217–220. Zarathustra is taught by the animals to accept and to proclaim the eternal return.
84. Nietzsche, *Thus Spoke Zarathustra*, pt. 3, sect. 16, "The Seven Seals (Or: The Yes And Amen Song)," pp. 228–231.
85. Nietzsche, *Thus Spoke Zarathustra*, pt. 2, sect. 2, "Upon the Blessed Isles," p. 86.
86. Sigmund Freud, *The Future of an Illusion*, trans. and ed. James Strachey (New York: Norton, 1961), 49 (emphasis his).
87. Freud, *Future of an Illusion*, 50.
88. Sigmund Freud, *Civilization and its Discontents*, trans. and ed. James Strachey (New York: Norton, 1961), 21.
89. Sigmund Freud, *New Introductory Lectures on Psychoanalysis*, newly trans. and ed. James Strachey (New York: Norton, 1965), 160.
90. Freud, *Future of an Illusion*, 53 (emphasis his).
91. Thomae Aquinatis, *Quaestio disputata de Veritate*, in *Questiones Disputatae*, ed. E. Spiazzi (Taurini: Marietti, 1964), 1.1.
92. Kenneth Schmitz, "Towards a Metaphysical Restoration of Natural Things," in *An Etienne Gilson Tribute* (Milwaukee: Marquette University Press, 1959), 254.
93. This is one of the similar ways in which Aquinas ends each of the *quinque viae:* "et hoc omnes intelligunt Deum" or "causam efficientem primam, quam omnes Deum nominant," "quod omnes dicunt Deum," etc. (*Summa theologiae* 1.2.3).
94. See Buckley, *Motion and Motion's God*, 220.
95. Feuerbach, *Essence of Christianity*, 272.
96. Feuerbach, *Essence of Religion*, 282–283 (emphasis his).
97. Feuerbach, *Essence of Religion*, 283. See Feuerbach, *The Essence of Faith According to Luther*, trans. Melvin Cherno (New York: Harper and Row, 1967), 31–33, 38–43.
98. Feuerbach, *Essence of Faith According to Luther*, 46–47.
99. Feuerbach, *Essence of Christianity*, 29 n. 1.
100. Thomas Nagel, *The Last Word* (New York: Oxford University Press, 1997), 131.
101. Ibid., 130.

Chapter 5. *The Radical Finitude of Religious Ideas*

1. James E. Faulconer, "Deconstruction," <http://jamesfaulconer.byu.edu/deconstr.htm>, 15 June 1998. I have quite deliberately resisted using the vocabulary of "deconstruction" because of its variations in meaning. Much that has been stated here,

however, about inadequacies and contradictions would echo many of the reserves of deconstruction.

2. G. W. F. Hegel, "How Common Sense Takes Philosophy, shown through an analysis of the works of Herr Krug," in Walter Kaufmann, *Hegel: A Reinterpretation* (Garden City, N.Y.: Doubleday, 1966), 60.

3. Sidney Hook, *From Hegel to Marx: Studies in the Intellectual Development of Karl Marx* (Ann Arbor: University of Michigan, 1962), 248–249. Cf. also de Lubac, *The Drama of Atheistic Humanism*, 8; N. Lobkowicz, "Marx's Attitude toward Religion," *Review of Politics* 26 (July 1964), 92.

4. Ludwig Feuerbach, *Essence of Religion*, 255.

5. Ibid., 254.

6. Xenophanes, fr. 15 (Clement of Alexandria, Strom. 5, 109, 3), in G. S. Kirk and J. E. Raven, *The Presocratic Philosophers: A Critical History with a Selection of Texts* (Cambridge: University Press, 1963), 169 n. 172.

7. David Hume, *An Enquiry concerning Human Understanding and Other Essays* (New York: Washington Square, 1963), 23.

8. Xenophanes, fr. 23 (Clement, Strom. 5, 109, 1), in Kirk–Raven, 169 n. 173.

9. David Hume, *Dialogues concerning Natural Religion* (Indianapolis: Bobbs–Merrill, 1946), pt. 12, p. 227. For Hume's "augmenting without bound or limit," see Collins, *God in Modern Philosophy*, 114–122.

10. Kamenka, *The Philosophy of Ludwig Feuerbach*, 167 n. 43.

11. Ralph Waldo Emerson, *Nature*, in *The Complete Essays and Other Writings of Ralph Waldo Emerson*, ed. Brooks Atkinson (New York: Random House, 1940), sect. 7, "Spirit," p. 36.

12. Ludwig Feuerbach, *The Essence of Christianity*, xxxvi.

13. Ibid., xxxiii, xxxv, xli.

14. Ibid., 3–5.

15. Ibid., 29–30. See 213–214.

16. Ibid., 25. See 14–21.

17. Max Jammer, *The Conceptual Development of Quantum Mechanics* (New York: McGraw-Hill, 1966), 370–371. This paragraph is little more than a paraphrase of this section of Jammer.

18. Isaac Newton, "Preface to the First Edition," in *Mathematical Principles of Nature Philosophy*, xviii; Jammer, *Conceptual Development*, 373.

19. John von Neumann, *Mathematical Foundations of Quantum Mechanics*, trans. R. T. Beyer (Princeton, N.J.: Princeton University Press, 1955), 420, cited in Jammer, *Conceptual Development*, 373.

20. W. Heisenberg, "The representation of nature in contemporary physics," *Daedalus* 87, no. 3 (1958): 99, cited in Jammer, *Conceptual Development*, 373.

21. Sigmund Freud, "Obsessive Acts and Religious Practices," in *The Standard Edition of the Complete Psychological Works of Sigmund Freud*, 24 vols. (London: Hogarth Press and the Institute of Psycho-Analysis, 1953–74), 9:116ff.

22. Freud, *Future of an Illusion*, 17.

23. Freud, *Future of an Illusion*, 24.

24. Freud, *Future of an Illusion*, 30–33.

25. Freud, *Future of an Illusion*, 43 and n. 3.

26. Freud, *Future of an Illusion*, 16.

27. Sigmund Freud, *Totem and Taboo* (New York: Norton, 1965), 75.

28. Sigmund Freud, *Leonardo da Vinci and a Memory of His Childhood*, trans. Alan

Tyson, ed. James Strachey (New York: Norton, 1989), 103. See Sigmund Freud, *Moses and Monotheism*, trans. Katherine Jones (New York: Vintage, 1939), pt. 3, sect. 1, pp. 102–110.

29. Freud, *Future of an Illusion*, 24.

30. Paul Ricoeur, *Freud and Philosophy: An Essay on Interpretation* (New Haven: Yale University Press, 1977), 203 n. Ricoeur maintains that Freud worked out the theory of projection in the third section of the Schreber case and that "this text is his most important contribution to the study of projection, and more precisely of projection in a religious theme" (Ibid., 238 n).

31. Kamenka, *The Philosophy of Ludwig Feuerbach*, 69.

32. Pseudo-Dionysius, *The Mystical Theology*, 135. For the Greek text, see *PG* 3:998.

33. Pseudo-Dionysius, *The Mystical Theology*, 2:1001A, p. 137. I am greatly indebted throughout this chapter to the directions and reflections of Denys Turner, *The Darkness of God: Negativity in Christian Mysticism* (Cambridge: Cambridge University Press, 1995).

34. Gregory of Nyssa, *The Life of Moses*, trans. Abraham Malherbe and Everett Ferguson (New York: Paulist Press, 1978), no. 163, p. 95.

35. Gregory of Nyssa, *The Life of Moses*, no. 164, p. 95. The source of this argument lies in the Johannine Gospel (1:18). This, in turn, grounded the doctrine of the incomprehensibility of God, which found its own speculative foundation in the infinite nature of God. See ibid., 178 n. 200.

36. John of the Cross, *The Ascent of Mount Carmel*, in *The Collected Works of John of the Cross*, trans. Kieran Kavanaugh and Otilio Rodriguez, with revisions and introductions by Kieran Kavanaugh, rev. ed. (Washington, D.C.: Institute of Carmelite Studies, 1991), "Theme," p. 113. All subsequent references to John of the Cross in English are taken from this edition. For the Spanish text, see Crisógono de Jesús, O.C.D., Matias del Niño Jesús, O.C.D., and Lucinio de SS. Sacramento, O.C.D., eds., *Vida y obras de San Juan de la Cruz*, 5th ed. (Madrid: BAC, 1964).

37. See, for example, Harvey Egan, S.J., "Christian Apophatic and Kataphatic Mysticisms," *Theological Studies* 39 (1978): 399–426; John F. Teahan, "The Dark and Empty Way," *Journal of Religion* 58 (1978): 263–287.

38. John of the Cross, *Ascent of Mount Carmel*, "Theme," p. 113; *Vida y obras*, 363.

39. John of the Cross, *The Living Flame of Love*, "Prologue," no. 2, pp. 638–639. Cf. *Ascent of Mount Carmel*, "Prologue," no. 4: "With God's help, then, we shall propose doctrine and counsel for beginners and proficients that they may understand or at least know how to practice abandonment to God's guidance when He wants them to advance" (p. 116).

40. William James, *The Varieties of Religious Experience* (New York: New American Library of World Literature, 1961), 240.

41. Cf. Edgar Allison Peers, *St. John of the Cross* (Freeport, N.Y.: Books for Libraries, 1970), 25.

42. John of the Cross, *Ascent of Mount Carmel*, "Prologue," no. 8, pp. 117–118.

43. Ibid., bk. 1, ch. 13, no. 11, pp. 150–151.

44. John of the Cross, *Living Flame of Love*, bk. 1, no. 3, p. 642.

45. John of the Cross, *The Dark Night of the Soul*, bk. 2, ch. 16, no. 4, p. 431.

46. John of the Cross, *Dark Night of the Soul*, bk. 2, ch. 16, no. 4, p. 431; bk. 1, ch. 4, no. 2, p. 368; *Living Flame of Love*, bk. 3, no. 34, p. 686. The transformation worked in the soul is just reverse of this maxim: "The receiver should act according to the mode of what is received, and not otherwise, in order to receive and keep it [the communication of God] in the way it is given" (*Living Flame of Love*, bk. 3, no. 34, p. 686).

47. Cf. John of the Cross, *Vida y obras*, p. 546, no. 6.

48. Thomas Aquinas, *Commentary on the Metaphysics of Aristotle* (Chicago: Regnery, 1961), vol. 1, lect. 10, no. 167.

49. Otto Bardenhewer, *Die pseudo–aristotelische Schrift Über das reine Gute: Liber de causis* (Freiburg: Herder, 1882), prop. ix, p. 174. I am grateful for the labors of Robert W. Schmidt, S.J., of Xavier University in Cincinnati, who researched this history of the Scholastic dictum. For the best single source, cf. Robert Henle, S.J., *St. Thomas and Platonism* (The Hague: Nijhoff, 1956), ch. 4, sect. c, "The Reception Principle."

50. John of the Cross, *Dark Night of the Soul*, bk. 1, ch. 4, no. 2, p. 368.

51. Ibid., bk. 2, ch. 16, no. 4, pp. 431–432.

52. Georg Wilhelm Friedrich Hegel, *The Logic of Hegel, Translated from the Encyclopedia of the Philosophical Sciences*, trans. William Wallace, 2d ed., revised and augmented (Oxford: Oxford University Press, 1959), xxi.

53. John of the Cross, *Dark Night of the Soul*, no. 5, p. 432.

54. John of the Cross, *Ascent of Mount Carmel*, bk. 2, ch. 5, no. 7, p. 165; *Living Flame of Love*, bk. 2, no. 34, p. 671; bk. 3, no. 8, p. 677; bk. 3, no. 78, p. 706.

55. John of the Cross, *Ascent of Mount Carmel*, bk. 1, ch. 14, no. 2, pp. 151–152.

56. Ibid., bk. 1, ch. 4, no. 1, p. 123.

57. John of the Cross, *Dark Night of the Soul*, bk. 1, ch. 10, no. 6, p. 382.

58. John of the Cross, *Ascent of Mount Carmel*, bk. 2, ch. 3, no. 1, p. 158.

59. Ibid., bk. 2, ch. 4, no. 2, p. 160.

60. Ibid., bk. 2, ch. 4, no. 3, p. 160.

61. John of the Cross, *Dark Night of the Soul*, bk. 2, ch. 6, no. 2, p. 404.

62. John of the Cross, *Living Flame of Love*, bk. 3, no. 48, p. 692.

63. John of the Cross, *Ascent of Mount Carmel*, bk. 2, ch. 1, no. 1, p. 154.

64. Karl Rahner, "What Is a Dogmatic Statement?" *Theological Investigations*, vol. 5 (New York: Seabury, 1966), 18–19.

65. John of the Cross, *Ascent of Mount Carmel*, bk. 1, ch. 13, no. 3, p. 148.

66. Ibid., bk. 2, ch. 7, no. 9, p. 172.

67. John of the Cross, *Living Flame of Love*, bk. 2, no. 17, p. 664.

68. Ibid., bk. 1, no. 19, p. 648.

69. Thomas Aquinas, *Summa theologiae* 2–28.2. Thomas is citing this definition from the *Moralia* of Gregory the Great. English translation (Blackfriars 32:7): "Understanding enlightens the mind on things it has heard."

70. Thomas Aquinas, *Summa theologiae* 2–2.8.7; also *In 3 Sent.*, dist. 34, q. 1, a. 4.

71. Jacques Maritain, ed., *Raissa's Journal* (Albany, N.Y.: Magi, 1974), xvi.

Chapter 6. The Negation of Atheism

1. I have traced this dialectical pattern in the development and the significance of the study of religion; see Michael J. Buckley, "Atheism and the Scientific Study of Religion," to appear in a *Festschrift* in honor of Nicholas Lash.

2. It will be perhaps helpful to call attention to the specific way in which "religion" is used throughout this book in, for example, "bracketing the religious." There is no attempt to give a genus so extensive as to include all of the accepted means and forms designated by "religion." "Religion" and "the religious" here bear the weight of their Judeo–Christian heritage and denote the interpersonal relationship with God that is realized in worship, prayer, morality, contemplation, faith, love, etc.

3. Pseudo–Dionysius, *The Mystical Theology*, ch. 1, 1000B, p. 136 (numeration added).

4. G. W. F. Hegel, *The Science of Logic*, 2:479.
5. G. W. F. Hegel, *Phenomenology of Spirit*, trans. A. V. Miller (Oxford: Oxford University Press, 1977), "Preface," no. 2, pp. 1–2.
6. Aristotle *Physics* 1.7.191a3–22.
7. See above, chapter 2, pp. 35ff.
8. Federick Copleston, *A History of Philosophy*, vol. 2, *Medieval Philosophy*, (Westminster, Md.: Newman, 1952), 195–196.
9. See Armand A. Maurer, *Medieval Philosophy* (New York: Random House, 1962), 100–101.
10. G. W. F. Hegel, *The Philosophy of Right*, translated with notes by T. M. Knox (Oxford: Clarendon Press, 1952). For a perceptive summary of this last stage of the Hegelian dialectic, see James Collins, *A History of Modern European Philosophy* (Milwaukee: Bruce Pub. Co., [1954]), 652–655.
11. Christopher Norris, *Derrida* (Cambridge, Mass.: Harvard University Press, 1987), 15.
12. Maurice O'C. Drury, "Conversations with Wittgenstein," in Rush Rhees, ed., *Ludwig Wittgenstein: Personal Recollections* (Totowa, N.J.: Rowman and Littlefield, 1981), 129, cited in Norman Malcolm, *Wittgenstein: A Religious Point of View*, ed. with a response by Peter Winch (Ithaca, N.Y.: Cornell University Press, 1994), 11.
13. Henri Bergson, *The Two Sources of Morality and Religion*, trans. R. Ashley Audra and Cloudesley Brereton, with the assistance of W. Horsfall Carter (Garden City, N.Y.: Doubleday, 1954), 240–241.
14. Maurice O'C. Drury, "Conversations with Wittgenstein," 117. See ibid., 101.
15. W. Donald Hudson, *Wittgenstein and Religious Belief* (London: Macmillan, 1975), 178–179. Hudson is basing his own summary remarks upon the lectures of Wittgenstein in *Lectures and Conversations on Aesthetics, Psychology and Religious Belief*, ed. Cyril Barrett (Oxford: Blackwell, 1966).
16. Hudson, *Wittgenstein and Religious Belief*, 161, citing Ludwig Wittgenstein, "Lectures on Religious Belief," in *Lectures and Conversations*, 56.
17. Drury, "Conversations with Wittgenstein," 123 (emphasis added).
18. Wittgenstein, *Lectures and Conversations*, 53.
19. Drury, "Some Notes on Conversations with Wittgenstein," in *Ludwig Wittgenstein: Personal Recollections*, 101.
20. Ludwig Wittgenstein, *Tractatus Logico–Philosphicus*, trans. D. F. Pears and B. F. McGuinness (London: Routledge and Paul, 1961), 6.522.
21. Alfred North Whitehead, *Symbolism: Its Meaning and Effect* (1927; reprint, New York: Capricorn Books, 1959), 16; Hans-Georg Gadamer, *Truth and Method*, trans. Joel Weinsheimer and Donald C. Marshall, 2d rev. ed. (New York: Crossroad, 1989), 346ff.
22. George P. Schner, "The Appeal to Experience," *Theological Studies* 53, no. 1 (March 1992): 40–59. See Owen C. Thomas, "Theology and Experience," *Harvard Theological Review* 78, no. 1–2 (1985): 179.
23. For the following analysis and the subsequent range of "experience" in Western thought, I am indebted to Richard P. McKeon, "Experience and Metaphysics," in *Expérience et Métaphysique*, vol. 4 of *Actes du XIème Congrès International de Philosophie: Bruxelles, 20–26 Août, 1953* (Amsterdam, North-Holland Publishing, 1953), 83–89, especially 84–86.
24. Aristotle, *Metaphysics* 1.1.980b25–981b9; *Posterior Analytics* 2.19.100a3–9; *Prior Analytics* 1.30.46a17–21; *Nicomachean Ethics* 1.1.1094b28–1095a13, 6.11.1143b6–14 (these references can be located in McKeon, ed., *The Basic Works of Aristotle*).

25. Immanuel Kant, "The Transcendental Deduction of the Pure Concepts of Under-standing," in *Critique of Pure Reason*, B166–167, pp. 173–174.

26. Kant, *Critique of Pure Reason*, B75, p. 93 (punctuation slightly altered).

27. John Dewey, *Experience and Nature*, Open Court Paperbacks (La Salle, Ill.: Open Court, 1971), 10–11.

28. John Dewey, *Reconstruction in Philosophy*, enlarged edition with a new introduction by the author (Boston: Beacon Press, 1966), 86.

29. Freda Mary Oben, "Edith Stein the Woman," in *Edith Stein Symposium: Teresian Culture*, ed. John Sullivan, O.C.D., Carmelite Studies, vol. 4 (Washington: ICS Publications, 1987), 12–14; for the description of her involvement with the phenomenological method, see Mary Catherine Baseheart, "Edith Stein's Philosophy of Person," ibid., 34–42; cf. also Sr. Teresia a Matre Dei, *Edith Stein: Auf der Suche nach Gott* (Ratisbon: Butzon and Bercker Kevelaer, 1963), 58–59.

30. Raïssa Maritain, *We Have Been Friends Together*, trans. Julie Kernan (New York: Longmans, Green, 1943), 150.

31. John Henry Newman, "Discourse 5. Saintliness the Standard of Christian Principle," *Discourses Addressed to Mixed Congregations* (London: Longmans, Green, and Co., 1916), 99–100, 102.

32. Simone Weil, *Waiting for God*, introduction by Leslie Fiedler, trans. Emma Cranford (New York: Harper and Row, 1951), 74.

33. See Ray Monk, *Ludwig Wittgenstein: The Duty of Genius* (New York: Free Press, 1990), 115–116 and 51.

34. Waltraud Herbstrith, *Edith Stein: A Biography*, trans. Bernard Bonowitz (San Francisco: Ignatius Press, 1985), 10.

35. Ibid., 38 and 70.

36. Maritain, *We Have Been Friends Together*, 80.

37. Weil, *Waiting For God*, 69.

38. See Aquinas *Summa theologiae* 2-2.1–7. For *veritas prima* as the formal object of faith, see 2-2.1.1. For the nature of "truth" in Aquinas, see 1.16.

39. Monk, *Ludwig Wittgenstein*, 410.

40. Rainer Maria Rilke, "Archaïscher Torso Appolos," in *The Selected Poetry of Rainer Maria Rilke*, ed. Stephen Mitchell (New York: Random House, 1982), 67. The original reads: "Du muß dein Leben ändern."

41. For personal "closeness to" or "distance from", understood as likeness or unlikeness of nature or grace, see *Summa theologiae* 1.8.1.ad 3; 1.115.1.ad 4.

42. Gerard Manley Hopkins, "The Wreck of the Deutschland," 29, in *A Hopkins Reader*, ed. John Pick (Garden City, NY: Doubleday, 1966), 43.

43. Cf. Col. 1:15–17.

44. In conversation with Simone de Beauvoir, Sartre remarked: "All the great philosophers have been believers more or less. That means different things at different times. Spinoza's belief in God is not the same as Descartes' or Kant's, but it seemed to me that a great atheist, truly atheist philosophy was something philosophy lacked. And that it was in this direction that one should now endeavor to work" (Simone de Beauvoir, *Adieux: A Farewell to Sartre* [New York: Pantheon, 1984], 436).

45. For this index of postmodernity, cf. José María Mardones, "Le fe cristiana ante la modernidad, la postmodernidad y la cultura neo-conservadora," in *Pluralismo socio-cultural y fe cristiana*, ed. Facultades de Teología de Vitoria y Oeusto (Bilbao: Vitoria, 1990), 36–41.

46. See Friedrich von Hügel, *Mystical Element of Religion*, 50–82.

Index of Names

Index of Subjects

accommodation, doctrine of, 7–8
Al-Ghazáli, Abú Hamíd, *The Incoherence of the Philosophers*, 122
alienation, xiv, 71, 84–86, 87–88, 93. *See also* God, as alienation
Also sprach Zarathustra. See Thus Spoke Zarathustra
American Enlightenment, 40
animism, 107
apologetics, theological: grounded in sciences, xii–xiii, xi, 5–6, 18, 20–22, 23–24, 36, 75–78, 81, 82–83, 121; exclusion of religious experience from, 36–38, 120–121, 123–126, 130–131, 135–138; dependence upon mechanics in, xi, 5–6, 18, 20–22, 23–24, 36, 121; grounded in human nature, xiv, 75–78, 82–83, 121; grounded in nature, 75–78, 81, 82–83, 121. *See also* theology, religion, religious
apophatic theology. *See* negative theology
a priori, theological, 12–17; and Einstein's impersonal God, 16–17
Aquinas, Thomas, 49–69; and origins of atheism, xii, xiii–xiv, 46–47, 50–51; Christology in, 51, 62–68; on faith, 118, 131, 134–135; on knowledge of God, 52–62; on truth, 134–135; *quinque viae*, xiii, 47, 49, 51; Tillich on, xii, xiii–xiv, 49–51, 56, 62. Works: *Commentary on the Sentences*, 57–58, 66, 151n25; *Compendium theologiae*, 65–66; *Expositio super librum Boethii de Trinitate*, 61–62; *In octo libros Physicorum expositio*, 152n40; *Quaestio disputata de Anima*, 152n40; *Quaestio disputata de*

Veritate, 58, 94, 132, 151n24; *Summa contra Gentiles*, 58; *Summa theologiae*, xiv, 46–47, 52–57, 134; *Super Epistolas S. Pauli lectura*, 153n41
Aristotle: on experience, 126. Works: *Metaphysics*, 162n24; *Nicomachean Ethics*, 162n24; *Politics*, 65; *Posterior Analytics*, 162n24; *Prior Analytics*, 162n24
Ascent of Mount Carmel, The (John of the Cross), 110, 111, 112, 114–115, 116–117
Astronomia nova (Kepler), 143n46
astronomy: and creation, 15; and scripture, 15; and theology, 11–14, 17; Galileo on, 7; Kepler on, 10–16
atheism, xiv, 1, 24, 42, 70–71, 121, 124; and Aquinas, 48– 51; and contemplation, 99–100; and humanism, 71; and modern science, 2; as anti-theism, 71; as epithet, 30; as philosophical problem, 30, 33; emergence of, x, xiv, 28, 36, 37–38, 42–43, 45, 48–49, 122; d'Holbach and, 35–36; Diderot and, 35–36; Feuerbach and, 84–86, 101–104, 107–108; Freud and, 92–93, 105–108; in ancient philosophy, 30–32; in France, 43–46; in the United States, 42, 44; Lessius on, 30–32; Marx and, 87–89; Mersenne on, 32–33; negation of, xii, 121, 124–125; Nietzsche on, 90–92; origins in mechanics, 36, 37–38; origins in physics, 36; origins in theory of human nature, 93–98. *See also* God; theism; theology
Atheism in France, 1650–1729 (Kors). *See Orthodox Sources of Disbelief*
atheists, 30–31, 32–33. *See also* atheism